DISCARD

The Female Spectator

The
Female Spectator

୬ଟ୍ଟ

ENGLISH WOMEN WRITERS
BEFORE 1800

Edited by

Mary R. Mahl

and

Helene Koon

Indiana University Press BLOOMINGTON & LONDON

The Feminist Press OLD WESTBURY, NEW YORK

Published in Canada by Fitzhenry & Whiteside Limited, Don Mills, Ontario
Manufactured in the United States of America

Library of Congress Cataloging in Publication Data
Main entry under title:
The female spectator.
Bibliographies.
1. English literature—Women authors.   I. Mahl, Mary R.
II. Koon, Helene, 1925–
PR1110.W6F4   1977   820'.9'9287   76–026430
ISBN 0–253–32166–2   1 2 3 4 5 81 80 79 78 77

Contents

In Appreciation

We wish to express our sincere appreciation to those individuals and institutions that have encouraged and assisted us in the preparation of this book. The staff at the British Museum Library and Students' Room, at the Folger Shakespeare Library, and above all, at the Henry E. Huntington Library have given us access to those rare books and manuscripts that make this anthology unique. And we gratefully acknowledge all the suggestions and comments, facetious and otherwise, made by that incomparable collection of brilliant scholars—our friends, the registered readers at the Huntington.

We would like to thank Captain Maurice E. Butler-Bowdon, O. B. E., Royal Navy (the eldest son of the late Colonel William E. Butler-Bowdon, who first translated the original text for the edition first published in 1936 by Jonathan Cape Ltd. of London) for permission to use herein several chapters from that edition of *The Book of Margery Kempe.*

"To the Thrice Sacred Queen Elizabeth," by Mary Sidney Herbert, Countess of Pembroke, is reprinted from *Two Poems by the Countess of Pembroke,* edited by Bent Juel-Jensen, Oxford University Press, 1962, by permission of the publisher.

The following selections are reproduced by permission of The Huntington Library, San Marino, California: HM 349595, *The Lamentation of a Sinner,* by Catharine Parr, 1548; HA 8799, "Upon the much lamented death of the Right Honorable, the Lady Elizabeth Langham," by Bathsua Makin, May 2, 1664; HM 58029, *The Malady and the Remedy of Vexations and Unjust Arrests and Actions,* by Bathsua Makin, 1646; MO 505, 508, 510, 512, 514, 519, 531, 532, Frances Glanville Boscawen letters; MO 3986–3992, Hannah More letters; JE 758–9, 762–5, 768, Anna Seward letters.

The Female Spectator

INTRODUCTION

This book began as the result of a conversation in the Henry E. Huntington Library Footnote, that corner where scholars retreat to rest their eyes and relax over a cup of coffee. That afternoon it happened that both of us had coincidentally met with the same problem: the extreme sparseness of information concerning women writers. Not only is material about them wanting, but very often their work has not been reissued since the first edition. With such a lack of availability, it comes as no surprise that they have been so far out of the mainstream of scholarly and critical evaluation that even our own colleagues did not know of more than one or two names of early women writers. Indeed, when our friends were told that we were preparing this anthology, the standard response was, "Women writers? Were there any?" spoken in a tone of utter disbelief.

Our first task was to determine the size of the undertaking. We examined the *Short Title Catalogue* (1476–1640 edited by Pollard and Redgrave, and 1641–1700 by Wing), which listed books published in England or in English before the eighteenth century, copies of which are available in selected libraries. Before long our list grew so rapidly that we arbitrarily decided to limit our study to works available at the Huntington Library. Even with this limitation we were unprepared for the mass of works almost untouched in the archives. Next we searched the manuscript catalogue and found a vast body of unpublished material: letters, stories, plays, and poems—every traditional genre is represented. Some, of course, deserve oblivion; many do not, and it was a great pleasure to find that the task we had set ourselves was not to try to locate acceptable works, but to select the best for our purpose from a rich mine of neglected worth. The library catalogues provided dozens of eighteenth-century women writers to complete our project.

We found it necessary to restrict our choices to English women only, partly because their works were within our own fields of scholarship, and also because the inclusion of continental and American writers extended the range too far for careful examination. While both these areas offer a wealth of possibilities, work is being done on early American women, and translations require time-consuming preparation that we did not deem worthwhile at this time. We have, therefore, elected to let English writers speak for themselves in their own vernacular.

Our criteria were threefold. The first was quality: no one has been included simply because she was a woman. We have chosen only from among those who made coherent and cogent statements. Second, we sought the representation of many viewpoints: as with modern women, some writers accepted social conventions without question, others protested, and many adapted for survival. The third criterion was accessibility: the increasing interest in women writers has brought about such recent editions as Lady Mary Wortley Montagu's *Letters* and Fanny Burney's *Diary*. We have avoided works readily available in general libraries and bookstores in favor of those found only in collections of rare books or in out-of-print editions.

We have reached back to a remote past, letting women speak for themselves in private letters, in diaries, in public memoirs, and in literary works, the voices of those who lived, worked, and thought before 1800. That there are differences between male and female perceptions of the world has become a standard observation. Today, as women assume their full role in society, it is clear that the differences are well worth examining. These varied voices are concerned with their immediate world, but they have larger concerns as well, and their acceptance or rejection of contemporary values provides a distinctive insight into a past world from which the present has emerged.

It is not as if women had never spoken. In fact, one of the most frequent stereotypes has been the chattering female whose tongue wags constantly without producing significant substance. If this is a standard masculine image, it is no less so than other visions of history, for the broad panoply of political events, social change, and artistic developments has been recorded by the men involved or interested in the proceedings. Yet even granting that women were seldom allowed active participation, one cannot ignore their influence. If they had neither the education nor the opportunity to express themselves publicly, they nonetheless spoke, and their awareness of the world was not merely that of passive observers. The concerns of the early women writers were the concerns of the individual rather than of society. Before the mid-seventeenth century few expected to reach a wide audience; the authors apparently believed that their writings would be useful records of experience available nowhere else. Outside the convents and the wealthy homes the literacy rate among women in England was extremely low, and the literature produced for female enlightenment was largely religious in nature. Dame Julian of Norwich was writing of her personal experiences while Walter Hilton was presenting instructions for those who aspired to spiritual excellence. Margery Kempe was incorporating the story of her life in a travel book, while Sir John Mandeville, whoever he was, was attempting to enlarge the horizons of the general public by writing his *Travels*, which comprise geographical and social facts and fancies. The amount of anonymous literature actually written by women will never be known.

It is often assumed that modern woman is the first to challenge the mythical tradition of masculine superiority. After all, it was a modern woman who coined the phrase "male chauvinist." Yet it is perfectly obvious that the movement from chattel to full citizenship began long before the first results became visible. When did women begin to regard themselves as individuals with the capacity to perceive and share the full range of human experience? Clearly they did not begin recently; just as clearly, the capacity was known and fully developed before the nineteenth century.

Sex roles have been differentiated even by the most primitive societies, but, as Margaret Mead points out, whether the differences were innate or imposed has not been finally determined. In any case, the roles, hardened by tradition, became cultural imperatives in Europe and America. Men were characterized by action and received glory for it; physical prowess, later translated into intellectual and artistic terms, was recognized and rewarded. Women, deterred from physical achievement for whatever reason, were debarred from intellectual and artistic opportunities as well. A good many rationalizations were given: as their bodies were weaker, so were their intellects; they were incapable of the single-mindedness demanded by stern intellectual disciplines; their creative faculties were spent in producing and rearing children; their place as guardian of the home was nobler than that of men struggling in the public arena; their power was properly exercised behind the scenes—"the hand that rocks the cradle rules the world." Essentially the argument was simple: women were inferior to that splendid creature, man. This is, of course, a generality, and exceptions to it are easily found from Hippolyta the Amazon to Anne, the last Stuart on the English throne. The factors behind the generality and its exceptions are too complex to analyze here, but a brief résumé might identify a number of them and account for some of the conflicting attitudes that have persisted in our own culture.

One of two major influences, the Graeco-Roman tradition clearly put woman in a secondary position; as Edith Hamilton once said, if the Greeks could have found babies in the temple they would have been happy to dispense with females entirely. Greek women were chattel who were either trained, professional entertainers or who lived out their lives in the *gynaceum* (women's quarters) to produce legitimate and healthy children. The Romans paid a kind of lip-service honor to women, but their actual practice was almost identical to that of the Greeks; in fact the *pater familias* held the power of life and death over all his dependents. On the other hand these same people worshipped goddesses like Hera/Juno (motherhood and the home), Athena/Minerva (wisdom), the virgin Artemis/Diana (hunting), and laughing Aphrodite/Venus (love), and regarded their power as awesome and as worthy of respect as any god's. The discrepancy does not appear to have concerned them unduly: the principle of female beauty and power could be worshipped, but in practice the need for male physical strength dominated society.

The other main influence, the Judeo-Christian, involves similar discrepancies in dissimilar ways. In the nomadic life of the early tribes of Israel, men and women shared equally in the burdens and responsibilities of survival. Even so, there is the suggestion that women are weak vessels—after all, it was Eve who caused the Fall, and today the orthodox Jew, following the ancient ritual begun by these nomads, daily thanks God that he was not born a woman. With the coming of Christianity further conflicts were introduced. The soul of a woman was as precious in the sight of God as the soul of a man, but in the emerging church only supporting roles were assigned to women. Although Christ, born of the Virgin Mary, died to redeem the world from sin, the church tacitly accepted the suffering of women as proper to the daughters of Eve, inheritors of the curse upon her.

Such conflicts, under pressure from evolving philosophies and changing social conditions, were usually resolved in practice by using the old standards of superiority. In fact, for centuries it was almost inconceivable that anyone would doubt this premise. Religious doctrine, governmental regulations, and cultural patterns combined to reinforce the concept, even though it abounded in anomalies. Women were helpless dependents without civil rights, yet they could be prosecuted for crime as responsible adults; barely educated, they could not support themselves, yet they were charged with caring for the next generation. In spite of these paradoxes, many, if not most, women believed themselves to have been born inferior, and if they did not subscribe wholeheartedly to the idea, they seldom jeopardized their positions by saying so.

The Middle Ages were the last period in which women enjoyed lives that were nearly parallel to those of men. With the rise of religious orders we find that most of the early monasteries provided convents for nuns nearby. These nuns were drawn almost entirely from the upper classes and were given an education similar to that given the men; in addition to the regular curriculum, housewifery was added. But these women did not actually engage in manual labor: servants looked after menial tasks under their supervision. Many nuns became highly proficient in Latin as well as in several modern languages and prepared manuscripts in the scriptoria with great skill. Highly literate, they conducted schools for gentlewomen and occasionally taught boys as well. In time of civil conflict it is probable that more women than men received formal education; while men were engaged in warfare, husbandry, and government, reading and writing were frequently thought of as the works of enclosed clerics and women. The Crusades led to the involvement of women in industry and commerce. Even some of the early craft guilds were not exclusively male. Brewing was almost entirely undertaken by women—the term "brewster" is the female form of "brewer." Chaucer's portrait of the Wife of Bath in the *Canterbury Tales* depicts a woman who was an expert weaver, a woman who had had five husbands, a woman who had participated in many pilgrimages, even to the Holy Land. By the fourteenth century women's roles were less sharply differentiated from men's; they paralleled and supplemented them. On the Continent, especially in Italy and Germany, women were not only students at the early universities, but they were also professors.

Dame Julian of Norwich was undoubtedly a well-educated woman. She was enclosed in her anchorhold in the late fourteenth century but was not cut off from the world in the strict sense. She entertained visitors, wrote her *Revelations of Divine Love*, and was widely known for her piety and her practical advice. A contemporary of Chaucer, she employed a clear, simple, yet highly polished vernacular in her writing. She was well versed in the Bible and in the teachings of the church fathers. As an anchoress, set apart for meditation and prayer, she exerted an influence far beyond her modest rooms.

One of Dame Julian's visitors was Margery Kempe, a woman of King's Lynn who had been a brewster before setting out on pilgrimages. Margery Kempe was wholly illiterate, but was bright enough to dictate her autobiography, in which she describes not only her life but also her spiritual quest, her thoughts about society as she saw it, and her aspirations. Her book was among the early works printed in England, but had to wait nearly four hundred years for a second edition.

Education in England before the Reformation was largely in the hands of the church. With the dissolution of the monasteries and convents went the closing of the schools; when church schools no longer afforded elementary instruction to the upper and middle classes, private schools could not fill the gap. Schools organized by the craft guilds, such as Merchant Taylor's, or the religious guilds, such as Corpus Christi at Oxford, restricted their enrollments to boys. Girls were tutored at home or perhaps allowed to attend small village schools that gave instruction in reading, writing, basic arithmetic, and perhaps household arts. Only wealthy citizens provided classical training in Latin, languages, and fine arts for their female children.

In the sixteenth century Henry VIII founded 50 schools, Queen Mary founded 19, and Queen Elizabeth founded 138. Most of them were situated in towns and villages and provided basic education for both boys and girls; however, while all boys had to study Latin, only the brightest girls were admitted to that program. Until the nineteenth century university education was restricted to men only; Oxford University did not grant degrees to women until 1920, and Cambridge followed in 1948.

Nearly all the women who wrote in the sixteenth and seventeenth centuries were of the upper classes. Of course royal princesses were well educated and wrote well—private tutors supervised the lessons of Mary and Elizabeth, daughters of Henry VIII and future queens; in fact, Elizabeth's tutor, Roger Ascham, was one of the most learned men of his age. All of Henry's queens were literate, as were most of the wives and daughters of the peers. Letters, diaries, poems, conduct books, speeches—all were produced by these women. Mary Sidney Herbert, Countess of Pembroke, a fine poet in her own right, has been eclipsed by her famous brother, Sir Philip Sidney, although her renditions of the Psalms are superior to his. In fact, she was using the so-called Spenserian sonnet form before the publication of Edmund Spenser's poems. Yet most scholars have ignored her work and have honored her only as a patron of poets and other writers.

Elizabeth Grymeston wrote a book of instruction for her son as a legacy. Published by him in 1604, the year after her death, the little devotional volume went through several editions within ten years, but almost nothing has been heard of it since that time. Her family belonged to the landed gentry and apparently her education was supplied by tutors, probably Jesuits who had to work secretly because of the religious temper of the time.

Ascham, Bacon, and Milton, like other pre-eighteenth-century champions of education, commented on the education of women, but none advocated that both sexes should—or could—learn the same subjects. Such equality of opportunity was still more than two hundred years in the future.

The first woman to write a treatise on the education of members of her own sex was Bathsua Makin. Daughter of a clergyman and sister of the famous mathematician John Pell, she was known as one of the most learned women of her day; Charles I recognized her impeccable credentials and employed her as tutor to Princess Elizabeth, who achieved a wide reputation for brilliance in languages. Makin's appeal to Parliament regarding the laws that demanded imprisonment for debt apparently had no effect on that body, but it is an outstanding document nevertheless, outlining every cogent reason for repealing those laws. Her appeal for the establishment of a school in which women could receive an education equivalent to that of men also went unheeded.

Margaret Cavendish, Duchess of Newcastle, firmly believed in the inferiority of women, and early in her life she prided herself on having had little education. A contemporary of Makin, she later deplored this lack of formal training and wondered why women were not well educated when the training of the next generation was to be entrusted to them. She wrote voluminously, works of uneven quality but wide variety, and published everything she wrote. Her best-known work is the life of her husband, William Cavendish, but her most interesting publications consist of her comments on the life and thought of her times. A woman of wit and imagination, she was alternately jeered and cheered by the reading public of her day, when the writings of women were judged by the standards set by classical training.

In spite of the dramatic political changes brought about by the restoration of the Stuarts in 1660, the status of women was generally unchanged. The one new factor, an exuberant young court bent on pleasure, has perhaps received undue attention, and the stories of the court's amours tend to give the misleading impression that women had considerable power in political as well as social matters. Actually such court favorites were given lip-service fealty, extravagant praise, and generous gifts of titles, lands, and gold. But the "power" playfully assigned them in poetry and prose was not real and lasted no longer than a successful courtship.

The court may have been the most visible segment of Restoration society, but it was only a very small part of the whole. The majority, the respectable middle-class women, were brought up to be a man's humble helpmeet, and such education as they were given was designed to prepare them as housewives and mothers. Under these circumstances few had time or qualification to record their impressions. Both the production and consumption of literature were for the most part confined to the leisured class, the aristocracy, nobility, and wealthy commoners; even among them, there were few competent writers. The exceptions like Aphra Behn were driven to write by the necessity to be self-supporting. The well-bred woman unprotected by a husband or a fortune was in a dangerous position. Unlike her lower-class sisters she had no means of survival. Unequipped to go into service or work at hard labor, she had few resources other than the stage or the street. Even if she had the wit and skill to write, she faced the social stigma of being "unfeminine," particularly if she were successful, and her enemies increased with her earnings.

In spite of this, writing was almost the only means for a woman to express herself outside the home, and the early years of the eighteenth century saw a number of women following in the footsteps of Aphra Behn. Catherine Trotter and Susannah Centlivre wrote plays, as did the prolific Delariviere Manley, who also wrote short stories, essays for *The Examiner*, and verses. Elizabeth Haywood published a magazine for women, *The Female Spectator*, from which we drew the name of our book. The poet Anne Finch, Countess of Winchilsea, was an exception to the rule of necessity, but even the security of titled wealth did not protect her from attack, and she frequently apologized for her temerity in entering the male domain.

Writing and publishing were symptoms of unrest. The records left by the eighteenth-century woman indicate that while life on the surface remained stabilized in the centuries-old patterns, women were not content to remain in the position of slaves, dolls, or children at the discretion of their male "protectors." The ideal state, said some, was widowhood, the only time a woman was given control of her life and her fortune. Edward Cave's *The Gentleman's Magazine*, one of the most popular and influential of all eighteenth-century periodicals, reflected some of these feelings. From its founding in 1730 until the end of the century there were frequent articles, letters, and other comments from women trapped in bad situations and from conservative old gentlemen who claimed women who did not cry at sad plays, who rode horses astride, or who occasionally said "damn" were desensitized and unfeminine. The arguments grew in depth and range, leading to Mary Wollstonecraft's clarion call at the end of the century. Fundamental change, however, had to wait for other generations to produce the Pankhursts and the Anthonys.

What brought about a good share of the discontent was the lack of education, and the eighteenth century saw the first female academies established. They could not be compared, of course, to the boys' schools, for the curricula were designed to produce ornamental wives, not political leaders. The classics, the basic ingredient of male education, were ignored in favor of more practical courses: a little French; a taste of the arts—music, painting, and fine sewing; enough mathematics to do household accounts; enough English to write a badly spelled letter. The primary emphasis was on ladylike behavior in society. The academies were for the upper classes; poor girls slipped in on scholarships were taught the same things in the expectation that they would be governesses and teach the children of the rich.

For most girls, the academies provided what they needed for their limited section of the world; they accepted and believed in the inferiority of women and were hesitant to undergo the rigors of learning for fear their minds would collapse under the strain. For others, however, the academy was not enough. Once they had learned to read, they began to realize the handicaps they faced without sufficient education. They watched their brothers go on to University and careers in government, knowing that they themselves were just as capable but would be forever shut away from the center of power. Even of this group, only a few protested. The majority exercised such power as they could behind the scenes. Some, like Georgiana, Duchess of Devonshire, actively campaigned for the politicians they favored and were hotly criticized for their efforts. A rare few wanted to be in the arena themselves, but they never had the slightest glimmer of hope for such glory. The forces against them were too great; woman had become the guardian of the moral standard,

she was too "pure" for politics, too "good" for the marketplace, too weak
for the battle. She should be protected in her padded and gilded cage,
leaving the work of the world to men. Even the women themselves
believed it.

In the light of such overwhelming pressure, it is extraordinary that
any women at all resisted. Yet on every level, there is evidence that some
did, either from physical necessity or from intellectual principle. Among
the working class, widows often continued their husbands' work as
printers, drapers, pub-keepers, and the like. Hannah Snell, left completely alone, disguised herself as a man, joined the army, then the navy,
and only when she was retired and claimed a pension did she reveal
herself. She received her pension, invested in a profitable tavern, and
operated it for the rest of her life. Charlotte Charke, abandoned and with
a child, appeared sometimes as a man, sometimes as a woman, enduring
the extreme physical hardships of the strolling player.

Upper-class women of intellect found the life of tea-table gossip,
intrigue, and cards unutterably boring and turned to reading, writing,
and literary meetings for relief. The major figure in this area was
Elizabeth Robinson Montagu, who formed the first "salon" in England.
Later ridiculed as "Queen of the Blues" (i.e. bluestockings or intellectual
women), she entertained every literary figure of note during the years of
her reign, and women who usually hid their minds under cascades of
frothy chatter came to her home in London's South Audley Street to share
their ideas with others who could give intelligent and respectful attention.
Here Hester Chapone read her translations from the Greek, which Dr.
Johnson considered among the best; the success of Hannah More's
tragedy *Regulus* was celebrated; and young Fanny Burney, after her
Evelina had become the rage, amused herself by baiting the older women.
For the first time, these women unashamedly enjoyed the stimulus of
intellectual give-and-take. It was a greater luxury than may be supposed
today, for in eighteenth-century London, women, like children, were
expected to be seen and not heard. In mixed company women listened,
their contribution limited to such expressions or questions as would lead
men on to pontificate and enlighten from their vast store of knowledge.

The attitudes of previous centuries were not erased overnight. Indeed,
many of them are with us today and form the basis for problems we are
still trying to solve. Some of the women we have included in our selections
could be speaking today, others reflect the attitudes of their own times,
attitudes rooted in our culture and thought, but now slowly, confusedly,

beginning to be examined for the values they represent. It is our hope that through these varied voices can be heard both the ephemeral and the constant, what was accepted or rejected by succeeding generations, and what has remained the distinctive viewpoint of *The Female Spectator.*

Mary R. Mahl
University of Southern California

Helene Koon
California State College,
San Bernardino

DAME JULIAN OF NORWICH

1342–1417(?)

DAME JULIAN OF NORWICH, Anchoress at the Church of St. Julian in Conisford, Norwich, has been called the "first English woman of letters." Her book, *Sixteen Revelations of Divine Love,* is the earliest literary work in English known to have been written by a woman; no doubt many earlier works that are listed under "Anonymous" or "Author Unknown" were composed by women. Dame Julian never even hints that she was a pioneer in this field.

We do not know the legal name of Julian, who adopted the name of the patron saint of the church beside which her anchorhold was built. Born about 1342, contemporary to Chaucer, Gower, Langland, Wycliffe, and Walter Hilton, Julian received her education at the convent at Carrow, a Benedictine establishment to which many noble families sent their daughters. At the time of Julian's residence, at least seven of the nuns were daughters of former bailiffs (municipal magistrates) or members of Parliament; all came from wealthy homes. We are inclined to regard the Prioress and the nun depicted in Chaucer's *Canterbury Tales* as models of medieval women who entered religious orders. And like Madam Eglantyne, who was so graphically described in Chaucer's "Prologue," Dame Julian was well aware of the "courtesy" or aristocratic manners and living conditions; in her descriptions of God she constantly uses the language appropriate to a noblewoman who would picture her father and his influence as lord of the manor. But there the comparison ends.

Deeply religious, Julian prayed for three gifts: to have the mind of Christ's passion, to suffer bodily illness, and to have God's gift of three wounds. Her second wish was granted while she was in the convent in May 1373. Dangerously ill, she received the last rites of the Church with her mother, her priest, and several nuns in attendance. Fifteen "shewings" or visions occurred to her between four and nine in the morning, and the sixteenth on the following night. Apparently this experience moved her to decide upon her recovery to live the life of an anchoress, enclosed in the tiny house or anchorhold that was under the control of the Carrow convent at the Church of St. Julian. From time to time a nun who chose such enclosure would be assigned to this residence in order to spend time in contemplation and prayer undistracted. Here Julian entered at the age of thirty.

A window in the living room of the anchorhold opened into the chancel of the church so that the recluse might enter into the worship and the sacraments; another window opened on the courtyard so that she might have contact, when she chose, with the outside world. Standard rules for this kind of life are found in *The Ancrene Riwle*, a medieval handbook for anchoresses that describes in detail the kind of life Julian chose. Two servants attended her—one cared for household duties indoors, and the other, "a plain, older woman," did the marketing and other chores that required her to engage in business outside. We know from contemporary accounts that Julian counseled many inquirers and was renowned for her piety and for her intelligent, practical advice. One visitor was Margery Kempe, whose life and work are treated elsewhere in this book.

Julian lived the contemplative life of an anchoress for twenty years before she called for the help of a scribe to record the visions that had never been far from her thoughts. By this time the first two gifts she had sought—to have the mind of Christ's passion and to suffer bodily illness—had been abundantly granted, and she had learned that the third, the gift of three wounds, was a spiritual one. Her book of instruction for the faithful is written in lively, colloquial language, incorporating figures of speech that betray the social position and personality of the author. She claims to be a "simple creature," unlearned, but in twentieth-century terms these claims are unjustified. She meant only that she was untrained in theology and knew little or no Latin. It is possible that after 1396 she obtained a copy of Wycliffe's translation of the epistles of St. Paul, as she quotes from them freely in her advice to Margery Kempe. Although the Church forbade the clergy to use this English translation, many had copies made and believed that this work was "intelligible, accurate, and unbiased," a boon to those who struggled with St. Jerome's Vulgate, the official Latin text.

Several recluses, including at least one man, occupied the anchorhold after Julian's death, up to the time of the Reformation; then the little house fell into ruin. On June 7, 1942, a German bomb completely destroyed the Church of St. Julian, but ten years later it was rebuilt with great care.

The French Benedictine, Serenus de Cressy, published an edition of *Sixteen Revelations of Divine Love* in 1670, one copy of which is in the Folger Shakespeare Library, Washington, D.C. All other known editions have been published in the twentieth century.

BIBLIOGRAPHY

Manuscripts

British Museum, Additional Ms., 37790, the Amherst Ms., 1413.
Westminster Cathedral Library, late fifteenth or early sixteenth century. (This contains only extracts from the expanded version.)
Bibliotheque Nationale, Paris, Fonds Anglais No. 40, sixteenth century.
British Museum, Sloane Ms. 2499, mid-seventeenth century.
British Museum, Sloane Ms. 3705, late seventeenth or early eighteenth century.

Editions

Julian of Norwich. *XVI Revelations of Divine Love*. Published by R. F. S. Cressy, 1670. (No editor or place on title page.)
Harford, Rev. Dundas, ed. *Comfortable Words for Christ's Lovers*. London: H. K. Allenson, 1911. (Transcription of the short version, B. M. Add. Ms. 37790.)
Hudleston, Dom. R., ed. *Revelations of Divine Love*. London: Burns & Oates, 1927. 2d ed., Westminster, Md.: Newman Press, 1952. (Long version, from Sloane Ms. 2499.)
Reynolds, Sister Anna Maria, ed. *A Shewing of God's Love*. London: Longmans, 1958. (Short version, B. M. Add. Ms. 37790.)
Walsh, James, S. J., ed. and trans. *Revelations of Divine Love*. St. Meinrad, Indiana: Abbey Press, 1974. (Paris Ms., basically.)
Warrack, Grace, ed. *Revelations of Divine Love*. London: Methuen & Co., 1901. 14th ed., 1952. (Long version, from Sloane Ms. 2499.)
Wolters, Clifton, ed. *Revelations of Divine Love*. Bungay, England: Penguin Books, 1966. (Long version, from Sloane Ms. 2499.)

Related Readings

Chambers, P. Franklin. *Juliana of Norwich*. London: Gollancz, 1955.
Jewson, Charles B. *People of Medieval Norwich*. Norwich, England: Jarrold & Sons Ltd., 1956.
Knowles, David. *The English Mystical Tradition*. New York: Harper, 1961.
Molinari, Paul, S. J. *The Teaching of a Fourteenth-Century English Mystic*. London: Longman's, 1958. (Quotations are from the Reynolds and Hudleston editions.)

Stone, Robert. *Middle English Prose Style: Margery Kempe and Julian of Norwich.* The Hague and Paris: Mouton, 1970.

Thouless, Robert Henry. *The Lady Julian.* London: Society for the Propagation of Christian Knowledge; New York and Toronto: Macmillan Co., 1924.

Walsh, James. *Pre-Reformation English Spirituality.* Bronx, N.Y.: Fordham University Press, 1966.

❦

XVI Revelations of Divine Love

DAME JULIAN OF NORWICH

[1670 edition]

Here beginneth the first chapter.

This is a Revelation of Love, that Jesu Christ our endless bliss made in xvi. shewings: of which,

The first is of his precious crowning of thorns, and therein was contained and specified the Blessed Trinity, with the Incarnation and the uniting between God and man's soul, with many fair shewings and teachings of endless wisdom and love: in which all the shewings that follow be grounded and joined.

The second is of the discoloring of his fair face, in tokening of his dear-worthy passion.

The third is that our Lord God Almighty, all wisdom and all love, right also verily as he hath made all things that are right, also verily he doth and worketh all things that are done.

The fourth is scourging of his tender body with plenteous shedding of his precious blood.

The fifth is that the field is overcome by the precious passion of Christ.

The sixth is the worshipful thanking of our Lord God, in which he rewardeth all his blessed servants in heaven.

The seventh is oftentimes feeling of weal and woe: feeling of weal is gracious touching and lightening with true sikerness [security] of endless joy. The feeling of woe is of temptation by heaviness, and weariness of our fleshly living with ghostly understanding, that we be kept also verily in love, in woe as in weal, by the goodness of God.

The eighth is the last pains of Christ and his cruel dying.

The ninth is of the liking which is in the Blessed Trinity of the hard passion of Christ after his rueful and sorrowful dying, in which joy and liking he will that we be in solace and mirth with him, till that we come to the glory in heaven.

The tenth is our Lord Jesu Christ by love his blessed heart even cloven in two.

The eleventh is an high and ghostly shewing of his dear-worthy Mother.

The twelfth is that our Lord God is all Sovereign being.

The thirteenth is that our Lord God will that we have great regard to all the deeds which he hath done in the great nobility of all things making, and of the excellency of man's making, the which is above all his works, and of the precious amends that he hath made for man's sin, turning all our blame into endless worship. Then meaneth he thus, "Behold and see, for by the same Might, Wisdom and Goodness that I have done all this, by the same Might, Wisdom and goodness I shall make well all that is not well, and thou shalt see it." And in this he will that we keep us in the faith and truth of Holy Church, not willing to wit [know] his privities, not but as it longeth to us in this life.

The fourteenth is that our Lord God is the ground of our beseeching. Herein was seen two fair properties, that one is rightful prayer; that other is very trust, which he wills both [to] be alike large, and thus our prayer liketh [pleaseth] him, and he of his goodness fulfilleth it.

The fifteenth is that we should suddenly be taken from all our pain, and from all our woe, and of his goodness we shall come up above, where we shall have our Lord Jesu to our meed [reward], and for to be fulfilled with joy and bliss in heaven.

The sixteenth is that the Blessed Trinity, our Maker in Christ Jesu our Savior, endlessly dwelleth in our soul, worshipfully rewarding and commanding all things, us mightly and wisely saving and keeping for love, and we shall not be overcome of our Enemy.

THE THIRTEENTH REVELATION

The xxvii Chapter

And after this our Lord brought to my mind the longing that I had to him before; and I saw nothing letted [hindered] me but sin: and so I beheld generally in us all; and methought, if sin had not been, we should all have been clean and like to our Lord as he made us. And thus in my folly before this time, often I wondered why by the great foresaid wisdom of God, the beginning of sin was not letted, for then thought me that all should have been well. This stirring was much to be forsaken; and nevertheless, mourning and sorrow I made therefore, without reason and discretion. But Jesu, that in this vision, informed me of all that we needed, answered by this word, and said, "Sin is behovely [must needs be], but all shall be well, and all shall be well, and all manner of thing shall be well." In this naked word sin, our Lord brought to my mind generally all that is not good; and the shameful despite and the uttermost tribulation that he bear for us in this life, and his dying and all his pains and passion bodily and ghostly, and the pains of all his creatures ghostly and bodily. For we be all in part troubled, and we shall be troubled following our Master Jesu, till we be full purged of our deadly flesh, and of all our inward affections, which be not very good. And the beholding of this with all the pains that ever were, or ever shall be. And with all this I understood the passion of Christ, for the most pain and over-passing. And all this was shewed in a touch and readily passed over into comfort; for our good Lord would not that the soul were afraid of this ugly sight, but I saw not sin; for I believe it had no manner of substance, nor no part of being, nor it might not be known but by the pain that is caused thereof. And this pain is something as to my sight for a time, for it purgeth and maketh us to know our self, and ask mercy; for the passion of our Lord is comfort to us against all this, and so is his blessed will; and for the tender love that our good Lord hath to all that shall be saved, he comforteth readily and sweetly, meaning thus: "It is true, that sin is cause of all this pain, but all shall be well, and all manner of thing shall be well." These words were shewed full tenderly, shewing no manner of blame to me, nor to none that shall be safe. Then were it great unkindness of me to blame or wonder on God of my sin, sithen [since] he blameth not me for sin. And in these same words I saw an high marvelous privity hid in God, which privity he shall openly make, and shall be known to us in heaven. In which knowing we shall verily see the cause why he suffered sin to come. In which sight, we shall endlessly have joy.

THE SIXTEENTH REVELATION

The lxvii Chapter

And in my sleep at the beginning methought the fiend set him in my throat, putting forth a visage full near my face, like a young man. And it was long and wonder lean, I saw never none such. The color was red like the tile stone when it is new brent, with black spots therein, like freckles, fouler than the tile stone; his hair was red, as rust not scoured; afore with side locks hanging down in flakes; he grinned upon me with a shrewd look, and shewed me white teeth. And so mykill [much] me thought it the more ugly; body, nor hands had he none, shapely; but with his paws he held me in the throat, and would have stopped my breath, and killed me, but he might not. This ugly shewing was made sleeping, and so was none other. And in all this time I trusted to be saved and kept by the mercy of God. And our courteous Lord gave me grace to wake, and I unnethes [scarcely] had any life. The persons that were with me beheld me, and wet my temples, and my heart began to comfort. And anon a little smoke came in at the door, with a great heat, and a foul stench; and then I said, "Benedicite dominus, is it all on fire that is here?" And I went [thought] it had been a bodily fire, that should burn us all to death. I asked them that were with me, if they felt any stench; they said nay, they felt none; I said, "Blessed be God," for then wist I well it was the fiend that was come only to tempt me. And anon I took me to that our Lord had shewed me on the same day, with all the faith of Holy Church; for I beheld it as both in one, and fled thereto as to my comfort. And anon all vanished away, and I was brought to great rest and peace, without sickness of body, or dread of conscience.

The lxviii Chapter

And then our good Lord opened my ghostly eye, and shewed me my soul in the midst of my heart. I saw the soul so large as it were an endless world, and also as it were a blessed kingdom. And by the conditions that I saw therein, I understood that it is a worshipful city. In midst of that city our Lord Jesu, very God and very man, a fair person and of large stature, highest Bishop, most solemn King, worshipful Lord. And I saw him clothed solemnly in worship; he sitteth in the soul, even right in peace and rest. And he ruleth and giveth heaven and earth, and all that is. The Man-hood with the God-head sitteth in rest: the God-head ruleth and giveth without any instrument or busy-ness. And the soul is all occupied with the blessed God-head: that is, sovereign Might, sovereign Wisdom, and sovereign Goodness. The place that Jesu taketh in our soul he shall never remove without end, as to my sight; for in us is his homeliest home, and his endless dwelling. And in this he sheweth the liking that he hath of the making of man's soul; for as well as the Father might make a creature, and as well as the Son might make a creature, so well would the Holy

Ghost that man's soul were made, and so it was done. And therefore the blessedful Trinity enjoyed without end in the making of man's soul. For he saw without beginning, what should like him without end. All thing that he hath made sheweth his Lordship, as understanding was given in the same time by example of a creature, that is led to see great nobleness, and kingdoms longing [belonging] to a Lord. And when it had seen all the nobleness beneath, then marveling, it was stirred to seek up above to that high place where the Lord dwelleth, knowing by reason that his dwelling is in the worthiest place. And thus I understand truly that our soul may never have rest in things that is beneath it self. And when it cometh above all creatures into it self, yet may it not abide in the beholding of it self, but all the beholding is blessedly set in God; that is, the Maker dwelling therein; for in man's soul is his very dwelling. And the highest light and the brightest shining of the City is the glorious love of our Lord God, as to my sight. And what may make us more enjoy in God, than to see in him that he enjoyeth in us highest of all his works? For I saw in the same shewing that if the blessed Trinity might have made man's soul any better, any fairer, any nobler than it was made, he should not have been full pleased with making of man's soul. But for he made man's soul as fair, as good, as precious, as he might make it a creature, therefore the blessed Trinity is full pleased without end in the making of man's soul. And he will that our hearts be mightily raised above the deepness of the earth, and all vain sorrows, and enjoy in him. This was a delectable sight, and a restful shewing that is without end. And the beholding of this whiles we are here, it is full pleasant to God, and full great speed to us. And the soul that thus beholdeth, it maketh him like to him that is beholden, and oned it [made it whole] in rest and in peace by his grace. And this was a singular joy and bliss to me that I saw him sitting: for the truth of sitting shewed endless dwelling. And he gave me knowing truly that it was he that shewed me all before: and when I had beholden all this with advisement, then shewed our good Lord's words full meekly, without voice, and without opening of lips, right as he had done afore, and said full sweetly: "Wit it now well, it was no raving that thou sawest today; but take it and believe it, and keep thee therein, and comfort thee therewith, and trust thereto, and thou shalt not be overcome." These last words were said for learning of true sikerness [assurance]; that is, our Lord Jesu that shewed me all. And right as in the first word, that our good Lord shewed, meaning his blessed Passion, herewith is the fiend overcome; right so he said in the last word with full true faithfulness meaning us all: "Thou shalt not be overcome." And all this learning and this true comfort is general to all mine even Christian, as it is aforesaid; and so is God's will. And this word, "Thou shalt not be overcome," was said full sharply, and full mightily for sickness and comfort against all tribulations that may come. He said not, "Thou shalt not be troubled, thou shalt not be travailed, thou shalt not be diseased;" but he said, "Thou shalt not be overcome." God will that we take heed at this word, and that we be ever mighty in faithful trusting in weal and woe; for he loveth us, and liketh us: and so will he that we love him and like him, and mightily trust in him, and all shall be well: and soon all was close, and I saw no more after this.

DAME MARGERY KEMPE

1373–1438(?)

A LTHOUGH BORN INTO the prosperous family of John Brunham, who became mayor of Lynn (now King's Lynn), Norfolk, five times, Margery Brunham Kempe apparently received little or no formal education. The few Latin and French words that she incorporated in her autobiography were doubtless learned in church or acquired in her travels. At the age of twenty she married John Kempe, one of the four chamberlains (tax collectors) of Lynn from 1394 to 1395. She bore him fourteen children and engaged unsuccessfully in the businesses of brewing and milling before she became famous—or infamous—as a religious enthusiast.

Her *Book* provides an earthy account of her life and includes not only records of visions and revelations, but also homely personal anecdotes that enable the reader to sense the tenor of the times. She writes of her visits to Dame Julian in Norwich and the maid of St. Birgitta in Rome with dignity and reverence; then she describes the last months of her husband's life with all the candor of a Wife of Bath.

Comparisons of Kempe with Chaucer's character are too numerous to be ignored, but she also bears an interesting resemblance to St. Birgitta of Sweden, who died the year of Kempe's birth and was canonized in 1391. Kempe was probably familiar with St. Birgitta's *Revelations*; both women produced books that describe strikingly similar experiences. Both women had a great propensity for weeping; both claimed to have been present (at least in visions) at the birth of Christ; both recounted similar events in the life of Christ, frequently in similar detail; both advised prelates but refused to accept advice they believed to be contrary to the will of God as revealed to them in private; each had a son who proved to be a sore trial.

Kempe's first amanuensis, or scribe, is humorously described in the Preface to the *Book*: he could write neither English nor Dutch well. He died ca. 1431, and nearly four years later a literate priest reluctantly consented to continue the work. The second amanuensis was probably responsible for the uniformity of phonology, morphology, and spelling. Later, another scribe named Salthows, or Salthouse, prepared the fair copy of the manuscript that is owned by Captain Butler-Bowdon. This copy probably dates before 1450. The events recorded are not necessarily in strict chronological order, but Kempe claims absolute accuracy and truth for every part of the *Book* except the chronology.

Until 1936 only brief excerpts of the *Book of Margery Kempe* were known. These had first been printed in 1501 by Wynkyn de Worde and then modernized and reprinted by Henry Pepwell in 1527. In 1910 Edmund Gardner further modernized Pepwell's edition (which contained six other mystical treatises besides Kempe's) and identified the author as "perhaps Margeria filia Johannis Kemp," fl. 1298. "The revelations show that she was (or had been) a woman of some wealth and social position, who had abandoned the world to become an ancress, following the life prescribed in that gem of early English devotional literature, the *Ancren Riwle*. It is clearly only a fragment of her complete book (whatever that may have been); but it is enough to show that she was a worthy precursor of that other great woman mystic of East Anglia: Juliana of Norwich." The discovery and identification of the complete manuscript of the *Book of Margery Kempe* by Col. Butler-Bowdon in 1936 proved Gardner's dating wrong by more than a century, and his assessment of the whole work seriously in error. The work of Sanford Meech, Hope Emily Allen, R. W. Chambers, and Col. W. Butler-Bowdon in editing and evaluating the newly discovered manuscript has radically altered the earlier identification and criticism.

In the *Book of Margery Kempe*, as one critic puts it, "we feel the pulse of the age," and we have the first autobiography in English—dictated by an illiterate woman.

BIBLIOGRAPHY

Manuscript

The Book of Margery Kempe. Scribe: Salthows, ca. 1440–50. Owned by Captain M. E. Butler-Bowdon.

Editions

Butler-Bowdon, Col. W. E. I., ed. *The Book of Margery Kempe*. London, 1936. Reprinted in World Classics, London: Oxford University Press, 1952. Modernized text.

de Worde, Wynkyn, ed. *A Shorte Treatyse of Contemplacyon . . . out of the boke of Margerie kempe of Lynn.* London: Wynkyn de Worde, 1501. Only extant copy known is in the Cambridge University Library. Contains excerpts, with archaic words changed and modernized.

Gardner, Edmund G., ed. *The Cell of Self-Knowing.* New York and London: New Medieval Library, 1910. A reprint and further modernization of Pepwell.

Meech, Sanford Brown, ed., with prefatory note by Hope Emily Allen. *The Book of Margery Kempe.* London: Early English Text Society, 1940. Transcription of Butler-Bowdon Ms.

Pepwell, Henry, ed. *A Shorte treatyse of Contemplacyon. . . .* London, 1521. Contains six other mystical treatises as well.

Related Readings

Cholmeley, Katharine. *Margery Kempe, Genius and Mystic.* London: Longmans, Green & Co., 1947.

Collis, Louise. *An Apprentice Saint.* London: Michael Joseph, 1964.

Stone, Robert K. *Middle English Prose Style: Margery Kempe and Julian of Norwich.* The Hague and Paris: Mouton, 1970.

Thornton, Martin. *Margery Kempe: An Example in the English Pastoral Tradition.* London: Society for the Propagation of Christian Knowledge, 1960. Provides "classified skeleton commentary."

The Book of Margery Kempe

*[ca. 1436. From a Modern Version by
W. Butler-Bowdon, London, 1936]*

THE PREFACE

A short treatise of a creature set in great pomp and pride of the world, who later was drawn to Our Lord by great poverty, sickness, shames and great reproofs in many divers countries and places, of which tribulations some shall be shewn hereafter, not in the order in which they befell, but as the creature could have mind of them, when they were written. For it was twenty years and more from the time she had forsaken the world and busily cleft unto Our Lord, ere this book was written.

Notwithstanding, this creature had great counsel to have written her tribulations and her feelings, and a White Friar proferred her to write freely, if she would. And she was warned in her spirit that she should not write so soon; and many years after, she was bidden in her spirit to write.

And then it was written first by a man who could neither well write English nor Dutch, so it was unable to be read save only by special grace, for there was so much obloquy and slander of this creature that but few men would believe this creature.

So, at the last, a priest was sore moved to write this treatise, and he could not well read it for four years together. Later, at the request of this creature and compelled by his own conscience, he essayed again to read it, and it was much more easy than it was aforetime.

And so he began to write in the year of Our Lord 1436, on the day next after Mary Magdalene, for the information of this creature.

CHAPTER I

When this creature was twenty years of age, or some deal more, she was married to a worshipful burgess (of Lynne) and was with child within a short time, as nature would. And after she had conceived, she was belaboured with great accesses [fits] till the child was born, and then, what with the labour she had in childing, and the sickness going before, she despaired of her life, weening she might not live. And she sent for her ghostly father, for she had a thing on her conscience which she had never shown before that time in all her life. For she was ever hindered by her enemy, the devil, evermore saying to her that whilst she was in good health she needed no confession, but to do penance by herself alone and all should be forgiven, for God is merciful enough. And therefore this creature oftentimes did great penance in fasting in bread and water, and other deeds of alms with devout prayers, save she would not show that in confession.

And when she was at any time sick or diseased, the devil said in her mind that she would be damned because she was not shriven of that default. Wherefore after her child was born, she, not trusting to live, sent for her ghostly father, as is said before, in full will to be shriven of all her lifetime, as near as she could. And when she came to the point for to say that thing which she had so long concealed, her confessor was a little too hasty and began sharply to reprove her, before she had fully said her intent, and so she would no more say for aught he might do. Anon, for the dread she had of damnation on the one side, and his sharp reproving of her on the other side, this creature went out of her mind and was wondrously vexed and laboured with spirits for half a year, eight weeks, and odd days.

And in this time she saw, as she thought devils opening their mouths all inflamed with burning waves of fire, as if they would have swallowed her in, sometimes ramping [wildly clutching] at her, sometimes threatening her, pulling her and hauling her, night and day during the aforesaid time. Also the devils cried upon her with great threatenings, and bade her that she should forsake Christendom, her faith, and deny her God, His Mother and all the Saints in Heaven, her good works and all good virtues, her father, her mother, and all her friends. And so she did. She slandered her husband, her friends, and her own self. She said many a wicked word, and many a cruel word; she knew no virtue nor goodness; she desired all wickedness; like as the spirits tempted her to say and do, so she said and did. She would have destroyed herself many a time at their stirrings and have been damned with them in Hell, and in witness thereof, she bit her own hand so violently, that the mark was seen all her life after.

And also she rived the skin on her body against her heart with her nails spitefully, for she had no other instruments, and worse she would have done, but that she was bound and kept with strength day and night so that she might not have her will. And when she had long been laboured in these and many other temptations, so that men weened she should never have escaped or lived, then on a time as she lay alone and her keepers were from her, Our Merciful Lord Jesus Christ, ever to be trusted, worshipped be His Name, never forsaking His servant in time of need, appeared to His creature who had forsaken Him, in the likeness of a man, most seemly, most beauteous and most amiable that ever might be seen with man's eye, clad in a mantle of purple silk, sitting upon her bedside, looking upon her with so blessed a face that she was strengthened in all her spirit, and said to her these words:—

"Daughter, why has thou forsaken Me, and I forsook never thee?"

And anon, as He said these words, she saw verily how the air opened, as bright as lightning. And He rose up into the air, not right hastily and quickly, but fair and easily, so that she might well behold Him in the air till it was closed again.

And anon this creature became calmed in her wits and reason, as well as ever she was before, and prayed her husband as soon as he came to her, that she might have the keys of the buttery to take her meat and drink as she had done before. Her maidens and her keepers counselled him that he should deliver her no keys, as they said she would but give away such goods as there were, for she knew not what she said, as they weened.

Nevertheless, her husband ever having tenderness and compassion for her, commanded that they should deliver to her the keys; and she took her meat and drink as her bodily strength would serve her, and knew her friends and her household and all others that came to see how Our Lord Jesus Christ had wrought His grace in her, so, blessed may He be, Who ever is near in tribulation. When men think He is far from them, He is full near by His grace. Afterwards, this creature did all other occupations as fell to her to do, wisely and soberly enough, save she knew not verily the call of Our Lord.

CHAPTER II

When this creature had thus graciously come again to her mind, she thought that she was bound to God and that she would be His servant. Nevertheless, she would not leave her pride or her pompous array, which she had used beforetime, either for her husband, or for any other man's counsel. Yet she knew full well that men said of her full much villainy, for she wore gold pipes on her head, and her hoods, with the tippets, were slashed. Her cloaks also were slashed and laid with divers colours between the slashes, so that they should be the more staring to men's sight, and herself the more worshipped.

And when her husband spoke to her to leave her pride, she answered shrewdly and shortly, and said that she was come of worthy kindred—he should never have wedded her—for her father was sometime Mayor of the town of N . . . [Lynne] and afterwards he was alderman of the High Guild of the Trinity in N . . . And therefore she would keep the worship of her kindred whatever any man said.

She had full great envy of her neighbours, that they should be as well arrayed as she. All her desire was to be worshipped by people. She would not take heed of any chastisement, nor be content with the goods that God had sent her, as her husband was, but ever desired more and more.

Then for pure covetousness, and to maintain her pride, she began to brew, and was one of the greatest brewers in the town of N . . . for three years or four, till she lost much money, for she had never been used thereto. For, though she had ever such good servants, cunning in brewing, yet it would never succeed with them. For when the ale was as fair standing under barm [froth that forms on top of fermenting malt liquors] as any man might see, suddenly the barm would fall down, so that the ale was lost, one brewing after another, so that her servants were ashamed and would not dwell with her.

Then this creature thought how God had punished her aforetime—and she could not take heed—and now again, by the loss of her goods. Then she left and brewed no more.

Then she asked her husband's mercy because she would not follow his counsel aforetime, and she said that her pride and sin were the cause of all her punishing, and that she would amend and that she had trespassed with good will.

Yet she left not the world altogether, for she now bethought herself of a new housewifery. She had a horse-mill. She got herself two good horses and a man to grind men's corn, and thus she trusted to get her living. This enterprise lasted not long, for in a short time after, on Corpus Christi Eve, befell this marvel. This man, being in good health of body, and his two horses sturdy and gentle, had pulled well in the mill beforetime, and now he took one of these horses and put him in the mill as he had done before, and this horse would draw no draught in the mill for anything the man might do. The man was sorry and essayed with all his wits how he should make this horse pull. Sometimes he led him by the head, sometimes he beat him, sometimes he cherished him and all availed not, nor he would rather go backward than forward. Then this man set a sharp pair of spurs on his heels and rode on the horse's back to make him pull, and it was never the better. When the man saw it would work in no way, he set up this horse again in the stable, and gave him corn, and he ate well and freshly. And later he took the other horse and put him in the mill, and like his fellow did, so did he, for he would not draw for anything the man might do. Then the man forsook his service and would no longer remain with the aforesaid creature. Anon, it was noised about the town of N . . . that neither man nor beast would serve the said creature.

Then some said she was accursed; some said God took open vengeance on her; some said one thing and some said another. Some wise men, whose minds were more grounded in the love of Our Lord, said that it was the high mercy of Our Lord Jesus Christ that called her from the pride and vanity of the wretched world.

Then this creature, seeing all these adversities coming on every side, thought they were the scourges of Our Lord that would chastise her for her sin. Then she asked God's mercy, and forsook her pride, her covet-

ousness, and the desire that she had for the worship of the world, and did
great bodily penance, and began to enter the way of everlasting life as
shall be told hereafter.

CHAPTER VI

Another day, she gave herself up to meditation as she had been bidden
and lay still, not knowing what she might best think of. Then she said to
Our Lord Jesus Christ:

"Jesus, of what shall I think?"

Our Lord answered to her mind:—"Daughter, think of My Mother,
for she is the cause of all the grace that thou hast."

Then, anon, she saw Saint Anne, great with child, and she prayed
Saint Anne that she might be her maiden, and her servant. And anon, Our
Lady was born, and then she arranged to take the child to herself and
keep it till it was twelve years of age, with good meat and drink, with fair
white clothing and white kerchiefs.

Then she said to the blessed child:—"Lady, you shall be the Mother
of God."

The blessed child answered and said:—"I would I were worthy to be
the handmaiden of her that should conceive the Son of God."

The creature said:—"I pray you, Lady, if that grace befall, you
renounce not my service."

The blessful child passed away for a certain time, the creature being
quiet in contemplation, and afterwards came again and said:—

"Daughter, now am I become the Mother of God."

And then the creature fell down on her knees with great reverence and
great weeping and said:—

"I am not worthy, Lady, to do you service."

"Yes, daughter," said she, "follow thou me, thy service liketh me
well."

Then went she forth with Our Lady and with Joseph, bearing with
her a pottle of wine and honey, and spices thereto. Then went they forth
to Elizabeth, Saint John the Baptist's mother, and when they met together, each worshipped the other, and so they dwelt together, with great
grace and gladness twelve weeks. And Saint John was born, and Our
Lady took him up from the earth with all manner of reverence, and gave
him to his mother, saying of him that he should be a holy man, and
blessed him. Afterwards they took leave of each other with compassion-

ate tears. Then the creature fell down on her knees to Saint Elizabeth, and begged her to pray for her to Our Lady that she might do her service and pleasure.

"Daughter," said Elizabeth, "me-seemeth thou does right well thy duty."

Then went the creature forth with Our Lady to Bethlehem and purchased her shelter every night with great reverence, and Our Lady was received with glad cheer. Also she begged for Our Lady fair white cloths and kerchiefs to swathe her Son in, when He was born; and when Jesus was born, she provided bedding for Our Lady to lie in with her Blessed Son. Later she begged meat for Our Lady and her Blessed Child, and she swathed Him with bitter tears of compassion, having mind of the sharp death He would suffer for love of sinful men, saying unto Him:—

"Lord, I shall fare fair with You. I will not bind You tight. I pray You be not displeased with me."

CHAPTER VII

And afterwards on the twelfth day, when three Kings came with their gifts, and worshipped Our Lord in His Mother's lap, this creature, Our Lady's handmaiden, beholding all the process in contemplation, wept wondrous sore.

And when she saw that they would take their leave to go home again into their country, she could not bear that they should go from the Presence of Our Lord, and for wonder that they should go, she cried wondrous sore. Soon after came an angel, and bade Our Lady and Joseph to go from the country of Bethlehem into Egypt. Then went this creature forth with Our Lady, day by day finding her harbourage with great reverence and many sweet thoughts and high meditations, and also high contemplation, sometimes continuing in weeping two hours and often longer in mind of Our Lord's Passion without ceasing, sometimes for her own sin, sometimes for the sin of the people, sometimes for the souls in Purgatory, sometimes for them that were in poverty and dis-ease, for she desired to comfort them all.

Sometimes she wept full plenteously and full boisterously for desire of the bliss of Heaven, and because she was so long deferred therefrom. She greatly coveted to be delivered out of this wretched world. Our Lord Jesus Christ said to her mind that she should abide and languish in love, "for I have ordained thee to kneel before the Trinity, to pray for all the world, for many hundred thousand souls shall be saved by thy prayers. So ask, daughter, what thou wilt, and I will grant thee thine asking."

The creature said:—"Lord, I ask mercy and preservation from everlasting damnation for me and all the world. Chastise us here how Thou wilt and in Purgatory also, and of Thy great mercy, keep us from damnation."

CHAPTER XVIII

This creature was charged and commanded in her soul that she should go to a White Friar, in the same city of Norwich, called William Sowthfeld, a good man and a holy liver, to show him the grace that God wrought in her, as she was commanded and came to the friar on a forenoon, and was with him in a chapel a long time, and showed him her meditations, and what God had wrought in her soul, to find out if she were deceived by any illusion or not.

This good man, the White Friar, ever whilst she told him her feelings, holding up his hands, said:—"Jesu mercy and gramercy."

"Sister," he said, "dread not for your manner of living, for it is the Holy Ghost working plenteously His grace in your soul. Thank Him highly for His goodness, for we all be bound to thank Him for you, Who now in our days will inspire His grace in you, to the help and comfort of us all, who are supported by your prayers and by such others as ye be. And we are preserved from many mischiefs and diseases which we should suffer, and worthily, for our trespass. Never were such good creatures amongst us. Blessed be Almighty God for His goodness. And therefore, sister, I counsel you that ye dispose yourself to receive the gifts of God as lowly and meekly as ye can, and put no obstacle or objection against the goodness of the Holy Ghost, for He may give His gifts where He will, and of unworthy He maketh worthy, of sinful He maketh rightful. His mercy is ever ready unto us, unless the fault be in ourselves, for He dwelleth not in a body subject to sin. He flieth all false feigning and falsehood: He asketh of us a lowly, a meek and a contrite heart, with a good will. Our Lord sayeth Himself:—'My Spirit shall rest upon a meek man, a contrite man, and one dreading My words.'

"Sister, I trust to Our Lord that ye have these conditions either in your will or your affection, or else in both, and I believe not that Our Lord suffereth them to be deceived endlessly, that set all their trust in Him, and seek and desire nothing but Him only, as I hope ye do. And therefore believe fully that Our Lord loveth you and worketh His grace in you. I pray God to increase it and continue it to His everlasting worship, for His mercy."

The aforesaid creature was much comforted both in body and in soul by this good man's words, and greatly strengthened in her faith.

Then she was bidden by Our Lord to go to an anchoress in the same city, named Dame Jelyan [Julian], and so she did, and showed her the grace that God put into her soul, of compunction, contrition, sweetness and devotion, compassion with holy meditation and high contemplation, and full many holy speeches and dalliance [chat, friendly converse] that Our Lord spake to her soul; and many wonderful revelations, which she showed to the anchoress to find out if there were any deceit in them, for the anchoress was expert in such things, and good counsel could give.

The anchoress, hearing the marvellous goodness of Our Lord, highly thanked God with all her heart for His visitation, counselling this creature to be obedient to the will of Our Lord God and to fulfil with all her might whatever He put into her soul, if it were not against the worship of God, and profit of her fellow Christians, for if it were, then it were not the moving of a good spirit, but rather of an evil spirit. "The Holy Ghost moveth ne'er a thing against charity, for if He did, He would be contrary to His own self for He is all charity. Also He moveth a soul to all chasteness, for chaste livers are called the Temple of the Holy Ghost, and the Holy Ghost maketh a soul stable and steadfast in the right faith, and the right belief.

"And a double man in soul is ever unstable and unsteadfast in all his ways. He that is ever doubting is like the flood of the sea which is moved and born about with the wind, and that man is not likely to receive the gifts of God.

"Any creature that hath these tokens may steadfastly believe that the Holy Ghost dwelleth in his soul. And much more when God visiteth a creature with tears of contrition, devotion, and compassion, he may and ought to believe that the Holy Ghost is in his soul. Saint Paul saith that the Holy Ghost asketh for us with mourning and weeping unspeakable, that is to say, he maketh us to ask and pray with mourning and weeping so plenteously that the tears may not be numbered. No evil spirit may give these tokens, for Saint Jerome saith that tears torment more the devil than do the pains of Hell. God and the devil are ever at odds and they shall never dwell together in one place, and the devil hath no power in a man's soul.

"Holy Writ saith that the soul of a rightful man is the seat of God, and so I trust, sister, that ye be. I pray God grant you perseverance. Set all your trust in God and fear not the language of the world, for the more despite shame and reproof that ye have in the world, the more is your merit in the sight of God. Patience is necessary to you, for in that shall ye keep your soul."

Much was the holy dalliance that the anchoress and this creature had by communing in the love of Our Lord Jesus Christ the many days that they were together.

This creature showed her manner of living to many a worthy clerk, to worshipful doctors of divinity, both religious men and others of secular habit, and they said that God wrought great grace with her, and bade her she should not be afraid—there was no deceit in her manner of living. They counselled her to be persevering, for their greatest dread was that she should turn and not keep her perfection. She had so many enemies and so much slander, that they thought she might not bear it without great grace and a mighty faith.

Others who had no knowledge of her manner of governance, save only by outward sight or else by jangling of other persons perverting the judgment of truth, spoke full evil of her and caused her much enmity and much distress, more than she would otherwise have had, had their evil language never been spoken. Nevertheless the anchorite of the Preaching Friars in Lynne, who was the principal ghostly father of the creature, as is written before, took it on charge of his soul that her feelings were good and pure, and that there was no deceit in them, and he by the spirit of prophecy, told her that, when she should go Jerusalem-ward, she would have much tribulation with her maiden, and how Our Lord would try her sharply and prove her full straitly.

Then she said to him:—"Ah! Good sir, what shall I do when I am far from home, and in strange countries, and my maiden is against me? Then is my bodily comfort gone, and ghostly comfort from any confessor such as ye be, I wot not where to get."

"Daughter, dread ye nothing, for Our Lord Himself shall comfort you His own self, Whose comfort surpasseth all other, and when all your friends have forsaken you, Our Lord will make a broken-backed man lead you forth whither ye will go."

And so it befell as the anchorite had prophesied in every point, and as, I trust, shall be written more fully afterwards.

CHAPTER LXXVI

It happened, on a time, that the husband of the said creature, a man in great age, passing three score years, as he would have come down from his chamber bare-foot and bare-legged, he slithered, or else failed of his footing, and fell down to the ground from the stairs, his head under him grievously broken and bruised, insomuch that he had in his head five linen plugs for many days, whilst his head was healing.

And, as God willed, it was known to some of his neighbors how he had fallen down from the stairs, peradventure through the din and the rush of his fall. So they came to him and found him lying with his head under him, half alive, all streaked with blood, and never likely to have spoken with priest or clerk, but through high grace and a miracle.

Then the said creature, his wife, was sent for and so she came to him. Then was he taken up and his head sewn, and he was sick a long time after, so that men thought he should have been dead.

Then the people said, if he died, his wife was worthy to be hanged for his death, forasmuch as she might have kept him and did not. They dwelt not together nor lay together, for, as is written before, they both with one assent and with the free will of each, had vowed to live chaste. Therefore, to avoid all perils, they dwelt and sojourned in divers places where no suspicion could be had of their inconvenience. For, at first, they dwelt together after they had made their vow, and then people slandered them, and said they used their lust and their pleasure, as they did before making their vow. And when they went out on pilgrimage, or to see and speak with other ghostly creatures, many evil folk, whose tongues were their own, failing the dread and love of Our Lord Jesus Christ, deemed and said they went rather to the woods, groves, and valleys, to use the lust of their bodies, so that people would not espy it or know it.

Having knowledge how prone people were to deem ill of them, and desiring to avoid all occasion for it as much as they rightly might, they, of their own free will and common consent, parted asunder, as touching their board and their chambers, and went to board in divers places. And this was the cause that she was not with him; and also that she should not be hindered from her contemplation. And therefore when he had fallen, and grievously was hurt, as is said before, the people said, if he died, it was worthy that she should answer for his death. Then she prayed to Our Lord that her husband might live a year, and she be delivered out of slander, if it were His pleasure.

Our Lord said to her mind:—"Daughter, thou shalt have thy boon, for he shall live, and I have wrought a great miracle for thee in that he was not dead, and I bid thee take him home and keep him for My love."

She said:—"Nay, good Lord, for I shall then not attend to Thee as I do now."

"Yes, daughter," said Our Lord, "thou shalt have as much reward for keeping him and helping him in his need at home, as if thou were in church, making thy prayers. Thou has said many times thou wouldst fain keep Me. I pray thee now keep him for the love of Me, for he hath some time fulfilled thy will and My will, both. And he hath made thy body free to Me, so that thou shouldst serve Me, and live chaste and clean, and I will that thou be free to help him at his need in My name."

"Ah! Lord," said she, "for Thy mercy grant me grace to obey and fulfil Thy will, and let never my ghostly enemies have any power to hinder me from fulfilling Thy will."

Then she took home her husband with her and kept him years after, as long as he lived, and had full much labor with him; for in his last days he turned childish again, and lacked reason, so that he could not do his own easement by going to a seat, or else he would not, but, as a child, voided his natural digestion in his linen clothes, where he sat by the fire or at the table, whichever it were; he would spare no place.

And therefore was her labor much the more in washing and wringing, and her costage in firing; and it hindered her full much from her contemplation, so that many times she would have loathed her labor, save she bethought herself how she, in her young age, had full many delectable thoughts, fleshly lusts, and inordinate loves to his person.

And therefore she was glad to be punished with the same person, and took it much the more easily, and served him, and helped him, as she thought, as she would have done Christ Himself.

QUEEN CATHARINE PARR

1513–1548

QUEEN CATHARINE PARR was born at Kendal Castle in Westmoreland in 1513, daughter of Sir Thomas Parr and his wife, the former Maud Green. Parr was Master of the Wards and Controller of the Household to Henry VII. He died when Catharine, the eldest of three children, was about four years old. His widow never remarried but spent the remainder of her life managing the estates and looking after the education of the children. Catharine could read and write Latin fluently at an early age, and was also proficient in Greek, French, Italian, and probably Spanish.

In 1525 Catharine was married to Edward, Lord Brough of Gainsborough, Lancashire, who died when she was fifteen. Technically the young widow was stepmother to children older than herself. Although inheriting a sizable fortune, she chose to live with her stepson Henry Brough at Sizergh Castle until, in 1533, she became the third wife of another older man, Sir John Nevill, Lord Latimer, an ardent, militant Roman Catholic. He too had children, a boy and a girl, whose education Catharine supervised and encouraged.

Between 1530 and 1534 Henry VIII gradually, through a series of investigations, decrees, and parliamentary acts, undertook to erode the authority of the Roman Church in his domains, until the parliament of 1534 finally passed a series of acts that completed and confirmed the independence of the Church of England. The articles and injunctions passed in 1536 and 1538 affirmed most Catholic doctrines but denied those relating to papal supremacy, purgatory, images, relics, pilgrimages, and distrust of the Bible in the vernacular. The king, excommunicated by Rome, was now authorized to dissolve the ancient abbeys and monasteries and to "sequester" or acquire church properties in the name of the Crown. No general uprising or protest took place in 1534, but by 1536 the confiscation of ancient church property began to stir resentment and opposition in several places.

One of these dissident movements, known as the Pilgrimage of Grace, was sponsored by Catharine's husband, Sir John Nevill, Lord Latimer, along with Aske and others. The band of dissenters gathered in Yorkshire and moved toward London as far as Doncaster, where they were met by the Duke of Norfolk. They attempted to prove to him that they were not political rebels in a military sense, but were devout patriots who believed that the king and parliament had erred in sending representatives to plunder churches and religious houses. Norfolk agreed to take their pleas to the king and later promised a just settlement, but eventually Aske and others were executed and the sequestrations continued. The king undoubtedly needed the money thus acquired, but a tide of resentment swelled along with the wealth.

When Latimer died in 1543 and was buried in St. Paul's, he left Catharine another sizable fortune; contemporary records list her as "exceedingly rich." She was apparently an adherent to the Roman Church until this time, but shortly after Latimer's death she became an ardent follower of Miles Coverdale, Hugh Latimer, and John Pankhurst (her future chaplain), reformers who sought to return the English church to its early simplicity. She was later called England's first Protestant queen, and the most learned woman in the land.

Almost at once Catharine was wooed by Thomas Seymour, brother of Jane Seymour, Henry's fourth queen. He was gruff, hotheaded, and heartless, but Catharine, free at last to choose a husband on purely personal and emotional grounds, was captivated. However, before they could be married, and shortly after the execution of Catherine Howard, Henry was strongly attracted to this mature, lovely lady, whose fondness for children was coupled with intellectual brilliance, and he decided to marry her. Her first reaction—only half in jest as she recalled the fates of her predecessors—was, "It would be better to be your mistress than your wife," but eventually she was persuaded to accept him. Seymour discreetly departed for Flanders, where he remained until several years after this marriage.

Catharine's influence on Henry VIII was great. She persuaded him to restore Princess Mary, daughter of Catherine of Aragon, to the royal line of succession, so that Edward, Mary, and Elizabeth would constitute the heirs to the throne. Henry later insisted that any child born to Catharine would enter the line directly after Edward, but no such children were produced. After the wedding Catharine gave elaborate gifts to Edward and Elizabeth, and made a special point of being kind to Mary by presenting her with costly jewels and also a sizable amount of money to assist her in maintaining a proper household. Mary and her new stepmother shared a love for learning and a talent for languages. From time to time Catharine ordered clothing and other necessities for her grave, withdrawn stepdaughter, charging them to Henry marked "for your daughter"—the daughter he had once bastardized by nullifying his marriage to her mother. Elizabeth and Edward were bright, outgoing youngsters who delighted their tutors and enjoyed the attentions of their new mother.

From July to September, 1544, while Henry was fighting in France, Catharine actually served as Regent. During this year she wrote the *Lamentation of a Sinner*, a small book that went through at least four editions before 1600. An excellent specimen of English prose of this age, the *"Lamentations* collect the elements of almost all the sermons that have been leveled against Catholicism. . . . She is nearly as severe on those who call themselves 'gospellers' and separate faith and works, as she is on the pope, and she evidently considers them in equal or greater error," according to her biographer Strickland. Catharine favored the middle way between Roman and Lutheran practice.

Her *Prayers, or Meditations*, after the manner of Thomas à Kempis, was published in 1545 and edited and revised at least five more times in the sixteenth century. Some of the prayers in the volume were anthologized in books of devotion compiled during this period. Edward, Mary, and Elizabeth all mention her letters with delight, but these have not been collected.

In 1547 Henry died. He acknowledged only two of his wives as queens—Jane Seymour and Catharine Parr—and banners with their coats of arms were carried at his funeral. Several months after Henry's death Sir Thomas Seymour, now Lord High Admiral, soon to be created Baron Sudeley of Sudeley, became Catharine's fourth husband. The marriage was not a happy one, as Seymour proved irascible, improvident, and irresponsible. Catharine bore him a daughter, but died six days later, on September 4, 1548. She was buried with great pomp at Sudeley Castle, but her stepchildren were not permitted to attend the funeral.

In her short life of thirty-five years, Catharine Parr was married four times, became a stepmother and widow three times, and mother once —for six days. A woman of great wealth, extraordinary intelligence, genuine religious faith, and deep compassion, she exerted a positive, benign influence on four British monarchs: Henry VIII, Edward VI, Mary, and Elizabeth I.

BIBLIOGRAPHY

Editions

The Lamentation of a Sinner. London: House of T. Barthelet, 1545. There were at least four editions before 1600.
Prayers and Meditations. London: House of T. Barthelet, 1545. There were at least six editions before 1600.

Related Readings

Garnett, Fred. Brooksbank. *Queen Katherine Parr and Sudeley Castle.* London: Transactions of the Cumberland & Westmoreland Antiquarian & Archaeological Society, 1878. See pp. 9–19.
Gordon, Marian A. *Life of Queen Katharine Parr.* Kendal, England: Wilson, 1951.
Strickland, Agnes. *Lives of the Queens of England from the Norman Conquest.* 12 vols. London: Colburn & Co., 1842. Abridged ed., 1 vol., London: Colburn & Co., 1878.

The Lamentation of a Sinner

CATHARINE PARR

[*London, 1548. First edition, 1545*]

A LAMENTATION ON OR
COMPLAINT OF A SINNER

When I consider the bethinking of mine evil and wretched former life, mine obstinate, stony and untractable heart, to have so much exceeded in evilness that it hath not only neglected, yea contemned [held in contempt] and despised God's holy precepts and commandments: but also embraced, received and esteemed vain, foolish and feigned trifles: I am partly by the hate I owe to sin, who hath reigned in me, partly by the love I owe to all Christians, whom I am content to edify, even with the example of mine own shame, forced and constrained with my heart and words to confess and declare to the world, how ingrate, negligent, unkind, and stubborn I have been to God my Creator; and how beneficial, merciful and gentle he hath been always to me his creature, being such a miserable and wretched sinner. Truly I have taken no little small thing upon me, first to set forth my whole stubborness and contempt in words the which is incomprehensible in thought (as it is in the Psalm [XII]) who understandeth his faults? Next this to declare the excellent beneficence, mercy and goodness of God which is infinite, unmeasurable: neither can all the words of angels and men make relation thereof, as appertaineth to his most high goodness. Who is he that is not forced to confess the same, if he consider what he hath received of God, and doeth daily receive? Yea if men would not acknowledge and confess the same, the stones would cry it out. Truly I am constrained and forced to speak and write thereof to mine own confusion and shame, but to the glory and praise of God. For he as a loving father, of most abundant and high goodness, hath heaped upon me, innumerable benefits: and I contrary, have heaped manifold sins, despising that which was good, holy, pleasant, and acceptable in his sight, and choosing that which was delicious, pleasant, and acceptable to my sight. And no marvel it was that I so did, for I would not learn to know the Lord and his ways, but loved darkness better than light. I embraced ignorance as perfect knowledge, and knowledge seemed to me superfluous and vain. I regarded little God's word, but gave myself to vanities and shadows of the world. I forsook him, in whom is all truth, and followed the vain foolish imaginations of my heart. I would have covered my sins with the pretence of holiness, I called superstition, godly meaning, and true holiness, error; the Lord did speak many pleasant and sweet words unto me, and I would not hear; he called me diversly but through frowardness I would not answer. Mine evils and miseries be so many and great, that they accuse me even to my face. Oh how miserably and wretchedly am I confounded? When for the multitude and greatness of my sins I am compelled to accuse myself. Was it not a marvelous unkindness when God did speak to me, and also call me, that I would not answer him? What man so called would not have heart, or what man hearing, would not have answered? If an earthly Prince had spoken, either called him, I suppose there be none but would willingly have done both. Now therefore what a wretch and caitiff am I, that when the Prince of princes, the King of kings, did speak many pleasant and gentle words unto me, and also called me so many and sundry times, that they cannot be numbered; and yet notwithstanding these great signs and tokens of love, I would not come unto him, but hid myself out of his sight, seeking many crooket and by ways wherein I walked so long that I had clean lost his sight. And no marvel or wonder, for I had a blind guide called Ignorance, who dimmed so mine eyes that I could never perfectly get any sight of the fair, goodly, straight, and right ways of his doctrine; but continually travailed uncomfortably in foul, wicked, and perverse ways. Yea and because they were so much haunted of many, I could not think but I walked in the perfect and right way, having more regard to the number of the walkers than to the order of the walking; believing also most surely with company to have walked to heaven, whereas I am most sure they would have brought me down to hell.

· · · ·

A goodly example and lesson for us to follow at all times and seasons, as well in prosperity as in adversity, to have no will but God's will, committing and leaving to him all our cares and griefs, and to abandon all our policies and inventions, for they be most vain and foolish, and indeed very shadows and dreams. But we be yet so carnal and fleshly, that we run headlong like unbridled colts, without snafle or bit.

If we had the love of God printed in our hearts, it would keep us back from running astray. And until such time as it please God to send us this bit to hold us in, we shall never run the right way, although we speak and talk never so much of God and his word. The true followers of Christ's doctrine hath always a respect and an eye to their vocation. If they be called to the ministry of God's word, they preach and teach it sincerely, to the edifying of others, and show themselves in their living, followers of the same. If they be married men, having children and family, they nourish and bring them up without all bitterness and fierceness, in the doctrine of the Lord, in all godliness and virtue, committing the instruction of others, which appertaineth not to their charge, to the reformation of God, and his ministers, which chiefly be kings and princes, bearing the sword even for that purpose, to punish evil doers. If they be children, they honor their father and mother, knowing it to be God's commandment, and that he hath thereto annexed a promise of long life. If they be servants, they obey and serve their masters with all fear and reverence, even for the Lord's sake, neither with murmuring nor grudging, but with a free heart and mind. If they be husbands, they love their wives as their own bodies, after the example as Christ loved the congregation, and gave himself for it, to make it to him a spouse, without spot or wrinkle. If they be women married, they learn of Saint Paul, to be obedient to their husbands and to keep silence in the congregation, and to learn of their husbands at home. Also they wear such apparel as becometh holiness and comely usage, with soberness, not being accusers or detracters, not given to much eating of delicate meats and drinking of wine, but they teach honest things, to make the young women sober minded, to love their husbands, to love their children, to be discreet, chaste, housewifely, good, obedient unto their husbands, that the word of God be not evil spoken of. Verily if all sorts of people would look to their own vocation and ordain the same according to Christ's doctrine, we should not have so many eyes and ears to other men's faults as we have. For we be so busy and glad to find and espy out other men's doings that we forget and can have no time to weigh and ponder our own, which after the word of God, we ought first to reform, and then we shall the better help another with the straw out of his eyes. But alas we be so much given to love and to flatter ourselves, and so blinded with carnal affections, that we can see and perceive no fault in ourselves. And therefore it is a thing very requisite and necessary for us to pray all with one heart and mind to God, to give us an heavenly light and knowledge of our own miseries, and calamaties, that we may see them and acknowledge them truly before him. If any man shall be offended at this my lamenting the faults of men, which be in the world fantasying with themselves, that I do it either of hatred or of malice to any sort or kind of people, verily in so doing they shall do me great wrong, for I thank God by his grace, I hate no creature: yea, I would say more to give witness of my conscience, that neither life, honor, riches, neither whatsoever I possess here, which appertaineth unto mine own private commodity, be it never so dearly beloved of me, but most willingly and gladly I would leave it to win any man to Christ, of what degree or sort soever he were. And yet is this nothing in comparison to the charity that God hath showed me in sending Christ to die for me; no, if I had all the charity of angels and apostles, it should be but like a spark of fire compared to a great heap of burning coals. God knoweth of what intent and mind I have lamented mine own sins and faults to the world. I trust nobody will judge that I have done it for praise or thank of any creature, since rather I might be ashamed than rejoice in rehearsal thereof. For if they know how little I esteem and weigh the praise of the world, that opinion were soon removed and taken away: for I thank God (by his grace) I know the world to be a blind Judge, and the praises thereof vain, and of little moment; and therefore I seek not the praises of the same, neither to satisfy it, none otherwise, than I am taught by Christ to do, according to Christian charity. I would to God we would all (when occasion doth serve) confess our faults to the world, all respects to our own commodity laid apart. But alas, self love doth so much reign amongst us that as I have said before, we cannot espy our own faults. And although sometime we find our own guilt, either we be favorable to interpret it no sin, or else we be ashamed to confess ourselves thereof. Yea and we be sore offended and grieved to hear our faults charitably and godly told us of other, putting no difference between charitable warning, and malicious accusing. Truly if we sought God's glory as we should do in all things, we should not be ashamed to confess ourselves to digress from God's precepts and ordinances, when it is manifest we have done, and daily do. I pray God our own faults and deeds condemn us not, at the last day, when every man shall be rewarded according to his doings. Truly if we do not redress and amend our living, according to the doctrine of the gospel, we shall receive a terrible sentence of Christ the Son of God when he shall come to judge and condemn all transgressors and breakers of his precepts and commandments, and to reward all his obedient and loving children, we shall have no man of law to make our plea for us, neither can we have the day deferred, neither will the just judge be corrupted with affection, bribes, or rewards, neither will he hear any excuse or delay, neither shall this saint or that martyr help us, be they never so holy, neither shall our ignorance save us from damnation. But yet willful blindness and obstinate ignorance shall receive greater punishment, and not without just cause. Then shall it be known who hath walked in the dark, for all things shall appear manifest before him. No man's deeds shall be hidden, no, neither words nor thoughts; the poor and simple observers of God's commandments shall be rewarded with everlasting life, as obedient children to the heavenly father. And the transgressors, adders, and diminishers of the law of God shall receive eternal damnation, for their just reward.

I beseech God we may escape this fearful sentence, and be found such faithful servants and loving children that we may hear the happy, comfortable, and most joyful sentence, ordained for the children of God, which is: Come hither ye blessed of my father, and receive the kingdom of heaven prepared for you before the beginning of the world. Unto the Father, the Son, and the holy Ghost be all honor and glory world without end.

Amen.

Finis.

❧

A Prayer for Men to Say Entering into Battle

CATHARINE PARR

[*from* Prayers or Meditations, *London, 1545*]

O Almighty king, and lord of hosts, which by thy angels thereunto appointed, dost minister both war and peace, and which didst give unto David both courage and strength, being but a little one, unarmed, and unexpert in feats of war, with his sling to set upon and overthrow the great huge Goliath: our cause now being just, and being enforced to enter into war and battle, we most humbly beseech thee (O Lord God of Hosts) so to turn the hearts of our enemies to the desire of peace, that no Christian blood be spilt, or else grant (O Lord) that with small effusion of blood, and to the little hurt and damage of innocents, we may to thy glory obtain victory and that the wars being soon ended, we may all with one heart and mind knit together in concord and unity, laud and praise thee: which livest and reigneth world without end. Amen.

QUEEN ELIZABETH
1533–1603

E LIZABETH TUDOR, daughter of Henry VIII and his second wife, Anne Boleyn, grew up under the care of four successive stepmothers: Jane Seymour, Anne of Cleves, Catherine Howard, and Catharine Parr. Her education was first supervised by her governess, Mrs. Katherine Ashley, who was succeeded by William Grindal and Roger Ascham. Proficient in French, Italian, Spanish, German, Latin, and Greek, she was also well schooled in music, science, the Bible, and the art of fine needlework. It is not necessary to provide a complete biographical sketch or bibliography for Queen Elizabeth here; many fine studies and collections are readily available. The superbly educated, highly intelligent royal princess was to become one of England's most brilliant and colorful monarchs.

When she came to the throne in 1558, Elizabeth's title was not a little suspect. Mary Stuart's claims were good: she was the great granddaughter of Henry VII, whereas Elizabeth had been declared illegitimate. The daughter of James V of Scotland and Mary of Guise, Mary was born on December 7 (?), 1542, and became queen of Scotland on the death of her father a week later. The infant was crowned on 9 September 1543. Five years later she was sent to France, where she was educated with the royal children. In April 1558 she married Francis, the dauphin, eldest son of Henry II and Catherine de Medici of France. Mary and the dauphin declared themselves king and queen of England, Scotland, and Ireland at the time of the death of Mary Tudor (1558). However, Francis died on 5 December 1560, shortly after the death of Henry II on 10 July 1559. Mary was practically excluded from the French court at this time, and returned to Scotland in 1561. Eventually she was acknowledged the rightful heir of James V and, in spite of her adherence to the Roman church, was accepted as queen of Scotland. Her marriage in 1565 to the English Catholic Lord Darnley was met with mixed reactions until her son James was born, 11 June 1566. On 24 July 1567 she was forced to abdicate in favor of James, who was reared a Protestant. Always considered a threat to Elizabeth's sovereignty, she was executed in 1587 for alleged complicity in a plot against the queen. Now all ties between the royal families of Catholic France and Protestant England were broken.

But what of Philip II of Spain? As the husband of Mary Tudor he had shared the throne of England; he also claimed descent from the House of Lancaster. In 1585 he began to plan an invasion of Britain that would result in the restoration of the Roman church there and would greatly strengthen his political position on the Continent, particularly against France. England's intervention in the Netherlands against the Spanish troops of the Duke of Parma served to strengthen his determination. He decided to solicit financial assistance and blessing from Pope Sixtus and eventually received a pledge of 1,000,000 crowns from the Holy See, 500,000 to be paid at once, in December 1586, and the remainder in installments of 100,000 crowns every four months thereafter. Pope Sixtus suspected that Philip's motives were not purely religious ones and was not willing to underwrite his scheme without a certain degree of caution.

Philip advised the Duke of Parma to be ready to send his army to England by the summer of 1587, and great preparation was made in the Low Countries to provide transports and enlarge the harbors in order to send the expeditionary forces abroad. The naval forces gathered in Cadiz harbor and other ports along the Spanish coast. Sir Francis Drake made several raids on these ships and on Spanish galleons off the Azores, creating such chaos in Philip's naval administration and such financial loss in the capture of one galleon laden with gold and silver that the projected invasion had to be postponed for one year. Drake's raids were carried out between April and June, 1587, rendering the summer scheme impossible.

Elizabeth had not been idle while Spain prepared its armada. Lord Howard of Effingham was appointed Lord Admiral, with Sir Francis Drake as Vice-Admiral of the naval forces. Elizabeth chose to command the land forces in person. Between 29 May 1588 and early August the English engaged the Spanish armada in several minor skirmishes and one major battle, in the Channel and off the eastern coast of Britain, until the Spanish fleet's commander, Medina Sidonia, was forced to flee northward past the Firth of Forth, around Scotland, past Ireland, and thence south to Spain. A storm took a toll of Sidonia's ships that was as great as the loss to the English, and about half of the armada's ships were sunk, damaged beyond repair, or abandoned. The English fleet lost not one ship.

On 18 August 1588 the queen sailed down the Thames on a barge to Tilbury, where the Earl of Leicester had prepared a camp for the land army which would repulse Parma, if necessary. (Actually, the English and Dutch forces had so bottled up the Duke's army in the Low Countries that they were never able to embark.) Garrett Mattingly describes Elizabeth's first appearance as she reviewed the troops:

> All eyes were on the queen. She rode a white gelding with a back like a barn door, and, if one may trust a portrait, a benignant, rather simpering expression. She was clad all in white velvet with a silver cuirass embossed with a mythological design, and bore in her right hand a silver truncheon chased in gold. Like the cavaliers on either side, she rode bareheaded, and there was a tuft of plumes, the sheen of pearls, and the glitter of diamonds in her hair.
>
> Perhaps an objective observer would have seen no more than a battered, rather scraggy spinster in her middle fifties perched on a fat white horse, her teeth black, her red wig slightly askew, dangling a toy sword and wearing an absurd little piece of parade armor like something out of a theatrical property box. But that was not what her subjects saw, dazzled as they were by more than the sun on the silver breastplate, or the moisture in their eyes. They saw Judith and Esther, Gloriana and Belphoebe, Diana the virgin Huntress and Minerva the wise protectress, and, best of all, their own beloved queen and mistress, come in this hour of danger, in all simplicity to trust herself among them. The touching rightness of the gesture whipped them to a pitch of enthusiasm which could find expression only in a wild babel of shouted blessings, endearments and protests of devotion. It must have been a long time since Elizabeth had enjoyed herself so much!
>
> [*The Armada* (Boston, 1959), pp. 348–49.]

The next day there was a review of the troops followed by a cavalry exercise that took on the character of a tournament. At the end of these ceremonies and entertainments, the queen made the famous speech reprinted here. However, before these festivities had been concluded, the Spanish armada had been soundly defeated—the news had not yet reached Tilbury. Spain, like France, was no longer a threat to the government and religion of England.

The great wave of patriotism that swept over England after the great victory climaxed the long reign of Elizabeth. But by the time the parliament of 1601 assembled on 27 October, successive expensive problems had so weakened the treasury that the country was on the verge of bankruptcy. Revenues from taxes were diminishing to an alarming degree, and the recent landing of a large Spanish force in Ireland made it imperative that funds and men be found for the defenses of that island. The sources of subsidies—parliamentary grants of funds to the queen for the conduct of the nation's affairs—were shrinking. A committee was formed in Parliament to visit the queen and to present to her a list of grievances, foremost of which was the existence of tax-free monopolies and patents which she had granted. On 28 November the queen issued a proclamation that "declared void the principal patents complained of in Parliament; authorized anyone grieved or wronged by other patents to seek ordinary remedy by the laws of the Realm; and—the crucial point—rescinded, and for the future forebade all letters of assistance from the Privy Council in support of patentees. As promised, it set people free to sow woad [a plant cultivated for the blue coloring matter it provided], with a proviso to save London and the royal palaces from its offensive smell. There was a clause warning subjects of the power and validity of the prerogative royal and the severe punishment awaiting offenders. It saved the principle from the wreck of the substance." (J. E. Neale, *Elizabeth I and her Parliaments*, II [London, 1957], pp. 387–88.)

The queen held an audience on 30 November and made the speech that is printed below. Before Christmas the parliament was dissolved, after having passed the subsidy bill along with thirty-seven other Acts, eight of which were vetoed. Elizabeth's last parliament had fulfilled her expectations in its demonstration of independence and loyalty. It is interesting to note that John Donne and John Davies of Hereford, who were to become famous poets, were members of this august body in 1601.

Queen Elizabeth died in 1603 and was succeeded by James VI of Scotland, son of Mary Queen of Scots; as James I he was the first of the Stuart kings in England.

BIBLIOGRAPHY

Selected Works

Ballard, George, ed. "Speech to the Troops at Tilbury." In *Memoirs of Several Ladies of Great Britain*, pp. 228–29. Oxford: Printed for the author by W. Jackson, 1752.

Bradner, Leicester, ed. *The Poems of Queen Elizabeth*. Providence, R. I.: Brown University Press, 1964.

Harrison, G. B., ed. *The Letters of Queen Elizabeth*. New York: Funk & Wagnalls, 1968.

Pemberton, Caroline, ed. *Queen Elizabeth's Englishings*. London: K. Paul, Trench, Truber, & Co., for Early English Text Society, 1899. Contains Elizabeth's translations of Boethius, *Consolation of Philosophy*, 1593; Plutarch, *De Curiositate*, 1598; and Horace, *De Arte Poetica* (in part), 1598.

Related Readings

Baker, Herbert Kendra. *Elizabeth and Sixtus, a Seventeenth-Century Sidelight on the Spanish Armada*. London: C. W. Daniel Co., Ltd., 1938.

Jenkins, Elizabeth. *Elizabeth the Great*. London: Coward-McCann, 1958. Contains bibliography.

Strickland, Agnes. *Lives of the Queens of England from the Norman Conquest*. 12 vols. London: Colburn & Co., Ltd., 1842. Abridged ed., 1 vol., London, 1878.

Williams, Neville. *All the Queen's Men: Elizabeth I and her Courtiers*. New York: Macmillan, 1972. Well illustrated.

✥

Speech to the Troops at Tilbury

QUEEN ELIZABETH

[*1588, before the battle with the Spanish armada. In* Memoirs of Several Ladies of Great Britain, *edited by George Ballard, Oxford, 1752, pp. 228–29.*]

My loving people,

We have been persuaded by some that are careful of our safety, to take heed how we commit our selves to armed multitudes, for fear of treachery; but I assure you I do not desire to live to distrust my faithful and loving people. Let tyrants fear, I have always so behaved my self that, under God, I have placed my chiefest strength and safeguard in the loyal hearts and good-will of my subjects; and therefore I am come amongst you, as you see, at this time, not for my recreation and disport, but being resolved, in the midst and heat of the battle, to live or die amongst you all; to lay down for my God, and for my Kingdom, and my People, my honour and my blood, even in the dust. I know I have the body but of a weak and feeble woman; but I have the heart and stomach of a King, and of a King of England too, and think foul scorn that Parma or Spain, or any Prince of Europe, should dare to invade the borders of my realm; to which rather than any dishonour shall grow by me, I my self will take up arms, I my self will be your general, judge, and rewarder of every one of your virtues in the field. I know already, for your forwardness you have deserved rewards and crowns; and We do assure you in the word of a Prince, they shall be duly paid you. In the mean time, my Lieutenant General shall be in my stead, than whom never Prince commanded a more noble or worthy subject; not doubting but by your obedience to my General, by your concord in the camp, and your valour in the field, we shall shortly have a famous victory over those enemies of my God, of my Kingdom, and of my People.

≈§

Queen Elizabeth's Speech to her Last Parliament

[Printed 1642]

[The 30 of November 1601, her Majesty being set under State in the Councell Chamber at Whitehall, the Speaker, accompanied with Privy Councellours, besides Knights and Burgesses of the lower House to the number of eight-score, presenting themselves at her Majesty's feet, for that so graciously and speedily she had heard and yielded to her Subjects' desires, and proclaimed the same in their hearing as followeth.]

Mr. Speaker,

We preceive your coming is to present thanks unto Us; know I accept them with no less joy than your loves can have desire to offer such a present, and do more esteem it than any treasure or riches, for those We know how to prize, but loyalty, love, and thanks, I account them invaluable; and though God hath raised Me high, yet this I account the glory of my Crown, that I have reigned with your loves. This makes that I do not so much rejoice that God hath made Me to be a Queen, as to be a Queen over so thankful a people, and to be the mean under God to conserve you in safety, and preserve you from danger, yea to be the instrument to deliver you from dishonor, from shame, and from infamy; to keep you from out of servitude, and from slavery under our enemies, and cruel tyranny, and vile oppression intended against Us: for the better withstanding whereof, We take very acceptably your intended helps, and chiefly in that it manifesteth your loves and largeness of heart to your Sovereign. Of My self I must say this, I never was any greedy scraping grasper, nor a strict fast-holding Prince, nor yet a waster; My heart was never set upon any worldly goods, but only for my subjects' good. What you do bestow on Me, I will not hoard up, but receive it to bestow on you again, yea Mine own properties I account yours to be expended for your good, and your eyes shall see the bestowing of it for your welfare.

Mr. Speaker, I would wish you and the rest to stand up, for I fear I shall yet trouble you with longer speech.

Mr. Speaker, you give me thanks, but I am more to thank you, and I charge you, thank them of the Lower House from Me, for had I not received knowledge from you, I might a fallen into the lapse of an error, only for want of true information.

Since I was Queen yet did I never put My pen to any grant but upon pretext and semblance made Me, that it was for the good and avail of my subjects generally, though a private profit to some of my ancient servants who have deserved well. But that my grants shall be made grievances to my people, and oppressions, to be privileged under color of Our patents, Our Princely Dignity shall not suffer it.

When I heard it, I could give no rest unto my thoughts until I had reformed it, and those varlets, lewd persons, abusers of my bounty, shall know I will not suffer it. And Mr. Speaker, tell the House from me, I take it exceeding grateful, that the knowledge of these things are come unto me from them. And though amongst them the principal members are such as are not touched in private, and therefore need not speak from any feeling of the grief, yet We have heard that other gentlemen also of the House, who stand as free, have spoken as freely in it; which gives Us to know that no respects or interests have moved them other than the minds they bear to suffer no diminution of our Honor, and our subjects' love unto Us. The zeal of which affection tending to ease my people, and knit their hearts unto us, I embrace with a Princely care far above all earthly treasures. I esteem my people's love more than which I desire not to merit:

and God that gave me here to sit, and placed me over you, knows that I never respected my self, but as your good was conserved in me; yet what dangers, what practises, and what perils I have passed, some, if not all of you know: but none of these things do move me, or ever made me fear, but it is God that hath delivered me.

And in my governing this land, I have ever set the last Judgment Day before mine eyes, and so to rule as I shall be judged and answer before a higher Judge, to whose Judgment Seat I do appeal in that never thought was cherished in my heart that tended not to my people's good.

And if my Princely bounty have been abused, and my grants turned to the hurt of my people, contrary to my will and meaning, or if any in authority under me have neglected, or converted what I have committed unto them, I hope God will not lay their culps to my charge.

To be a King, and wear a Crown, is a thing more glorious to them that see it, than it is pleasant to them that bear it: for my self, I never was so much inticed with the glorious name of a King, or the royal authority of a Queen, as delighted that God hath made me His Instrument to maintain His Truth and Glory, and to defend this kingdom from dishonor, damage, tyranny, and oppression. But should I ascribe any of these things unto my self, or my sexly weakness, I were not worthy to live, and of all most unworthy of the mercies I have received at God's hands, but to God only and wholly all is given and ascribed.

The cares and troubles of a Crown I cannot more fitly resemble than to the drugs of a learned physician, perfumed with some aromatical savour, or to bitter pills gilded over, by which they are made more acceptable or less offensive, which indeed are bitter and unpleasant to take; and for my own part, were it not for conscience sake to discharge the duty that God hath laid upon me, and to maintain His glory, and keep you in safety, in mine own disposition I should be willing to resign the place I hold to any other, and glad to be freed of the glory with the labors, for it is not my desire to live nor to reign longer than my life and reign shall be for your good. And though you have had and may have many mightier and wiser Princes sitting in this Seat, yet you never had nor shall have any that will love you better.

Thus Mr. Speaker, I commend me to your loyal loves, and yours to my best care and your further councels, and I pray you Mr. Controller, and Mr. Secretary, and you of my Councell, that before these Gentlemen depart into their countries, you bring them all to kiss my Hand.

ELIZABETH GRYMESTON

(d. 1603)

E LIZABETH GRYMESTON (or Grimston) was the daughter of Martin Bernye (or Barney, or Berney) and Margaret Flynte, of Gunton, Norfolk. Some years ago a disastrous fire at Gunton Hall, the family seat until 1614, destroyed all the Bernye's early family papers, including the registers that recorded dates of baptisms, weddings, and deaths. We do know that Grymeston's brother Francis predeceased her, and that his son Thomas was commended to her care in 1595.

At a time when recusancy (illegal adherence to Roman Catholicism) was common in Norfolk, Martin Bernye may well have sheltered Jesuits who provided his children's education. Elizabeth was well read in the Bible, the Church fathers, and contemporary poets, especially Robert Southwell, a Jesuit who was executed at Tyburn in 1595. All the biblical quotations in Grymeston's book derive from Jerome's Vulgate, and her Latin is classical and clerical. Personal allusions in her *Miscellanea* indicate that she also had training in music, particularly wind instruments.

Christopher Grymeston, of Grimston, Yorkshire, was at Caius College, Cambridge, when Elizabeth Bernye married him in 1584. Christopher remained there as Bursar after he had received his degree of Master of Arts. By 1592, when he was dismissed, Elizabeth had borne several children. Because the Bursar was supposed to reside at the college and remain unmarried, some scholars have assumed that the discovery of his marriage was cause for his dismissal, but there is no documentary proof of this. However, Caius was notorious for its "popish" leanings at this time, and efforts were continually being made to "purify" its ranks. In the Recusant Rolls of 1592/3 Elizabeth Grymeston was listed among those who were fined for failure to adhere to the Anglican faith. This conviction, and perhaps the discovery of the marriage, might have precipitated her husband's dismissal.

Recusancy was rampant among both families, the Bernyes and the Grymestons. In 1587 Martin Bernye was accused of recusancy and described by Bishop Scambler as "backwards in religion"; in 1595 he lost his commission as Justice of the Peace, which he had held since 1578, when a former servant testified that Bernye and Christopher Grymeston had attended mass in the manor house chapel at Gunton. While there is no direct evidence that the Grymestons and the Bernyes ever became public converts to the Roman Church, their leanings were unmistakable and directly affected their religious, social, and political lives.

Elizabeth Grymeston has provided a modicum of autobiography in the *Miscellanea*. She complains that her mother so abused her that she was ill most of her life; beyond this we know little. Her husband entered the law school Gray's Inn in 1593 and was admitted to the Bar in 1599—he and Elizabeth probably resided in London for most of those years, visiting Gunton Hall from time to time. Mother of nine, Elizabeth mourns the deaths of eight children; her little book was a legacy for Bernye, her remaining son. There is no evidence that she intended to publish the volume; she compiled a conduct book for the young man's guidance and consolation after her death. Bernye Grymeston may have died young—his name does not appear on the deeds to any of the properties that he logically might have inherited. The Gunton Hall fire no doubt destroyed the pertinent records.

The dedicatory poem in the *Miscellanea*, a Spenserian sonnet that begins, "Goe, famous thou, with ever-flying fame," was provided on the book's publication by Simon Grahame, a Scottish convert to the Roman church who eventually fled to the Continent. The "Epistle" contains a short poem, "Crush the serpent in the head," by Robert Southwell, whose works were published in 1595 and 1596. Another chapter consists of meditations on sixteen stanzas of Southwell's 112-stanza poem, "Peter's Complaint," in almost haphazard order. She quotes Stanza 5, then 7, followed by 3, 95, 94, 16, 8, 67, 91, 60, 62, 106, 110, and 112. Another chapter quotes in reverse (last stanza first, etc.) the poem on the seven penitential Psalms by another English recusant, Richard Rowlands, alias Verstegan. The remaining poems all appeared in *England's Parnassus*, an anthology published in 1600. Grymeston adroitly modifies her borrowings in order to make them conform to the ideas in her prose, which frequently paraphrases Gregory, Jerome, Ambrose, Augustine, Seneca, Virgil, Terence, Pindar, and others. She never claims originality and never mentions the names of the writers from whom she has borrowed so heavily, but her literary gifts and fine prose style have produced a worthy legacy for her son and for all subsequent readers. Either Bernye or his father had the book published in 1604, the year after her death, and revised editions appeared in 1606 (two), 1608, and 1610; it has not been reprinted since that time.

Hughey and Hereford summed up their appraisal of Grymeston's work as follows:

> No male writer of this period, if he had chosen her as the prototype for a fictitious feminine character, or if he had taken upon himself the writing of a book of remembrance on her, or even if he had intended merely to write about her as an actual individual, could have drawn for us so real a picture of the inner life of this sixteenth-century woman—her reading, her talents, her limitations, her prepossession with the moral and religious side of things, her consuming love for her son. She succeeded in weaving the writings of others ingeniously into a pattern of her own; and she thus was able to write a book that was read and republished. ["Elizabeth Grymeston and her *Miscellanea*," *The Library*, XV, No. 1 (June 1934), 91.]

BIBLIOGRAPHY

Editions

Miscelanea: Prayers, Meditations, Memoratives. London: M. Bradwood for F. Norton, 1604. Further editions: 1606, ca. 1609, 1618.

Related Readings

Ballard, George. *Memoirs of Several Ladies of Great Britain.* Oxford: Printed for the author by W. Jackson, 1752.

Hazlitt, W. C. *Prefaces, Dedications, and Epistles.* London: "Privately printed: only 50 copies," 1874.

Hughey, Ruth, and Hereford, Philip. "Elizabeth Grymeston and her *Miscellanea*." *The Library*, Fourth Series, XV (1934), pp. 61–91.

Miscelanea:
Prayers, Meditations, Memoratives

ELIZABETH GRYMESTON

[*London, 1604. From 1606 edition*]

To Her Loving Son, Bernye Grymeston.

My dearest son, there is nothing so strong as the force of love; there is no love so forcible as the love of an affectionate mother to her natural child: there is no mother can either more affectionately show her affection, than in advising her children out of her own experience, to eschew evil, and incline them to do that which is good. Out of these resolutions, finding the liberty of this age to be such, as that *Quicquid libet licet* [Whatever pleases is lawful], so men keep themselves from criminal offences; and my mother's undeserved wrath so virulent, as that I have neither power to resist it, nor patience to endure it, but must yield to this languishing consumption to which it hath brought me: I resolved to break the barren soil of my fruitless brain, to dictate some thing for thy direction; the rather for that as I am now a dead woman among the living, so stand I doubtful of thy father's life; which albeit God hath preserved from eight several sinister assaults, by which it hath been sought; yet for that I see that *Quem sæpe transit casus, aliquando invenit* [Misfortune will one day find him whom until then it has passed by], I leave thee this portable *veni mecum* [companion, or guide] for thy Counsellor, in which thou mayest see the true portraiture of thy mother's mind, and find something either to resolve thee in thy doubts, or comfort thee in thy distress; hoping, that being my last speeches, they will be better kept in the conservance of thy memory; which I desire thou wilt make a Register of heavenly Meditations. For albeit, if thou provest learned (as my trust is thou wilt; for that without learning man is but as an immortal beast) thou mayest happily think, that if every Philosopher fetched his sentence, these leaves would be left without lines; yet remember withall, that as it is the best coin that is of greatest value in fewest pieces, so is it not the worst book that hath most matter in least words.

The gravest wits, that most grave works expect,
The quality, not quantity respect.

And the spider's web is neither the better because woven out of his own breast, nor the bee's honey the worse for that gathered out of many flowers: neither could I ever brook to set down that haltingly in my broken style, which I found better expressed by a graver author.

God send thee too, to be a wit's Camelion,
That any author's color can put on.

I have prayed for thee, that thou mightest be fortunate in two hours of thy life time: in the hour of thy marriage, and at the hour of thy death. Marry in thine own rank, and seek expecially in it thy contentment and preferment: let her neither be so beautiful, as that every liking eye shall level at her; nor yet so brown, as to bring thee to a loathed bed. Defer not thy marriage till thou comest to be saluted with a "God speed you, Sir," as a man going out of the world after forty; neither yet to the time of "God keep you, Sir," whilst thou art in thy best strength after thirty; but marry in the time of "You are welcome, Sir," when thou art coming into the world: for seldom shalt thou see a woman out of her own love to pull a rose that is full blown, deeming them always sweetest at the first opening of the bud. It was Phædra her confession to Hippolytus, and it holds for truth with the most: *Thesei vultus amo illos priores quos tulit quondam iuvenis* [I love those former looks of Theseus which in early manhood once he wore]. Let thy life be formal, that thy death may be fortunate: for he seldom dies well that liveth ill. To this purpose, as thou hast within thee Reason as thy Counsellor, to persuade or dissuade thee, and thy Will as an absolute Prince with a *Fiat vel Evitetur*, with a Let it be done or neglected; yet make thy conscience thy *Censor morum* [guide to behavior], and chief commander in thy little world: let it call Reason to account whether she have subjected her self against reason to sensual appetites. Let thy Will be censured, whether her desires have been chaste, or as a harlot she have lusted after her own delights. Let thy thoughts be examined. If they be good, they are of the spirit (quench not the spirit), if bad, forbid them entrance: for once admitted, they straightways fortify; and are expelled with more difficulty, than not admitted.

Crush the serpent in the head,
Break ill eggs ere they be hatched.
Kill bad chickens in the tread,
Fledge they hardly can be catched.
In the rising stifle ill,
Lest it grow against thy will.

For evil thoughts are the Devil's harbingers; he never resteth, but where they provide his entertainment. These are those little ones whose brains thou must dash out against the rock of true judgment: for

As a false Lover that thick snares hath laid
T'intrap the honor of a fair young maid,
When she (though little) listening ear affords,
To his sweet, courting, deep affected words,
Feels some assuaging of his freezing flame,
And soothes himself with hope to gain his game,
And wrapt with joy, upon this point persists,
That parling City never long resists:
Even so the serpent that doth counterfeit
A guileful call, t'allure us to his net,
Perceiving us his flattering gloze disgest,
He prosecutes, and jocund doth not rest,
Till he have tri'd foot, hand, and head, and all,
Upon the breach of this new battered wall.

I could be content to dwell with thee in this argument: but I must confine my self to the limits of an Epistle, *Quæ non debet implere sinistram manum* [I will not fill up the letter with my left hand]. To which rule I do the more willingly submit my self, for that the discourses following are motives to the same effect: which I pray thee use to peruse, even in that my affectionate love, which diffused amongst nine children which God did lend me, is now united in thee, whom God hath only left for my comfort. And because God hath endued thee with so violent a spirit, as that *quicquid vis valdè vis* [whatever you want, you want very strongly]; therefore by so much the more it behooveth thee to deliberate what thou undertakest: to which purpose my desire is, that thou mightest be seasoned with the precepts in thy youth, that the practice of thy age may have a taste of them. And because that it is incident to quick spirits to commit rash attempts; as ever the love of a mother may challenge the performance of her demand of a dutiful child, be a bridle to thy self, to restrain thee from doing that which indeed thou mayest do; That thou mayest the better forbear that which in truth thou oughtest not to do: for, *haud cito progreditur ad maiora peccata, qui parua reformidat*; he seldomest commits deadly sin, that makes a conscience of a venial scandal.

Thou seest my love hath carried me beyond the list I resolved on, and my aching head and trembling hand have rather a will to offer, than ability to afford further discourse. Wherefore with as many good wishes to thee, as good will can measure, I abruptly end, desiring God to bless thee with sorrow for thy sins, thankfulness for his benefits, fear of his judgments, love of his mercies, mindfulness of his presence; that living in his fear, thou mayest die in his favor, rest in his peace, rise in his power, remain in his glory, for ever and ever.

Thine assured loving mother

Elizabeth Grymeston.

CHAPTER IV

Who lives most honestly will die most willingly.

Sweet (saith Chrysostom) is the end of the laborers: willingly doth the traveler question about his Inn: often casteth the hireling when his years will come out: the woman great with child will often muse of her delivery: and he that knows his life is but a way to death, will sit upon the threshold with the poor prisoner, expecting to have the door open to be let out of so loathsome a prison, looking for death without fear, desiring it without delight, and accepting it with devotion.

> For what's the life of man, but even a tragedy,
> Full of sad sighs, and sore catastrophes?
> First coming to the world with weeping eye,
> Where all his days like dolorous trophies
> Are heaped with spoils of fortune and of fear.

For it is only death that unlooseth the chains and sets us free from our domestical enemy. It is only he that wafts us forward in this sea of calamities, the danger whereof is shown by the multitude of those that perish by the gunshot of the devil's assaults, and by the rareness of those that escape shipwreck.

> Our frailties' doom is written in the flowers,
> Which flourisheth now, but fade ere many hours.

By death's permission th'aged linger here,
Straight after death, is due the fatal bier.

It is only death that brings us into harbor, where our repose is without
trouble, comfort without crosses, where our tears shall be turned into
triumph, our sadness into joy, and all our miseries into perfect felicity.

Death is the salve that ceaseth all annoy.
Death is the port by which we pass to joy.

It is for brutes to fear death, whose end of life is conclusion of their
being. It is for Epicures to fear death, whose death is the beginning of their
damnation. It is for such as traffic vanities, to look to gain grief; for such
as have sown sin, to look to reap misery; for those of a desperate life, to
look for a damnable disease: but the good man that did sow in tears, by
death shall reap in joy; for his judge he is who knows our weakness, and
will acknowledge our infirmities: his accusers are made dumb by former
repentance; his conscience is cleared by former confession; hope is his
staff, to keep him from sliding; grace is his guide, to keep him from erring;
faith is his assurance, to strengthen his resolution: and what doth he lose,
but frail and fickle life, a vapor that soon vanisheth, a dry leaf carried
with every wind, a sleep fed with imaginary dreams, a tragedy of transi-
tory things and disguised persons, that pass away like a post in the night,
like a ship in the sea, like a bird in the air, whose tract the air closeth?

Life is a bubble blown up with a breath,
Whose wit is weakness, and whose wage is death,
Whose way is wildness, and whose Inn is penance,
Stooping to crooked age the host of grievance.

Who can sit in his study and look on his hourglass, and say not to
himself, . . . That thy life is spent with the hour? Who can walk in the sun,
and look on his shadow, and not say with Pindar, . . . Man is but the
dream of a shadow? . . . Canst thou feel the wind beat on thy face, and
canst thou forget that thou holdest thy tenement by a puff of wind? Canst
thou sit by the river side, and not remember that as the river runneth, and
doth not return, so is the life of man? Canst thou shoot in the fields, and
not call to mind that as the arrow flieth in the air, so swiftly do thy days
pass? Or canst thou walk in the fields, and see how some grass is coming,
some newly withered, and some already come, and dost not remember
that all flesh is grass? . . . Miserable man, why dost thou not dispose

thyself to death, since thou are sure thou canst not live? . . . Our best life is
to die well: for living here we enjoy nothing: things past are dead and
gone: things present are always ending: things future always beginning:
while we live we die; and we leave dying when we leave living. Our life
was a smoke, and is vanished; was a shadow and is passed; was a bubble
and is dissolved. The poor man's life is led in want, and therefore
miserable. The rich man's joy is but vanity: for he is poor in his riches,
abject in his honors, discontented in his delights. This made Hilarion say,
. . . Thou hast served thy God four score years, and therefore fear not
now to go take thy wages. And Ambrose: . . . Who feared not to die,
knowing that he that came hither to buy us an inheritance, is gone before
us to prepare it for us.

> O who would live, so many deaths to try,
> Where will doth wish that wisdom doth reprove,
> Where nature craves that grace must needs deny,
> Where sense doth like, that reason cannot love,
> Where best in show in final proof is worst,
> Where pleasure's upshot is to die accursed?

CHAPTER XX

Memoratives [A selection]

The darts of lust are the eyes; and therefore fix not thy eye on that
which thou mayest not desire.

Epicurism is the fuel of lust; the more thou addest, the more she is
enflamed.

Think from whence thou camest, and blush; where thou art, and
sigh; and tremble to remember whither thou shalt go.

The whole world is as an house of exchange, in which Fortune is the
nurse that breeds alteration.

Mishap is the touchstone of friendship, and adversity the trial of
friends.

A malefactor hath Fear for his bedfellow, Care for his companion,
and the sting of Conscience for his torment.

If thou givest a benefit, keep it close; but if thou receivest one, publish
it, for that invites another.

He that leaves his wife a Goldfinch may at his return find her a
Wagtail.

On the anvil of upbraiding is forged the office of unthankfulness.

True nobility descending from ancestry proves base, if present life continue not thy dignity.

The longer we delay to show our virtue, the stronger is the presumption that we are guilty of base beginning.

Be not at any time idle. Alexander's soldiers should scale mole-hills rather than rest unoccupied; it is the woman that sitteth still that imagineth mischief; it is the rolling stone that riseth clean, and the running water that remaineth clear.

There be four good mothers have four bad daughters: Truth hath Hatred; Prosperity hath Pride; Security hath Peril, and Familiarity hath Contempt.

A fair woman is a paradise to the eye, a purgatory to the purse, and a hell to the soul.

What harm the heart doth think and the hand effect, that will the worm of conscience betray.

MARY SIDNEY HERBERT,
COUNTESS OF PEMBROKE
1561–1621

MARY SIDNEY HERBERT, Countess of Pembroke, was born at Tickenhill Palace near Bewdley, Worcestershire, October 27, 1561, the fifth of seven children. Her brother was the famous Sir Philip Sidney, courtier, soldier, statesman, and poet. Her father, Sir Henry Sidney, was the godson of Henry VIII and had been a close companion of Edward VI throughout that young man's childhood; in fact Edward had died in his arms. Sir Henry was made governor of Ireland, Lord President of the Marches of Wales, Knight of the Garter, and, in 1565, Lord Deputy of Ireland. Mary's mother was Lady Mary Dudley, daughter of John Dudley, Duke of Northumberland, Earl of Warwick and Baron Lisle.

Although the manor of Penshurst, granted to Sir Henry's father by Edward VI in 1552, was the official family seat, it appears that the family spent little time there during Mary's youth. In 1564 they resided at Ludlow Castle, and Philip attended Shrewsbury School a few miles to the north. Sir Henry returned to Ireland in 1569 and the family, except for Philip, joined him there in 1570, remaining until his return to England a year later. For the next four years they lived at Ludlow, Penshurst, and the court. In 1575 Mary's sister Ambrosia died and was buried in the church at Ludlow, leaving Mary the sole remaining daughter (two sisters had died in infancy). At this point Queen Elizabeth wrote a letter of condolence to Sir Henry and asked that Mary be permitted to come to the court as a Lady in Waiting. From 1575 until her marriage in 1577, Mary served the queen as her mother had done before her.

Little is known about the education of the Countess of Pembroke. She was proficient in French and Italian and apparently had a working knowledge of Latin. She and her brother Philip were close, although about seven years separated them; they shared a love of the arts, particularly poetry.

In 1577 Mary Sidney became the third wife of Henry Herbert, second

Earl of Pembroke, a man about twenty-seven years her senior. His mother was Anne, sister of Catharine Parr, sixth wife of Henry VIII. His previous wives were Catherine Grey, sister of the ill-fated Lady Jane Grey, who was executed when her supporters attempted to make her queen in place of Mary Tudor, and Catherine Talbot, daughter of the Earl of Shrewsbury. When he married Mary Sidney he received £1,000 in partial payment of the promised dowry, as Sir Henry was in severe financial straits at this time. (Sir Henry's requests to the queen for reimbursement of expenses incurred in her service in Ireland and Wales went unheeded; he even had to reject her offer of a peerage owing to the additional expenses such a position would incur.)

The seat of the Earls of Pembroke was Wilton House, in Wiltshire, near Salisbury. From time to time Mary resided for short periods in other houses that her husband owned at Ramsbury and Ivy Church; their London residence was Baynard's Castle, on St. Paul's wharf. It is highly likely that the Countess did not always travel with her husband or change her residence as frequently as he did; it appears that all four children were born at Wilton House. William, the first son, was born April 8, 1580; his godmother was Queen Elizabeth. Katherine was born October 15, 1581, and died three years later; she was buried in Wilton Church. Next came Anne, on March 9, 1583, and Philip, godson of Sir Philip Sidney, on October 16, 1584.

In 1580 Sir Philip incurred the displeasure of Queen Elizabeth and retreated to Wilton House, where he enjoyed long visits for the next five years. During his absence from the court he wrote *The Countess of Pembroke's Arcadia* and wrote or revised the *Apology for Poetry*; we know that the revised portion of the *Arcadia* and the Norwich Ms. of the *Apology* were copied by the same scribe at Wilton House about 1585, the year he was ordered by the queen to take part in the military action in the Netherlands.

Little is known about the life of the Countess between 1580 and 1590, apart from the births of her children. In 1586 tragedy struck: Sir Henry Sidney died in May, Lady Mary died in August, and Sir Philip died in October. Two brothers remained: Robert, who succeeded to his father's title and the ancestral lands, and Thomas, who did not long survive his parents. Robert's wife, Barbara Gamage, shared many of the interests and talents of his sister Mary, and the two women exchanged letters that indicate deep affection.

The Countess engaged Samuel Daniel as tutor to her sons in 1590,

and on March 9, 1593, both William, age 13, and Philip, age 9, entered
New College, Oxford. Both were awarded the degree of M. A. in August,
1605. William served as Chancellor of the University from 1616 until his
death in 1630 at Baynard's Castle, London; Pembroke College, Oxford,
was named for him. Philip, a favorite of James I, served as High Steward
of Oxford from 1615 to 1641, when he became Chancellor. Deprived of
his office in 1643, he was restored to it in 1647 and retained it until his
death in 1650.

About Anne we know little. She accompanied her mother to court
and visited with her at several estates, but the last reference to her in
official records is dated 1603. There is no record of her marriage, and we
do not know when or where she died.

During the 1590s the Countess was engaged in editing and publishing
Sir Philip's work and writing and translating on her own. The *Arcadia*
first appeared in print in 1590 in an unauthorized edition; the edition
sponsored by the Countess came out in 1593. In 1595 two versions of the
Apology were published; the Countess reprinted one of them in 1598.
Her English translations of DuPlessis Mornay's *Discourse of Life and
Death* and of Robert Garnier's *The Tragedy of Antonie* (in blank verse),
both from the original French, appeared in 1592. The Inner Temple
library in London houses her unpublished manuscript of Petrarch's
Triumph of Death, which retains the terza rima form of the original.

We do not know when she began to prepare the metrical version of
the Psalms that her brother had begun, but her work circulated in
manuscript and was praised by Samuel Daniel in 1593. Her renderings
begin with Psalm 44, her brother having completed the first forty-three.
She employed many stanza forms, always uniting form and theme, and
the resultant collection of poems is metrically fascinating. Psalm 100
takes the form of a Spenserian sonnet; Spenser's *Amoretti*, the sonnet
cycle in which he introduced this form, was published in 1595. It is
possible that the Countess had seen these poems in manuscript, as the
poet was a member of that literary circle which frequented Wilton House
and included Abraham Fraunce, Samuel Daniel, Nicholas Breton, Ga-
briel Harvey, John Donne, Thomas Nashe, Sir John Harrington, John
Davies of Hereford, Ben Jonson, and others; many of these men dedicated poems to her. Psalm 150 is written in the form of a Petrarchan
sonnet. She also uses rhyme royal, ottava rima, heroic couplets, ballad
stanzas, and other forms that she herself devised. Another woman,
Æmelia Lanier, praised her rendition of the Psalms in her *Salve Deus Rex
Judaeorum*, which was published in 1611.

The entire 150 Psalms were published in 1823 at the suggestion of James Boswell, famous biographer of Dr. Samuel Johnson. Only 250 copies were printed. A new edition appeared in 1963, admirably edited by J. A. C. Rathmell.

The manuscript that contains the poem "To the Angell Spirit of the Most Excellent Sir Philip Sidney" and another poem (printed below) dedicating the metrical psalms to Queen Elizabeth is owned by Dr. Bent Juel-Jensen, who published the texts in a very small edition in 1962. No doubt many other poems by the Countess exist in scattered manuscripts; a good edition of her *Works* is needed. Unfortunately a disastrous fire in 1647 destroyed the original Wilton House and its fine library, in which family records and original manuscripts would logically have been stored.

Whether or not the Countess of Pembroke was a patron of the theater and of dramatists is a matter for conjecture. She did attend performances of plays at Court, and may well have become acquainted with William Shakespeare. The first folio edition of Shakespeare's plays, published in 1623, bears a dedication to her two sons William and Philip.

Mary Herbert, Countess of Pembroke, died in 1621 in the house on Aldergate Street, London, and was buried beside her husband in Salisbury Cathedral, having outlived him by eighteen years.

BIBLIOGRAPHY

Works

The Psalmes of David, begun by . . . Sir Philip Sidney, Knt., and finished by . . . The Countess of Pembroke His Sister. Now first printed from a copy of the original manuscript, transcribed by John Davies of Hereford, in the Reign of James the First. Chiswick, England: Printed by C. Whittingham for R. Triphook, 1823.

Fraunce, Abraham, ed. *The Countess of Pembroke's Emanuell.* London: William Ponsonby, 1591.

Grosart, A. B., ed. "The Countess of Pembroke's Emanuell," in *Miscellanies.* London: Printed for private circulation, 1871.

Juel-Jensen, Bent, ed. *Two Poems by the Countess of Pembroke.* Oxford: Oxford University Press, 1962.

Rathmell, J. A. C., ed. *The Psalms of Sir Philip Sidney and the Countess of Pembroke.* New York: New York University Press, 1963.

Translations

Discourse of Life and Death, by DuPlessis Mornay, and Antonius, by R. Garnier. London: William Ponsonby, 1592, 1600, 1606, 1607.

The Tragedy of Antonie. From the French, by Robert Garnier. London: William
Ponsonby, 1595.

Related Readings

Ballard, George. *Memoirs of Several Ladies of Great Britain*. Oxford: Printed for
the author by W. Jackson, 1752.

Bulloch, M. M. *Mary Sidney, Countess of Pembroke, an Elizabethan Historiette*.
Aberdeen, Scotland: n.p., 1895.

Costello, Louisa. *Memoirs of Eminent Englishwomen*. London: R. Bentley,
1844.

Juel-Jensen, Bent. "A Highly Personal Affair." *The Book Collector* (Summer
1966), pp. 152–74.

Young, Frances B. *Mary Sidney, Countess of Pembroke*. London: D. Nutt, 1912.
Very useful.

To the Thrice Sacred Queen Elizabeth

MARY SIDNEY HERBERT, COUNTESS OF PEMBROKE

[*1599. From* Two Poems by the Countess of Pembroke, *printed
at Oxford, New Bodleian Library, 1962,
from the Ms. owned by Bent Juel-Jensen*]

1

Even now that Care which on thy Crown attends
and with thy happy greatness daily grows
Tells me thrice sacred Queen my Muse offends,
and of respect to thee the line out goes,
One instant will or willing can she lose
I say not reading, but receiving Rimes,
On whom in chief dependeth to dispose
what Europe acts in these most active times?

2

Yet dare I so, as humbleness may date
cherish some hope they shall acceptance find;

not weighing less thy state, lighter thy Care,
but knowing more thy grace, abler thy mind.
What heavenly powers thee highest throne assigned,
assigned thee goodness suiting that Degree:
and by thy strength thy burthen so designed,
To others toil, is Exercise to thee.

3

Cares though still great, cannot be greatest still,
Business must ebb, though Leisure never flow:
Then these the Posts of Duty and Goodwill
shall press to offer what their Senders owe;
Which once in two, now in one Subject go,
the poorer left, the richer* rest away:
who better might (O might, Ah word of woe.)
have given for me what I for him defray.

4

How can I name whom sighing signs extend,
and not unstop my tears' eternal spring?
but he did warp, I weaved this web to end;
the stuff not ours, our work no curious thing,
Wherein yet well we thought the Psalmist King
How English denizened, though Hebrew born,
would to thy music undispleased sing,
Oft having worse, without repining worn;

5

And I the Cloth in both our names present,
a livery robe to be bestowed by thee:
small parcel of the undischarged rent,
from which nor pains nor payments can us free.
And yet enough to cause our neighbors see
We will our best, though scanted in our will:
and those nigh fields where sown thy favors be
unwealthy do, not else unworthy till.

* Refers to her late brother, Sir Philip Sidney.

6

For in our work what bring we but thine own?
what English is, by many names is thine,
There humble Laurels in thy shadows grown
To garland others would, themselves repine.
Thy breast the Cabinet, thy seat the shrine,
Where Muses hang their vowed memories:
where Wit, where Art, where all that is divine
conceived best, and best defended lies.

7

Which if men did not (as they do) confess,
and wronging worlds would otherwise consent:
Yet here who minds so meet at Patroness
for Authors' state or writings' argument?
A King should only to a Queen be sent:
God's loved choice unto his chosen love:
Devotion to Devotion's President:
What all applaud, to her whom none reprove.

8

And who sees ought, but sees how justly square
his haughty Ditties to thy glorious days?
How well beseeming thee his Triumphs are?
his hope, his zeal, his prayer, plaint, and praise,
Needless thy person to their height to raise:
less need to bend them down to thy degree:
These holy garments each good soul assays,
some sorting all, all sort to none but thee.

9

For even thy Rule is painted in his Reign:
both clear in right: both nigh by wrong oppressed:
And each at length (man crossing God in vain)
Possessed of place, and each in peace possessed.
proud Philistines did interrupt his rest,
The foes of heaven no less have been thy foes;
He with great conquest, thou with greater blessed;
Thou sure to win, and he secure to lose.

10

Thus hand in hand with him thy glories walk:
but who can trace them where alone they go?
Of thee two hemispheres on honor talk,
and Lands and seas thy Trophies jointly show.
The very winds did on thy party blow,
and rocks in arms thy foe men eft defy:
But soft my muse, Thy pitch is earthly love;
forbear this heaven, where only Eagles fly.

11

Kings on a Queen enforced their states to lay;
Main-lands for Empire waiting on an Isle;
Men drawn by worth a woman to obey;
one moving all, herself unmoved the while:
Truth's restitution, vanity exile,
wealth sprung of want, war held without annoy,
let subject be of some inspired style,
Till then the object of her subjects' joy.

12

Thy utmost can but offer to her sight
Her handmaids task, which most her will endears;
and pray unto thy pains life from that light
Which lively light some, Court and Kingdom cheers,
What wish she may (far past her living Peers
and Rival still to Judas faithful King)
In more than he and more triumphant years,
Sing what God doth, and do What men may sing.

৵ঌ

The Psalmes of David

BEGUN BY THE NOBLE AND LEARNED GENT., SIR
PHILIP SIDNEY. KNT., AND FINISHED BY THE
RIGHT HONORABLE THE COUNTESS OF PEMBROKE,
HIS SISTER.

[*1823*]

PSALM LXI. *Exaudi, Deus*

To thee I cry,
My crying hear.
To thee my praying voice doth fly:
Lord, lend my voice a listening ear,
From country banished,
All comfort vanished,
To thee I run when storms are nigh.

Up to thy hill,
Lord, make me climb;
Which else to scale exceeds my skill:
For in my most distressed time
Thy eye attended me,
Thy hand defended me,
Against my foe, my fortress still.

Then where a tent
For thee is made,
To harbor still is my intent:
And to thy wings protecting shade
My self I carry will,
And there I tarry will,
Safe from all shot against me bent.

What first I crave
First grant to me,
That I the royal rule may have
Of such as fear and honor thee:
Let years as manifold,
As can be any told,
Thy king, O God, keep from the grave.

Before thy face
Grant ever he
May sit, and let thy truth and grace
His endless guard appointed be.
Then singing pleasantly,
Praising uncessantly,
I daily vows will pay to thee.

PSALM C. *Jubilate Deo*

O all you lands, the treasures of your joy
In merry shout upon the Lord bestow:
Your service cheerfully on him employ,
With triumph song into his presence go.
Know first that he is God; and after know
This God did us, not we our selves create:
We are his flock, for us his feedings grow:
We are his folk, and he upholds our state.
With thankfulness O enter then his gate:
Make through each porch of his your praises ring,
All good, all grace, of his high name relate,
He of all grace and goodness is the spring.
Time in no terms his mercy comprehends,
From age to age his truth it self extends.

PSALM CL. *Laudate Dominum*

O laud the Lord, the God of hosts commend,
Exalt his power, advance his holiness,
With all your might lift his almightiness:
Your greatest praise upon his greatness spend.

Make trumpets' noise in shrillest notes ascend,
  Make lute and lyre his loved fame express,
  Him let the pipe, him let the tabret bless,
Him organs' breath, that winds or waters lend.

Let ringing timbrels so his honor sound,
  Let sounding cymbals so his glory ring,
That in their tunes such melody be found,
  As fits the pomp of most triumphant king.
Conclude by all that air or life enfold,
Let high Jehovah highly be extold.

ÆMELIA LANIER

1570(?)–1640(?)

W HEN GEORGE BALLARD WROTE in 1752 that he had been forced to omit certain women "of distinguished parts and learning" from his *Memoirs of Several Ladies of Great Britain* because he had "been unable to collect very little else relating to them," his list included Elizabeth Grymeston, Bathsua Makin, and Æmelia Lanier. And today little more is known of Makin and Lanier.

Æmelia's maiden name is in doubt. She may have been the daughter of a member of the King's Music, Baptist Bassano, and Margaret Johnson, but we cannot be sure. We do know that she married Alphonso Lanier, a musician who played the recorder in the King's Music from 1594 until his death in 1613. Apparently Æmelia was well educated and had been trained in Latin and French. Her use of imagery from the field of music demonstrates her close familiarity with that art, either from personal training or from her association with the royal band at court. She was also well versed in classical mythology. Direct reference to the metrical version of the Psalms by the Countess of Pembroke reveals that she moved in that social group which circulated poetry in manuscript. The simple quatrains of her dedicatory poem are followed by the more sophisticated stanzas, ottava rima, of the *Salve Deus Rex Judæorum* itself.

Court records of the King's Music date back to the coronation of Edward IV in 1460. Queen Elizabeth's band seems to have been the first to include violins, in addition to the usual brasses, woodwinds, and timpani. Many of the musicians came from French and Italian families who arrived in England in the sixteenth century. Nicholas Lanier, father-in-law of Æmelia, was a member of the French Royal Music in the court of Henry II as late as 1561. Lanier appears to have moved that year to England, where he lived in London with Guillaume de Vache, another French musician. And that same year he joined the Queen's band. As was customary, his six sons eventually followed him in the Royal Music, as did many of their sons after them. Of his five daughters we know nothing.

The fifth child was Alphonso who, trained in flute and recorder, joined the band in 1594. He continued in his position at court until his death in 1613. He apparently held an army commission as well, and was known as Captain Lanier. In 1604 he was awarded a "grant of the office of weighing of hay and straw brought to London and Westminster, for 20 years," according to the *Grove Supplement*. This patent devolved upon Æmelia at his death but she made it over to his brother Innocent, who proposed to apply for a supplementary grant and to give her one-half of the joint proceeds. He failed to acquire the added grant, however, and never made any payments to her. At Innocent's death in 1625, another brother, Clement, held the patent, which had evidently been renewed. He also exploited Æmelia and withheld payment to her when she appealed to the courts for redress in 1635. No settlement was ever recorded.

Henry Lanier, the only son of Æmelia and Alphonso, pursued a career in the King's Music as a flutist, as his father had before him. He had one son, Andrea, whom he placed under the tutelage of an uncle so that the boy might be trained in flute and cornet. Henry died in 1633.

By 1635 Æmelia was left alone, her husband and her son having died, and her grandson having been placed with Alphonso's brother as ward and pupil. Her life had been spent in court circles during the reigns of Elizabeth, James I, and Charles I, all of whom had encouraged the development of music and drama. By 1635 court musicians were engaged in preparing music not only for plays but also for elaborate masques, and a new form of music drama, called "opera," was in its infancy. The term "orchestra" was now being used to describe the band that was located between the singers and the audience—a departure from the usual position behind or beside the stage. Within Æmelia's lifetime England had witnessed the development of the madrigal, the opera, and masques that required fantastic musical settings. Her brother-in-law, Nicholas, became Master of the King's Music, traveled on the Continent as agent for Charles I and the Duke of Buckingham to purchase paintings, and wrote what might be considered the first true English opera, entitled *Lovers Made Men* in 1617. His portrait was painted by Van Dyck. He was a friend of the famous Henry Lawes, and of John Milton, Sr., the poet's father.

We do not know when Æmelia Lanier died, but her name has not been found in official records after 1639. Her little book published in 1611 would seem to be too polished for a first attempt at writing poetry; it is highly possible that other works exist in manuscript, unidentified.

BIBLIOGRAPHY

Salve Deus Rex Judæorum. London: Printed by V. Simmes for R. Bonian, 1611.

Related Readings

Ballard, George. *Memoirs of Several Ladies of Great Britain.* Oxford: Printed for the author by W. Jackson, 1752.

Blom, Eric, ed. *Grove's Dictionary of Music and Musicians.* 9 vols. 5th ed. London: Macmillan, 1954. *Supplement*, 1961.

de la Fontaine, H. T. C. *The King's Musick.* London: Novello & Co., 1909.

Hughes, A. W., ed. *Miscellanea Genealogica et Heraldica.* 5th series. London: Mitchell Hughes & Clarke, 1926–28.

Salve Deus Rex Judæorum

ÆMELIA LANIER [LANYER]

[*London, 1611*]

Containing

1. The Passion of Christ.
2. Eve's Apology in defense of Women.
3. The Tears of the Daughters of Jerusalem.
4. The Salutation and Sorrow of the Virgin Mary.

With divers other things not unfit to be read.

The Author's Dream
to the Lady Mary, the Countess Dowager
of Pembroke.

Me thought I passed through th' Edalian Groves,
And asked the Graces if they could direct
Me to a Lady whom Minerva chose
To live with her in height of all respect.

Yet looking back into my thoughts again,
The eye of Reason did behold her there

Fast tied unto them in a golden chain,
They stood, but she was set in Honor's chair.

And nine fair virgins sat upon the ground,
With harps and viols in their lily hands;
Whose harmony had all my senses drowned,
But that before mine eyes an object stands,

Whose beauty shined like Titan's clearest rays,
She blew a brazen trumpet, which did sound
Through all the world that worthy Lady's praise,
And by eternal fame I saw her crowned.

Yet studying if I were awake or no,
God Morphy* came and took me by the hand,
And willed me not from slumber's bower to go,
Till I the sum of all did understand.

When presently the welkin that before
Looked bright and clear, me thought, was overcast,
And dusky clouds, with boisterous winds great store,
Foretold of violent storms which could not last.

And gazing up into the troubled sky,
Me thought a chariot did from thence descend,
Where one did sit replete with majesty,
Drawn by four fiery dragons, which did bend

Their course where this most noble Lady sat,
Whom all these virgins with due reverence
Did entertain, according to that state
Which did belong unto her Excellence.

When bright Bellona,† so they did her call,
Whom these fair nymphs so humbly did receive,
A manly maid which was both fair and tall,
Her borrowed chariot by a spring did leave.

* Morpheus, god of sleep.
† goddess of war.

With spear and shield and currat* on her breast
And on her head a helmet wondrous bright,
With myrtle, bays, and olive branches dressed,
Wherein me thought I took no small delight.

To see how all the Graces sought grace here,
And in what meek yet princely sort she came;
How this most noble Lady did embrace her,
And all humors unto hers did frame.

Now fair Dictina† by the break of day,
With all her damsels round about her came,
Ranging the woods to hunt, yet made a stay,
When harkening to the pleasing sound of Fame;

Her ivory bow and silver shafts she gave
Unto the fairest nymph of all her train;
And wondering who it was that in so grave
Yet gallant fashion did her beauty stain:

She decked herself with all the borrowed light
That Phoebus would afford from his fair face,
And made her virgins to appear so bright,
That all the hills and vales received grace.

Then pressing where this beauteous troop did stand,
They all received her most willingly,
And unto her the Lady gave her hand,
That she should keep with them continually.

Aurora rising from her rosy bed,
First blushed, then wept, to see fair Phoebe graced,
And unto Lady May these words she said,
Come, let us go, we will not be out-faced.

I will unto Apollo's wagoner,
A bid him bring his Master presently,

* cuirass: breastplate.
† variation of Diana.

That his bright beams may all her beauty mar,
Gracing us with the luster of his eye.

Come, come, sweet May, and fill their laps with flowers,
And I will give a greater light than she;
So all these Ladies' favors shall be ours,
None shall be more esteemed than we shall be.

Thus did Aurora dim fair Phoebe's light,
And was received in bright Cynthia's place,
While Flora all with fragrant flowers dight,
Pressed to show the beauty of her face.

Though these, me thought, were very pleasing sights,
Yet now these Worthies did agree to go,
Unto a place full of all rare delights,
A place that yet Minerva did not know.

That sacred spring where Art and Nature strived,
Which should remain as Sovereign of the place;
Whose ancient quarrel being new revived,
Added fresh beauty, gave far greater grace.

To which as unpires now these Ladies go,
Judging with pleasure their delightful case;
Whose ravished senses made them quickly know
'T would be offensive either to displace.

And therefore willed they should forever dwell,
In perfect unity by this matchless spring,
Since 'twas impossible either should excell,
Or her fair fellow in subjection bring.

But here in equal sovereignty to live,
Equal in state, equal in dignity,
That unto others they might comfort give,
Rejoicing all with their sweet unity.

And now me thought I long to hear her name,
Whom wise Minerva honored so much,

She whom I saw was crowned by noble Fame,
Whom Envy sought to sting, yet could not touch.

Me thought the meager elf did seek byways
To come unto her, but it would not be;
Her venom purified by virtue's rays,
She pined and starved like an Anatomy:

While beauteous Pallas with this Lady fair,
Attended by these nymphs of noble fame,
Beheld those woods, those groves, those bowers rare,
By which Pergusa, for so hight the name

Of that fair spring, his dwelling place and ground;
And through those fields with sundry flowers clad,
Of several colors, to adorn the ground,
And please the senses even of the most sad:

He trailed along the woods in wanton wise,
With sweet delight to entertain them all;
Inviting them to sit and to devise
On holy hymns; at last to mind they call

Those rare sweet songs which Israel's King did frame,
Unto the Father of Eternity,
Before his holy wisdom took the name
Of great Messias, Lord of unity.

Those holy sonnets they did all agree,
With this most lovely Lady here to sing;
That by her noble breast's sweet harmony,
Their music might in ears of angels ring.

While saints like swans about this silver brook
Should Hallelujah sing continually,
Writing her praises in th'eternal book
Of endless honor, true fame's memory,

Thus I in sleep the heavenliest music heard,
That ever earthly ears did entertain;

And durst not wake, for fear to be debarred
Of what my senses sought still to retain.

Yet sleeping, prayed dull Slumber to unfold
Her noble name, who was of all admired;
When presently in drowsy terms he told
Not only that, but more than I desired.

This nymph, quoth he, great Pembroke hight by name,
Sister to valiant Sidney, whose clear light
Gives light to all that tread true paths of Fame,
Who in the globe of heaven doth shine so bright;

That being dead, his fame doth him survive,
Still living in the hearts of worthy men;
Pale Death is dead, but he remains alive,
Whose dying wounds restored him life again.

And this fair earthly goddess which you see,
Bellona and her virgins do attend;
In virtuous studies of divinity,
Her precious time continually doth spend.

So that a Sister well she may be deemed,
To him that lived and died so nobly;
And far before him is to be esteemed
For virtue, wisdom, learning, dignity.

Whose beauteous soul hath gained a double life,
Both here on earth, and in the heavens above,
Till dissolution end all worldly strife:
Her blessed spirit remains, of holy love,

Directing all by her immortal light,
In this huge sea of sorrows, griefs, and fears;
With contemplation of God's powerful might,
She fills the eyes, the hearts, the tongues, the ears

Of after-coming ages, which shall read
Her love, her zeal, her faith, and piety;

The fair impression of whose worthy deed,
Seals her pure soul unto the Diety.

That both in heaven and earth it may remain,
Crowned with her Maker's glory and his love;
And this did Father Slumber tell with pain,
Whose dulness scarce could suffer him to move.

When I awaking left him and his bower,
Much grieved that I could no longer stay;
Senseless was sleep, not to admit me power,
As I had spent the night to spend the day:

Then had God Morphie showed the end of all,
And what my heart desired, mine eyes had seen;
For as I waked me thought I heard one call
For that bright claret lent by Jove's fair Queen.

But thou, base cunning thief, that robs our spirits
Of half that span of life which years doth give:
And yet no praise unto thyself it merits,
To make a seeming death in those that live.

Yea wickedly thou dost consent to death,
Within thy restful bed to rob our souls;
In Slumber's bower thou stealest away our breath,
Yet none there is that thy base stealths controls.

If poor and sickly creatures would embrace thee,
Or they to whom thou givest a taste of pleasure,
Thou fliest as if Acteon's hounds did chase thee,
Or that to stay with them thou hadst no leisure.

But though thou has deprived me of delight,
By stealing from me ere I was aware;
I know I shall enjoy the self-same sight,
Thou hast no power my waking spirits to bare.

For to this Lady now I will repair,
Presenting her the fruits of idle hours;

Though many books she writes that are more rare,
Yet there is honey in the meanest flowers:

Which is both wholesome and delights the taste:
Though sugar be more finer, higher prized,
Yet is the painful bee no whit disgraced,
Nor her fair wax, or honey more despized.

And though that learned damsel and the rest,
Have in a higher style her trophy framed;
Yet these unlearned lines being my best,
Of her great wisdom can no whit be blamed.

And therefore, first I here present my dream,
And next, invite her Honor to my feast;
For my clear reason sees her by that stream,
Where her rare virtues daily are increased.

So craving pardon for this bold attempt,
I here present my mirror to her view,
Whose noble virtues cannot be exempt,
My glass being steel, declares them to be true.

And Madam, if you will vouchsafe that grace,
To grace those flowers that springs from virtue's ground,
Though your fair mind on worthier works is placed,
On works that are more deep, and more profound;

Yet is it no disparagement to you,
To see your Savior in a shepherd's weed,
Unworthily presented in your view,
Whose worthiness will grace each line you read.

Receive him here by my unworthy hand,
And read his paths of fair humility;
Who though our sins in number pass the sand,
They are all purged by his Divinity.

(Here begins the Passion of Christ.)

That very Night our Saviour was betrayed,
Oh night! exceeding all the nights of sorrow,
When our most blessed Lord, although dismayed,
Yet would not he one Minute's respite borrow,
But to Mount Olives went, though sore afraid,
To welcome Night, and entertain the Morrow;
    And as he oft unto that place did go,
    So did he now, to meet his long nursed woe.

. . . .

Now when the dawn of day gins to appear,
And all your wicked counsels have an end,
To end his Life, that holds you all so dear,
For to that purpose did your studies bend;
Proud Pontius Pilate must the matter hear,
To your untruths his ears he now must lend:
    Sweet Jesus bound, to him you led away,
    Of his most precious blood to make your prey.

Which, when that wicked Caitiff did perceive,
By whose lewd means he came to this distress;
He brought the price of blood he did receive,
Thinking thereby to make his fault seem less,
And with these Priests and Elders did it leave,
Confessed his fault, wherein he did transgress:
    But when he saw Repentance unrespected,
    He hanged himself; of God and Man rejected.

By this Example, what can be expected
From wicked Man, which on the Earth doth live?
But faithless dealing, fear of God neglected;
Who for their private gain cares not to sell
The Innocent Blood of God's most dear elected,
As did that caitiff wretch, now damned in Hell:
    If in Christ's School, he took so great a fall,
    What will they do, that come not there at all?

Now Pontius Pilate is to judge the Cause
Of faultless Jesus, who before him stands;
Who neither hath offended Prince, nor Laws,
Although he now be brought in woefull bands:
O noble Governor, make thou yet a pause,
Do not in innocent blood imbrue thy hands;
  But hear the words of thy most worthy wife,
  Who sends to thee, to beg her Saviour's life.

Let barbarous cruelty far depart from thee,
And in true Justice take affliction's part;
Open thine eyes, that thou the truth mayest see,
Do not the thing that goes against thy heart,
Condemn not him that must thy Saviour be;
But view his holy Life, his good desert.
  Let not us Women glory in Men's fall,
  Who had power given to over-rule us all.

Till now your indiscretion sets us free,
And makes our former fault much less appear;
Our Mother Eve, who tasted of the Tree,
Giving to Adam what she held most dear,
Was simply good, and had no power to see,
The after-coming harm did not appear:
  The subtle Serpent that our Sex betrayed,
  Before our fall so sure a plot had laid.

That undiscerning Ignorance perceived
No guile, or craft that was by him intended;
For had she known, of what we were bereaved,
To his request she had not condescended.
But she (poor soul) by cunning was deceived,
No hurt therein her harmless Heart intended:
  For she alleged God's word, which he denies,
  That they should die, but even as Gods, be wise.

But surely Adam can not be excused,
Her fault though great, yet he was most to blame;
What Weakness offered, Strength might have refused,
Being Lord of all, the greater was his shame:

Although the Serpent's craft had her abused,
God's holy word ought all his actions frame,
    For he was Lord and King of all the earth,
    Before poor Eve had either life or breath.

Who being framed by God's eternal hand,
The perfectest man that ever breathed on earth;
And from God's mouth received that strait command,
The breach whereof he knew was present death:
Yea having power to rule both Sea and Land,
Yet with one Apple won to loose that breath
    Which God had breathed in his beauteous face,
    Bringing us all in danger and disgrace.

And then to lay the fault on Patience's back,
That we (poor women) must endure it all;
We know right well he did discretion lack,
Being not persuaded thereunto at all;
If Eve did err, it was for knowledge sake,
The fruit being fair persuaded him to fall:
    No subtle Serpent's falsehood did betray him,
    If he would eat it, who had power to stay him?

Not Eve, whose fault was only too much love,
Which made her give this present to her Dear,
That what she tasted, he likewise might prove,
Whereby his knowledge might become more clear;
He never sought her weakness to reprove,
With those sharp words, which he of God did hear:
    Yet men will boast of Knowledge, which he took
    From Eve's fair hand, as from a learned Book.

If any Evil did in her remain,
Being made of him, he was the ground of all;
If one of many Worlds could lay a stain
Upon our Sex, and work so great a fall
To wretched Man, by Satan's subtle train;
What will so foul a fault amongst you all?
    Her weakness did the Serpent's words obey,
    But you in malice God's dear Son betray.

Whom, if unjustly you condemn to die,
Her sin was small, to what you do commit;
All mortal sins that do for vengeance cry,
Are not to be compared unto it:
If many worlds would altogether try,
By all their sins the wrath of God to get;
      This sin of yours surmounts them all as far
      As doth the Sun, another little star.

Then let us have our Liberty again,
And challenge to your selves no Sovereignty;
You came not in the world without our pain,
Make that a bar against your cruelty;
Your fault being greater, why should you disdain
Our being your equals, free from tyranny?
      If one weak woman simply did offend,
      This sin of yours hath no excuse, nor end.

To which (poor souls) we never gave consent,
Witness thy wife (O Pilate) speaks for all;
Who did but dream, and yet a message sent,
That thou shouldest have nothing to do at all
With that just man; which, if thy heart relent,
Why wilt thou be a reprobate with Saul?
      To seek the death of him that is so good,
      For thy soul's health to shed his dearest blood.

Yea, so thou mayest these sinful people please,
Thou are content against all truth and right,
To seal this act, that may procure thine ease
With blood, and wrong, with tyranny, and might;
The multitude thou seekest to appease,
By base dejection of this heavenly Light:
      Demanding which of these that thou shouldst loose,
      Whether the Thief, or Christ, King of the Jews.

Base Barrabas the Thief, they all desire,
And thou more base than he, performest their will;
Yet when thy thoughts back to themselves retire,

Thou art unwilling to commit this ill:
Oh that thou couldst unto such grace aspire,
That thy polluted lips might never kill
> That Honour, which right Judgment ever graceth,
> To purchase shame, which all true worth defaceth.

. . . .

ELIZABETH CLINTON, COUNTESS OF LINCOLN

1574–1630(?)

E LIZABETH CLINTON was the daughter of Sir Henry Knyvet of Charl-
ton, Wiltshire, and Anne, daughter of Sir Christopher Pickering of
Killington, Westmoreland. The Knyvet family was prominent in East
Anglia as well as in Wiltshire, and, through marriage, was well represented in the noble households and at the court. Elizabeth's brother
Thomas was a member of the parliament of 1601 for Thetford, was
knighted in 1604, and was summoned to Parliament as Baron Knyvet of
Escrick, Yorkshire, in 1607. We know nothing of his sister's education
apart from allusions in her *Nurserie*.

Thomas Clinton, who was to become the third Earl of Lincoln and
the eleventh Baron Clinton, married Elizabeth Knyvet in 1584, when she
was ten years old and he was sixteen, still a student at Christ Church,
Oxford. He received his M.A. in 1588. Along with his brother-in-law, he
too was a member of the parliament of 1601 for Great Grimsby and
represented Lincolnshire from 1604 to 1610. In 1610, after the death of
his father, Thomas was summoned to Parliament "in his father's Barony,
and was placed accordingly," in the House of Lords. The full title and
major estates were now his.

Elizabeth and Thomas had seven sons and nine daughters, few of
whom survived childhood. The eldest son, Theophilus, succeeded to his
father's titles and estates in 1619. He was made Knight of the Bath in
1616, and was at Queen's College, Cambridge, in 1618. Two years later
he married Briget, daughter of William first Viscount Say and Sele.
Theophilus was active in military affairs, served as Speaker of the House
of Lords in 1647, was appointed Commissioner for the Colonies in 1660,
and assisted at the coronation of Charles II in 1661. He died in 1667.

As for the daughters, the names of six were listed in their father's will,
which was probated in 1620: Fraunces, Arabella, Susan, Dorcas, Sara,

and Elizabeth. The Lady Arabella married Isaac John, a Puritan, and emigrated to New England with the John Winthrop party in 1629. The flagship of the convoy was named *The Lady Arabella* in her honor. Her husband was a prime mover in the project for the settlement of Massachusetts Bay. Arabella died in 1630.

By the time *The Countess of Lincoln's Nurserie* was printed in 1622, Elizabeth had been Dowager Countess, a widow, for three years. She asserts in a letter to Briget, wife of Theophilus, that this is her first work to be printed and implies that she had written other items, although these have not been identified. She praises her daughter-in-law for nursing her own children, and expresses the hope that this treatise may persuade others to follow her example. Briget bore two sons, both of whom died young, and seven daughters before her own death in 1630.

Thomas Lodge, whose *Rosalind* was the source for Shakespeare's *As You Like It*, provided a prefatory note to the *Nurserie*, addressed "To the Courteous, chiefly most Christian, Reader," in which he stated three reasons why this book should be read: the eminence of the Countess, the rarity of the subject handled, and the brevity of its treatment.

In addition to its first publication in 1622, the little treatise was published in 1744, 1808 (two editions), and 1809.

BIBLIOGRAPHY

Editions

The Countess of Lincoln's Nurserie. Oxford: J. Lichfield & J. Short, 1622.
The Countess of Lincoln's Nurserie. Printed in *Harleian Miscellany* for R. Dutton. London, 1809.

Related Readings

Ballard, George. *Memoirs of Several Ladies of Great Britain.* Oxford: Printed for the author by W. Jackson, 1752.
British Museum, Additional Ms. 19138—for Knyvet pedigree. (Elizabeth Clinton was a member of the Knyvet family.)

The Countess of Lincoln's Nurserie

ELIZABETH CLINTON, COUNTESS OF LINCOLN

[Oxford, 1622]

Because it hath pleased God to bless me with many children, and so caused me to observe many things falling out to mothers and to their children, I thought good to open my mind concerning a special matter belonging to all child-bearing women seriously to consider of, and to manifest my mind the better, even to write of this matter, so far as God will please to direct me; in sum, the matter I mean is, the duty of nursing, due by mothers to their own children.

In setting down whereof I will, first, show that every woman ought to nurse her own child; and, secondly, I will endeavor to answer such objections as are used to be cast out against this duty, to disgrace the same.

The first point is easily performed, for it is the express ordinance of God that mothers should nurse their own children, and, being his ordinance, they are bound to it in conscience. This should stop the mouths of all repliers, for God is most wise and therefore must needs know what is fittest and best for us to do; and, to prevent all foolish fears or shifts, we are given to understand that he is also all-sufficient, and therefore infinitely able to bless his own ordinance and to afford us means in ourselves (as continual experience confirmeth) toward the observance thereof.

If this, as it ought, be granted, then how venturous are those women that dare venture to do otherwise, and so to refuse, and, by refusing, to despise that order which the most wise and Almighty God hath appointed, and instead thereof to choose their own pleasures? O what peace can there be to these women's consciences, unless, through the darkness of their understanding, they judge it no disobedience?

And then they will drive me to prove that this nursing and nourishing of their own children in their own bosoms is God's ordinance. They are very willful, or very ignorant, if they make a question of it. For it is proved sufficiently to be their duty, both by God's word and also by his works.

By his word it is proved, first, by examples: namely, the example of Eve. For who suckled her sons Cain, Abel, Seth, etc. but herself? Which she did not only of mere necessity, because yet no other woman was created, but especially because she was their mother, and so saw it was her duty; and because she had a true natural affection which moved her to do it gladly. Next, the example of Sarah, the wife of Abraham; for she both gave her son Isaac suck, as doing the duty commanded of God, and also took great comfort and delight therein, as in a duty well pleasing to herself; whence she spoke of it, as of an action worthy to be named in her holy rejoicing. Now if Sarah, so great a princess, did nurse her own child, why should any of us neglect to do the like, except (which God forbid) we think scorn to follow her, whose daughters it is our glory to be, and which we be only upon this condition, that we imitate her well-doing. Let us look therefore to our worthy pattern, noting withal, that she put herself to this work when she was very old, and so might the better have excused herself, than we younger women can, being also more able to hire and keep a nurse than any of us. But why is she not followed by most in the practice of this duty? Even because they want her virtue and piety. This want is the common hindrance to this point of the woman's obedience; for this want makes them want love to God's precepts, want love to his doctrine, and, like step-mothers, want due love to their own children.

But now to another worthy example: namely, that excellent woman Hannah, who having, after much affliction of mind, obtained a Son of God, whom she vowed unto God; she did not put him to another to nurse but nursed him her ownself, until she had weaned him, and carried him to be consecrated unto the Lord; as well knowing that this duty, of giving her child suck, was so acceptable to God, as, for the cause thereof, she did not sin in staying with it at home from the yearly sacrifice; but now women, expecially of any place, and of little grace, do not hold this duty acceptable to God because it is unacceptable to themselves; as if they would have the Lord to like and dislike, according to their vain lusts.

To proceed, take notice of one example more: that is, of the blessed Virgin; as her womb bare our blessed Savior, so her paps gave him suck. Now who shall deny the own mother's suckling of their own children to be their duty, since every godly matron hath walked in these steps before them: Eve, the mother of all the living; Sarah, the mother of all the faithful; Hannah, so graciously heard of God; Mary, blessed among women, and called blessed of all ages. And who can say but that the rest of holy women mentioned in the holy scriptures did the like, since no doubt that speech of that noble dame saying, Who would have said to Abraham, that Sarah should have given children suck? was taken from the ordinary custom of mothers in those less corrupted times?

And so much for proof of this office and duty to be God's ordinance, by his own word according to the argument of examples; I hope I shall likewise prove it by the same word from plain precepts. First, from that precept which willeth the younger women to marry and to bear children; that is, not only to bear them in the womb, and to bring them forth, but also to bear them on their knee, in their arms, and at their breasts; for this bearing a little before is called nourishing and bringing up; and to enforce it the better into women's consciences, it is numbered as the first of the good works for which godly women should be well reported of. And well it may be the first, because if holy ministers or other Christians do hear of a good woman to be brought to bed, and her child to be living, their first question usually is, whether she herself give it suck, yea or no? If the answer be she doth, then they commend her; if she doth not, then they are sorry for her.

And thus I come to a second precept. I pray you, who that judges aright, doth not hold the suckling of her own child the part of a true mother, of an honest mother, of a just mother, of a sincere mother, of a mother worthy of love, of a mother deserving good report, of a virtuous mother, of a mother winning praise for it? All this is assented to by any of good understanding. Therefore this is also a precept, as for other duties, so for this of mothers to their children, which saith: whatsoever things are true, whatsoever things are honest, whatsoever things are just, whatsoever things are pure, whatsoever things are worthy of love, whatsoever things are of good report, if there be any virtue, if there be any praise, think on these things; these things do, and the God of peace shall be with you.

So far for my promise to prove, by the word of God, that it is his ordinance that women should nurse their own children; now I will endeavor to prove it by his works: First, by his works of judgment; if it were not his ordinance for mothers to give their children suck, it were no judgment to bereave them of their milk; but it is specified to be a great judgment to bereave them hereof, and to give them dry breasts; therefore it is to be gathered, even from hence, that it is his ordinance, since to deprive them of means to do it is a punishment of them.

I add to this, The work that God worketh in the very nature of mothers, which proveth also that he hath ordained that they should nurse their own children; for by his secret operation the mother's affection is so knit by nature's law to her tender babe, as she finds no power to deny to suckle it, no not when she is in hazard to lose her own life by attending on it; for in such a case it is not said, Let the mother fly, and leave her infant to the peril, as if she were dispensed with; but only it is said, Woe to her, as if she were to be pitied, that for nature and her child she must be unnatural to herself; now if any then being even at liberty and in peace, with all plenty, shall deny to give suck to their own children, they go against nature; and show that God hath not done so much for them as to work any good, no not in their nature, but left them more savage than the dragons, and as cruel to their little ones as the ostriches.

Now another work of God, proving this point, is the work of his provision for every kind to be apt and able to nourish their own fruit; there is no beast that feeds their young with milk but the Lord, even from the first ground of the order of nature, Grow and multiply, hath provided it with milk to suckle their own young, which every beast takes so naturally unto, as if another beast come towards their young to offer the office of a dam unto it, they show, according to their fashion, a plain dislike of it, as if nature did speak in them and say it is contrary to God's order in nature, commanding each kind to increase and multiply in their own bodies, and by their own breasts, not to bring forth by one dam, and to bring up by another; but it is his ordinance that every kind should bring forth, and also nurse its own fruit.

Much more should this work of God prevail to persuade women made as man in the image of God, and therefore should be ashamed to be put to school to learn good nature of the unreasonable creature. In us also, as we know by experience, God provideth milk in our own breasts against the time of our children's birth, and this he hath done ever since it was said to us also, Increase and multiply; so that this work of his provision showeth that he tieth us likewise to nourish the children of our own womb, with our own breasts, even by the order of nature; yea it showeth that he so careth for and regardeth little children, even from the womb, that he would have them nursed by those that in all reason will look to them with the kindest affection, namely their mothers; and in giving them milk for it, he doth plainly tell them that he requires it.

Oh consider, how comes our milk? Is it not by the direct providence of God? Why provides he it but for the child? The mothers then that refuse to nurse their own children, do they not despise God's Providence? Do they not deny God's will? Do they not as it were say, I see, O God, by the means thou hast put into me, that thou wouldst have me nurse the child thou hast given me, but I will not do so much for thee. Oh impious and impudent unthankfulness; yea monstrous unnaturalness, both to their own natural fruit born so near their breasts and fed in their own wombs, and yet may not be suffered to suck their own milk.

And this unthankfulness and unnaturalness is oftener the sin of the higher and the richer sort than of the meaner and the poorer, except some nice and proud idle dames, who will imitate their betters, will they make their poor husbands beggars. And his is one hurt which the better rank do by their ill example egg and embolden the lower ones to follow them to their loss. Were it not better for us greater persons to keep God's ordinance and to show the meaner their duty in our good example? I am sure we have more helps to perform it and have fewer probable reasons to allege against it than women that live by hard labor and painful toil. If such mothers as refuse this office of love and of nature to their children should hereafter be refused, despised, and neglected of those their children, were they not just requited according to their own unkind dealing? I might say more in handling this first point of my promise, but I leave the larger and learneder discourse hereof unto men of art and learning; only to speak of so much as I read and know in my own experience, which, if any of my sex and condition do receive good by, I am glad; if they scorn it, they shall have the reward of scorners. I write in modesty, and can reap no disgrace by their immodest folly.

And so I come to my last part of my promise which is, to answer objections made by divers against this duty of mothers to their children.

First, it is objected that Rebecca had a nurse, and that therefore her mother did not give her suck of her own breasts, and so good women in the first ages did not hold them to this office of nursing their own children. To this I answer that if her mother had milk, and health, and yet did put this duty from her to another, it was her fault, and so proved nothing against me; but it is manifest that she that Rebecca called her nurse was called so either for that she most tended her while her mother suckled her, or for that she weaned her, or for that, during her nonage and childhood, she did minister to her continually such good things as delighted and nourished her up. For to any one of these the name of a nurse is fitly given; whence a good wife is called her husband's nurse; and that Rebecca's nurse was only such a one, appeareth, because afterwards she is not named a nurse but a maid, saying: Then Rebecca rose, and her maids;

now maids give not suck out of their breasts, never any virgin or honest maid gave suck, but that blessed one from an extraordinary and blessed power.

Secondly, it is objected that it is troublesome, that it is noisome to one's clothes, that it makes one look old, etc. All such reasons are uncomely and unchristian to be objected, and therefore unworthy to be answered; they argue unmotherly affection, idleness, desire to have liberty to gad from home, pride, foolish fineness, lust, wantonnesss, and the like evils. Ask Sarah, Hannah, the blessed Virgin, and any modest loving mother, what trouble they accounted it to give their little ones suck? Behold most nursing mothers, and they be as clean and sweet in their clothes and carry their age and hold their beauty as well as those that suckle not, and most likely are they so to do because, keeping God's ordinance, they are sure of God's blessing; and it hath been observed in some women that they grow more beautiful and better favored, by very nursing their own children.

But there are some women that object fear, saying that they are so weak, and so tender, that they are afraid to venture to give their children suck lest they endanger their health thereby. Of these I demand, why then did they venture to marry and so to bear children? And if they say they could not choose, and that they thought not that marriage would impair their health, I answer, that for the same reasons they should set themselves to nurse their own children, because they should not choose but to do what God would have them do; and they should believe that this work will be for their health also, seeing it is ordinary with the Lord to give good stomach, health, and strength to almost all mothers that take this pains with their children.

One answer more to all the objections that use to be made against giving children suck is this, that now the hardness, to effect this matter, is much removed by a late example of a tender young lady and you may all be encouraged to follow after, in that wherein she hath gone before you, and so made the way more easy, and more hopeful, by that which she findeth possible and comfortable by God's blessing, and no offence to her lord nor herself; she might have had as many doubts and lets as any of you, but she was willing to try how God would enable her, and he hath given her good success, as I hope he will do to others that are willing to trust in God for his help.

Now if any reading these few lines return against me, that it may be I myself have given my own children suck and therefore am bolder and more busy to meddle in urging this point, to the end to insult over and to make them to be blamed that have not done it. I answer, that whether I have or have not performed this my bounden duty, I will not deny to tell my own practice. I know and acknowledge that I should have done it and, having not done it, it was not for want of will in myself, but partly I was over-ruled by another's authority and partly deceived by some ill counsel, and partly I had not so well considered of my duty in this motherly office as since I did, when it was too late for me to put it in execution. Wherefore, being pricked in heart for my undutifulness, this way, I study to redeem my peace, first by repentance towards God, humbly and often craving his pardon for this my offence; secondly, by studying how to show double love to my children, to make them amends for neglect of this part of love to them, when they should have hung on my breasts and been nourished in my own bosom; thirdly, by doing my endeavor to prevent many Christian mothers from sinning in the same kind, against our most loving and gracious God.

And for this cause I add unto my performed promise this short exhortation: namely, I beseech all godly women to remember how we elder ones are commanded to instruct the younger, to love their children; now therefore love them so as to do this office to them when they are born, more gladly for love sake than a stranger, who bore them not, shall do for lucre sake. Also I pray you to set no more so light by God's blessing in your own breasts, which the Holy Spirit ranketh with other excellent blessings; if it be unlawful to trample under feet a cluster of grapes in which a little wine is found; then how unlawful is it to destroy and dry up those breasts in which your own child, and perhaps one of God's very elect, to whom to be a nursing father is a King's honor, and to whom to be a nursing mother is a Queen's honor, might find food of sincere milk, even from God's immediate providence, until it were fitter for stronger meat; I do know that the Lord may deny some women either to have any milk in their breasts at all, or to have any passage for their milk, or to have any health, or to have a right mind; and so they may be letted from this duty by want, by sickness, by lunacy, etc. But I speak not to these: I speak to you whose consciences witness against you, that you cannot justly allege any of those impediments.

Do you submit yourselves to the pain and trouble of this ordinance of God? Trust not other women whom wages hires to do it better than yourselves, whom God and nature tie to do it. I have found by grievous experience such dissembling in nurses, pretending sufficiency of milk,

when, indeed, they had too much scarcity; pretending willingness, to-
wardness, wakefulness, when, indeed, they have been most wilful, most
froward, and most slothful, as I fear the death of one or two of my little
babes came by the default of their nurses. Of all those which I had for
eighteen children, I had but two which were thoroughly willing and
careful; divers have had their children miscarry in the nurses' hands, and
are such mothers (if it were by the nurses' carelessness) guiltless? I know
not how they should, since they will shut them out of the arms of nature
and leave them to the will of a stranger; yea, to one that will seem to
estrange herself from her own child to give suck to the nurse-child: this
she may feign to do upon a covetous composition, but she frets at it in her
mind, if she has any natural affection.

Therefore, be no longer at the trouble and at the care to hire others to
do your own work; be not so unnatural as to thrust away your own
children; be not so hardy as to venture a tender babe to a less tender heart;
be not accessory to that disorder of causing a poorer woman to banish
her own infant for the entertaining of a richer woman's child, as it were,
bidding her unlove her own to love yours. We have followed Eve in
transgression; let us follow her in obedience. When God laid the sorrows
of conception, of breeding, of bringing forth, and of bringing up her
children upon her, and so upon us in her loins, did she reply any word
against it? Not a word; so I pray you all my own daughters, and others
that are still child bearing, reply not against the duty of suckling them
when God hath sent you them.

Indeed, I see some, if the weather be wet, or cold; if the way be foul, if
the church be far off, I see thay are so coy, so nice, so lukewarm, they will
not take pains for their own souls. Alas! No marvel if these will not be at
trouble and pain to nourish their children's bodies; but fear God; be
diligent to serve him; approve all his ordinances; seek to please him;
account it no trouble or pain to do anything that hath the promise of his
blessing; and then you will, no doubt, do this good, laudable, natural,
loving duty to your children. If yet you be not satisfied, inquire not of such
as refuse to do this, consult not with your own conceit, advise not with
flatterers; but ask counsel of sincere and faithful preachers. If you be
satisfied, then take this with you, to make you do it cheerfully: think
always that, having the child at your breast, and having it in your arms,
you have God's blessing there. For children are God's blessings. Think
again how your babe crying for your breast, sucking heartily the milk out
of it, and growing by it, is the Lord's own instruction, every hour, and

every day, that you are suckling it, instructing you to show that you are his new-born babes, by your earnest desire after his word, and the sincere doctrine thereof, and by your daily growing in grace and goodness thereby; so shall you reap pleasure and profit. Again, you may consider that, when your child is at your breast, it is a fit occasion to move your heart to pray for a blessing upon that work, and to give thanks for your child, and for ability and freedom unto that which many a mother would have done and could not; who have tried and ventured their health, and taken much pains, and yet have not obtained their desire. But they that are fitted every way for this commendable act have certainly great cause to be thankful; and I much desire that God may have glory and praise for every good work, and you much comfort, that do seek to honor God in all things. Amen.

ELIZABETH CARY,
VISCOUNTESS FALKLAND
1585–1639

ELIZABETH TANFIELD CARY was the only child of Sir Lawrence Tanfield, a prosperous lawyer who became Chief Baron of the Exchequer, and Elizabeth Symonds, granddaughter of Sir Anthony Lee. When their daughter was four or five years old, the Tanfields engaged a tutor to teach her French, but within a few weeks he was dismissed: Elizabeth refused to study with him. Later, when she became interested in French books, she taught herself to read them. Her parents soon found that no tutor could teach her anything: she insisted on being self-taught. Before her marriage at seventeen she was proficient in Spanish, French, Latin, Transylvanian, and possibly Italian and Hebrew, and her skill in the traditionally feminine art of needlework was astonishing. When she developed an interest in geography she translated an abridgement of Ortelius's *Le Miroir du Monde*, the manuscript of which is now in the possession of Burford parish church in Oxfordshire, where she grew up.

The story is told that she accompanied her father to court one day to observe the trial of a woman accused of witchcraft. Elizabeth's keen observation enabled her to suggest questions that her father incorporated in his examination. The result was an acquittal, in spite of prior confessions that had been made under duress. The child was then ten years old.

Two years later Tanfield gave her Calvin's *Institutes*, a monumental work of theology that had been translated from the Latin into English in 1562 and published in a volume of more than a thousand folio pages. The father was scandalized by her criticism of it and cried, "This girl hath a spirit averse to Calvin!"

When her parents forbade her to read in bed, the precocious Elizabeth soon bribed the servants, and by the time she was twelve she owed them £100 for eight hundred candles, and twice that amount for other items she required. These debts were paid at the time of her marriage.

Sir Henry Cary (or Carew), son of the Master of the Royal Jewel House, was twenty-six when he married Elizabeth Tanfield in 1602. He spent several years immediately after their marriage fighting in the Low Countries and was taken prisoner there. The ransom paid for his release reduced the family fortune to the extent that Sir Henry was in financial straits for many years afterwards. However, his service abroad brought him considerable renown, and he was honored as a hero on his return to London. During his absence Elizabeth had lived with his mother, an imperious matriarch whose attempts to command subservience only resulted in defiance on the part of her daughter-in-law and hatred on both sides.

Sir Henry established a home with his wife some time after 1606. Their first daughter was born in 1609, and the first son, Lucius, a year later. By 1624 nine more children had been "born alive," according to Elizabeth's record. Lucius was taken into the Tanfield household while still a small child, to be raised as the prospective heir.

Sir Henry was raised to the Scottish peerage in 1620 as Viscount Falkland, County of Fife. In 1622 he was appointed Lord Deputy of Ireland and took up residence on that island with his family. Without Elizabeth's funds, he could not have taken the post. She turned over to him the jointure settled upon her by her father as part of the marriage contract, and was disinherited as a result of her action. It is possible that the knowledge of Elizabeth's conversion to Roman Catholicism had some bearing on her father's decision to remove her name from his will, as this change of religion greatly offended him. Elizabeth returned to England in 1625, the year of her father's death.

For many years Catholicism had appealed to Lady Cary; she claimed conversion at the age of nineteen, but was not formally received into the Roman church until 1626. Then her problems multiplied. Estranged from her husband, she was denied her living allowance, stripped of most of her possessions, and denied access to her children. Even the king urged her to return to her mother's house. But she still had some friends in high places. The queen, herself a Catholic, took Elizabeth's eldest daughter into her service, and Lady Buckingham also supported her, as did others.

By 1627 the king had decided that the Falkland problem was a court scandal and that the Viscountess might well be starving. The Privy Council ordered Sir Henry to pay all of Elizabeth's debts, give her an allowance of £100 annually and supply all necessities for her, including nine servants; or he could give her an annual allowance of £500. Eventually he compromised, and agreed to pay her £300 per year. Two years later the queen brought about a reconciliation between the Falklands when Sir Henry returned from Ireland. They probably lived together for a short time that summer, shortly before Sir Henry's death, which resulted from a fall from a horse. There is a romantic tale that circulated about the manner of his death. He had been riding in the company of the king, and when the accident occurred, the king rode toward him to see what had happened. Sir Henry had always followed the tradition of standing in the presence of the sovereign, and, when he saw Charles, he forced himself to his feet in spite of his broken leg. The injury was thereby compounded, and a resulting infection caused his death.

Until her death in 1639 Elizabeth lived in dire poverty, although her son Lucius provided her with gifts from time to time. Her reputation for prodigality and for irresponsibility in financial matters made it difficult for her friends to help her. Six of her children became Roman Catholics—four daughters entered a convent at Cambray, and one son, Placid, took holy orders in the Roman church. She herself enjoyed a solid reputation as a theologian and scholar and was continually visited by the intellectuals of her day. Her translation of part of the *Reply of the Most Illustrious Cardinal of Perron to the Answer of the Most Excellent King of Great Britain*, dedicated to the queen, was published in Douay, France, in 1630. Most of the copies sent to England were ordered burnt by the Archbishop of Canterbury, but a few reached Elizabeth. She also wrote, in verse, lives of St. Mary Magdalen, St. Agnes Martyr, and St. Elizabeth of Portingall, as well as many verses on the Virgin Mary. None of these works is now extant.

The Tragedy of Mariam may have been inspired by the Countess of Pembroke's translation of the *Tragedy of Antonie*, from Garnier's French. We do not know just when Elizabeth wrote it, but when it was published in 1613 it was a landmark: this was the first play in English known to have been written by a woman. The dedicatory poem addressed to her sister-in-law, Elizabeth Cary (or Carew), is in the form of a Shakespearean sonnet. She also follows this form in the first fourteen lines of the first scene, after which she writes, for the most part, in quatrains that rhyme abab; from time to time the rhyme scheme is interlocking—abab, bcbc, etc.—reminiscent of Spenser. The iambic pentameter lines written for the chorus are in the form of sestets, rhyming ababcc. Frequently the speeches of the principals are concluded in a couplet. Apparently the blank verse of Marlowe and Shakespeare held no charms for the Viscountess, who chose the discipline of rhyme for her play.

BIBLIOGRAPHY

Works

The Reply of the Most Illustrious Cardinal Perron. Translated. Douay, France: Printed by Martin Bogart, 1630.

The Tragedie of Mariam, The Fair Queen of Jewry. London: Printed by Thomas Creede for Richard Hawkins, 1613.

Dunstan, A. C. and Greg, W. W., eds. *The Tragedy of Mariam, 1613.* Oxford: Printed by H. Hart at Oxford University Press for the Malone Society, 1914.

Related Readings

Dolman, Charles, ed. *The Lady Falkland: Her Life.* From a Ms. in the Imperial Archives, Lille, France. Probably written by one of Elizabeth Cary's daughters, revised by a son (according to Dolman). London: Catholic Publishing & Bookselling Co., 1861. Prime source for Fullerton and Murdock.

Dunstan, A. C. *Examination of Two English Dramas.* Königsberg, Germany: Hartungsche Buchdruckerei, 1908.

Fullerton, Lady Georgiana Charlotte. *The Life of Elizabeth Lady Falkland 1585–1639. Quarterly Series,* vol. 6. London: Burns & Oates, 1883.

Murdock, Kenneth Ballard. *The Sun at Noon.* New York: Macmillan, 1939. Also contains sketches of Lucius Cary and John Wilmot.

The Tragedie of Mariam, The Fair Queen of Jewry

ELIZABETH CARY, VISCOUNTESS FALKLAND

[*London, 1613*]

To Diana's Earthlie Deputesse, and my Worthy
Sister, Elizabeth Carew.

When cheerful Phoebus his full course hath run,
His sister's fainter beams our hearts doth cheer:
So your fair Brother is to me the Sun,
And you his Sister as my Moon appear.

You are my next belov'd, my second Friend,
For when my Phoebus' absence makes it night,
Whilst to th'Antipodes his beams do bend,
From you my Phoebe, shines my second light.

He like to Sol, clear-sighted, constant, free,
You Luna-like, unspotted, chaste, divine:
He shone on Sicily, you destin'd be
T'illumine the now obscured Palestine.
My first was consecrated to Apollo,
My second to Diana now shall follow.

E. C.

THE NAMES OF THE SPEAKERS

Herod, King of Judea.	Phaeroras, Herod's brother.
Doris, his first wife.	Graphina, his love.
Mariam, his second wife.	Babus, first son.
Salome, Herod's sister.	Babus, second son.
Antipater, his son by Salome.	Annanell, the High Priest.
Alexandra, Mariam's mother.	Sohemus, a Counsellor to Herod.
Silleus, Prince of Arabia.	Nuntio.
Constabarus, husband to Salome.	Bu, another messenger.

Chorus, a Company of Jews.

THE ARGUMENT

Herod the son of Antipater (an Idumean), having crept by the favor of the Romans into the Jewish monarchy, married Mariam, the daughter of Hircanus, the rightful King and Priest, and for her (besides her high blood, being of singular beauty) he repudiated Doris, his former wife, by whom he had children.

This Mariam had a brother called Aristobolus, and next him and Hircanus his grandfather, Herod in his wife's right had the best title.

Therefore to remove them, he charged the first with treason and put him to death, and drowned the second under color of sport. Alexandra, daughter to the one and mother to the other, accused him for their deaths before Anthony.

So when he was forced to go answer this accusation at Rome, he left the custody of his wife to Josephus his uncle, that had married his sister Salome, and out of a violent affection (unwilling any should enjoy her after him) he gave strict and private commandment, that if he were slain, she should be put to death. But he returned with much honor, yet found his wife extremely discontented, to whom Josephus had (meaning it for the best, to prove Herod loved her) revealed his charge.

So by Salome's accusation he put Josephus to death, but was reconciled to Mariam, who still bore the death of her friends exceeding hardly.

In this meantime Herod was again necessarily to revisit Rome, for Caesar having overthrown Anthony his great friend, was likely to make an alteration of his fortune.

In his absence, news came to Jerusalem that Caesar had put him to death; their willingness it should be so, together with the likelihood, gave this rumor so good credit, as Sohemus that had succeeded Josephus' charge, succeeded him likewise in revealing it. So at Herod's return, which was speedy and unexpected, he found Mariam so far from joy that she showed apparent signs of sorrow. He still desiring to win her to a better humor, she being very unable to conceal her passion, fell to upbraiding him with her brother's death. As they were thus debating, came in a fellow with a cup of wine, who, hired by Salome, said first, it was a love potion which Mariam desired to deliver to the King; but afterwards he affirmed that it was a poison, and that Sohemus had told her somewhat, which procured the vehement hate in her.

The King hearing of this, more moved with jealousy of Sohemus, than with this intent of poison, sent her away, and presently after by the instigation of Salome, she was beheaded. Which rashness was afterward punished in him with an intolerable and almost frantic passion for her death.

ACT I, SCENE I

Mariam sola.

How oft have I with public voice run on?
To censure Rome's last hero for deceit

Because he wept when Pompey's life was gone,
Yet when he liv'd, he thought his name too great.
But now I do recant, and Roman Lord,
Excuse too rash a judgment in a woman:
My sex pleads pardon, pardon then afford,
Mistaking is with us but too too common.
Now do I find by self experience taught,
One object only yields both grief and joy:
You wept indeed, when on his worth you thought,
But joyed that slaughter did your foe destroy.
So at his death your eyes true drops did rain,
Whom dead, you did not wish alive again.
When Herod liv'd, that now is done to death,
Oft have I wished that I from him were free:
Oft have I wished that he might lose his breath;
Oft have I wished his carcass dead to see.
Then rage and scorn had put my love to flight,
That love which once on him was firmly set:
Hate hid his true affection from my sight,
And kept my heart from paying him his debt.
And blame me not, for Herod's jealousy
Had power even constancy itself to change:
For he by barring me from liberty,
To shun my ranging, taught me first to range.
But yet too chaste a scholar was my heart,
To learn to love another than my Lord:
To leave his love, my lessons' former part,
I quickly learn'd, the other I abhorred.
But now his death to memory doth call
The tender love that he to Mariam bare:
And mine to him, this makes those rivers fall
Which by another thought unmoistened are.
For Aristobolus the loveliest youth
That ever did in Angel's shape appear,
The cruel Herod was not mov'd to ruth,
Then why grieves Mariam Herod's death to hear?
Why joy I not the tongue no more shall speak,
That yielded forth my brother's latest doom:
Both youth and beauty might thy fury break,

And both in him did ill befit a tomb.
And worthy Grandsire ill did he requite,
His high assent alone by thee procur'd,
Except he murdered thee to free the spright
Which still he thought on earth too long immur'd.
How happy was it that Sohemus' mind
Was mov'd to pity my distressed estate?
Might Herod's life a trusty servant find,
My death to his had been unseparate.
These thoughts have power, his death to make me bear,
Nay more, to wish the news may firmly hold:
Yet cannot this repulse some falling tear,
That will against my will some grief unfold.
And more I owe him for his love to me,
The deepest love that ever yet was seen:
Yet had I rather much a milkmaid be,
Than be the Monarch of Judea's Queen.
It was for naught but love, he wished his end
Might to my death but the vaunt-courier prove:
But I had rather still be foe than friend
To him that saves for hate, and kills for love.
Hard-hearted Mariam, at thy discontent,
What floods of tears have drenched his manly face?
How canst thou then so faintly now lament,
Thy truest lover's death, a death's disgrace:
I, now mine eyes you do begin to right
The wrongs of your admirer: and my Lord,
Long since you should have put your smiles to flight,
Ill doth a widowed eye with joy accord.
Why now methinks the love I bare him then,
When virgin freedom left me unrestrained,
Doth to my heart begin to creep again,
My passion now is far from being feigned.
But tears fly back, and hide you in your banks,
You must not be to Alexandra seen:
For if my moan be spied, but little thanks
Shall Mariam have, from the incensed Queen.

· · · ·

[End of Act III]

Chorus. Tis not enough for one that is a wife
To keep her spotless from an act of ill:
But from suspicion she should free her life,
And bare herself of power as well as will.
        Tis not so glorious for her to be free,
        As by her proper self restrained to be.

When she hath spacious ground to walk upon,
Why on the ridge should she desire to go?
It is no glory to forbear alone,
Those things that may her honor overthrow.
        But tis thank-worthy, if she will not take
        All lawful liberties for honor's sake.

That wife her hand against her fame doth rear,
That more than to her Lord alone will give
A private word to any second care,
And though she may with reputation live.
        Yet though most chaste, she doth her glory blot,
        And wounds her honor, though she kills it not.

When to their husbands they themselves do bind,
Do they not wholly give themselves away?
Or give they but their body, not their mind,
Reserving that thought best, for others' prey?
        No sure, their thoughts no more can be their own,
        And therefore should to none but one be known.

Then she usurps upon another's right,
That seeks to be by public language graced:
And though her thoughts reflect with purest light,
Her mind if not peculiar is not chaste.
        For in a wife it is no worse to find
        A common body, than a common mind.

And every mind though free from thought of ill,
That out of glory seeks a worth to show:

When any's ears but one therewith they fill,
Doth in a sort of pureness overthrow.
    Now Mariam had, (but that to this she bent)
    Been free from fear, as well as innocent.

ACT IV, SCENE I

Enter Herod and his attendants.

Herod. Hail, happy city, happy in thy store,
And happy that thy buildings such we see:
More happy in the Temple where w'adore,
But most of all that Mariam lives in thee.
Art thou returned? how fares by Mariam?
    Enter Nuntio.
Nuntio. She's well, my Lord, and will anon be here
As you commanded.
Herod. Muffle up thy brow,
Thy day's dark taper. Mariam will appear.
And where she shines, we need not thy dim light;
Oh haste thy steps, rare creature, speed thy pace,
And let thy presence make the day more bright,
And cheer the heart of Herod with thy face.
It is an age since I from Mariam went,
Methinks our parting was in David's days:
The hours are so increased by discontent,
Deep sorrow, Joshua-like the season stays.
But when I am with Mariam, time runs on,
Her sight can make months, minutes, days of weeks;
An hour is then no sooner come than gone,
When in her face mine eye for wonders seeks.
You world-commanding city, Europe's grace,
Twice hath my curious eye your streets surveyed,
And I have seen the statue-filled place,
That once if not for grief had been betrayed.
I all your Roman beauties have beheld,
And seen the shows your Aediles did prepare,
I saw the sum of what in you excelled,
Yet saw no miracle like Mariam rare.

The fair and famous Livia, Caesar's love,
The world's commanding Mistress did I see,
Whose beauties both the world and Rome approve,
Yet Mariam: Livia is not like to thee.
Be patient but a little, while mine eyes
Within your compassed limits be contained:
That object straight shall your desires suffice,
From which you were so long a while restrained.
How wisely Mariam doth the time delay,
Lest sudden joy my sense should suffocate:
I am prepared, thou needst no longer stay:
Who's there, my Mariam, more than happy fate?
Oh no, it is Pheroras. Welcome, brother;
Now for a while I must my passion smother.

· · · ·

ACT V, SCENE I

Nuntio. When, sweetest friend, did I so far offend
Your heavenly self, that you my fault to quit
Have made me now relator of her end,
The end of beauty? Chastity and wit,
Was none so hapless in the fatal place,
But I most wretched, for the Queen t'choose,
Tis certain I have some ill boding face
That made me culled to tell this luckless news.
And yet no news to Herod: were it new,
To him unhappy t'had not been at all:
Yet do I long to come within his view,
That he may know his wife did guiltless fall.
And here he comes. Your Mariam greets you well.
        Enter Herod.
Herod. What? lives my Mariam? joy, exceeding joy.
She shall not die.
Nuntio. Heav'n doth your will repell.
Herod. Oh do not with thy words my life destroy,
I prithee tell no dying-tale: thine eye
Without thy tongue doth tell but too too much:
Yet let thy tongue's addition make me die;

Death welcome, comes to him whose grief is such.
Nuntio. I went amongst the curious gazing troop,
To see the last of her that was the best:
To see if death had heart to make her stoop,
To see the sun admiring Phoenix nest.
When there I came, upon the way I saw
The stately Mariam not debased by fear:
Her look did seem to keep the world in awe,
Yet mildly did her face this fortune bear.
Herod. Thou dost usurp my right, my tongue was framed
To be the instrument of Mariam's praise:
Yet speak: she cannot be too often famed:
All tongues suffice not her sweet name to raise.
Nuntio. But as she came she Alexandra met,
Who did her death (sweet Queen) no whit bewail,
But as if nature she did quite forget,
She did upon her daughter loudly rail.
Herod. Why stopped you not her mouth? where had she words
To dark that, that Heaven made so bright?
Our sacred tongue no epithet affords
To call her other than the world's delight.
Nuntio. She told her that her death was too too good,
And that already she had lived too long:
She said, she shamed to have a part in blood
Of her that did the princely Herod wrong.
Herod. Base pick-thank devil! Shame, 'twas all her glory,
That she to noble Mariam was the mother:
But never shall it live in any story;
Her name, except to infamy, I'll smother.
What answer did her princely daughter make?
Nuntio. She made no answer, but she looked the while
As if thereof she scarce did notice take,
Yet smiled, a dutiful though scornful smile.
Herod. Sweet creature, I that look to mind do call,
Full oft hath Herod been amazed withall.
Nuntio. Go on, she came, unmoved, with pleasant grace,
As if to triumph her arrival were:
In stately habit and with cheerful face:
Yet every eye was moist but Mariam's, there.

When justly opposite to me she came,
She picked me out from all the crew;
She beckoned to me, called me by my name,
For she my name, my birth, and fortune knew.
Herod. What did she name thee? happy, happy man,
Wilt thou not ever love that name the better?
But what sweet tune did this fair dying Swan
Afford thine ear? tell me, omit no letter.
Nuntio. "Tell thou my Lord," said she.
Herod. Me, meant she me?
It's true, the more my shame. I was her Lord,
Were I not made her Lord, I still should be.
But now her name must be by me adored.
Oh say, what said she more? Each word she said
Shall be the food whereon my heart is fed.
Nuntio. "Tell thou my Lord thou saw'st me lose my breath."
Herod. Oh that I could that sentence now control.
Nuntio. "If guiltily eternal be my death,"
Herod. I hold her chaste ev'n in my inmost soul.
Nuntio. "By three days hence if wishes could revive,
I know himself would make me oft alive."
Herod. Three days, three hours, three minutes, not so much,
A minute in a thousand parts divided,
My penitency for her death is such,
As in the first I wished she had not died.
But forward in thy tale.
Nuntio. Why, on she went,
And after she some silent prayer had said,
She did as if to die she were content,
And thus to heaven her heavenly soul is fled.
Herod. But art thou sure there doth no life remain?
Is't possible my Mariam should be dead,
Is there no trick to make her breathe again?
Nuntio. Her body is divided from her head.
Herod. Why yet me thinks there might be found by art
Strange ways of cure, 'tis sure rare things are done
By an inventive head and willing heart.
Nuntio. Let not my Lord your fancies idly run.
It is as possible it should be seen

That we should make the holy Abraham live,
Though he entombed two thousand years had been.
As breath again to slaughtered Mariam give,
But now for more assaults prepare your ears.
Herod. There cannot be a further cause of moan,
This accident shall shelter me from fears:
What can I fear? already Mariam's gone.
Yet tell ev'n what you will.
Nuntio. As I came by,
From Mariam's death, I saw upon a tree
A man that to his neck a cord did tie,
Which cord he had designed his end to be.
When me he once discerned, he downwards bowed,
And thus with fearful voice he cried aloud,
"Go tell the King he trusted ere he tried,
I am the cause that Mariam causeless died."
. . . .

Herod. She's dead, hell take her murderers; she was fair,
She had not singly one of beauty rare,
But such a pair as here where Herod stands,
He dares the world to make to both compare.
Accursed Salome, hadst thou been still,
My Mariam had been breathing by my side.
Oh never had I—had I had my will,
Sent forth command, that Mariam should have died.
But Salome, thou didst with envy vex
To see thyself out-matched in thy sex;
Upon your sex's forehead Mariam sat,
To grace you all like an imperial crown;
But you, fond fool, have rudely pushed thereat,
And proudly pulled your proper glory down.
One smile of hers, nay, not so much: a look
Was worth a hundred thousand such as you;
Judea, how canst thou the wretches brook,
That robbed from thee the fairest of the crew?
. . . .

But can her eye be made by death obscure?
I cannot think but it must sparkle still:

Foul sacrilege to rob those lights so pure,
From out a Temple made by heavenly skill.
I am the Villain that have done the deed,
The cruel deed, though by another's hand;
My word, though not my sword, made Mariam bleed,
Hircanus's Grandchild died at my command.

· · · ·

If she had been like an Egyptian black,
And not so fair, she had been longer lived:
Her overflow of beauty turned back,
And drowned the spring from whence it was derived.
Her heavenly beauty 'twas that made me think
That it with chastity could never dwell:
But now I see that heaven in her did link
A spirit and a person to excel.
I'll muffle up myself in endless night,
And never let mine eyes behold the light.
Retire thyself, vile monster, worse than he
That stained the virgin earth with brother's blood,
Still in some vault or den inclosed be,
Where with thy tears thou mayest beget a flood,
Which flood in time may drown thee: happy day
When thou at once shalt die and find a grave,
A stone upon the vault, some one shall lay,
Which monument shall an inscription have,
And these shall be the words it shall contain,
"Here Herod lies, that hath his Mariam slain."
          Chorus.
      Who ever hath beheld with steadfast eye,
      The strange events of this one only day:
      How many were deceived? How many die,
      That once today did grounds of safety lay?
          It will from them all certainty bereave,
          Since twice six hours so many can deceive.

      This morning Herod held for surely dead,
      And all the Jews on Mariam did attend:
      And Constabarus rise from Salom's bed,

And neither dreamed of a divorce or end.
Pheroras joyed that he might have his wife,
And Babus sons for safety of their life.

Tonight our Herod doth alive remain,
The guiltless Mariam is deprived of breath:
Stout Constabarus both divorced and slain,
The valiant sons of Baba have their death.
Pheroras sure his love to be bereft,
If Salome her suit unmade had left.

Herod this morning did expect with joy,
To see his Mariam's much beloved face:
And yet ere night he did her life destroy,
And surely thought she did her name disgrace.
Yet now again so short do humor last,
He both repents her death and knows her chaste.

Had he with wisdom now her death delayed,
He at his pleasure might command her death:
But now he hath his power so much betrayed,
As all his woes cannot restore her breath.
Now doth he strangely lunatickly rave,
Because his Mariam's life he cannot save.

This day's events were certainly ordained
To be the warning to posterity:
So many changes are therein contained,
So admirably strange variety.
This day alone, our sagest Hebrews shall
In after times the school of wisdom call.

Finis.

BATHSUA MAKIN

1612(?)–1674(?)

A<small>N ART CRITIC</small> has described the painting of Bathsua Makin that hangs in the Woodburn Gallery in England as follows: "She is represented as old, without any remains of beauty. I should rather conclude that she never had any, as her figure is remarkably homely."

Few details of Makin's life can be verified in spite of the fact that during her lifetime she was frequently referred to as the most learned woman of her day. Her father was John Pell, a minister in the parish of Southwick, Sussex, and her mother's name was Holland. Although the names of her brothers John and Thomas appear in the Southwick parish register, hers does not; perhaps her father was preaching elsewhere at the time of her birth, as he never was a permanent rector. We find no records of her education, although her brothers attended school at Steyning, and the elder, John, proceeded to Trinity College, Cambridge.

Makin was employed by Charles I as tutor for his children. Princess Elizabeth became so proficient in mathematics and in languages—Greek, Latin, Hebrew, French, Italian, and Spanish—that her fame spread through Europe. However, when Makin petitioned the Council of State in 1655 for payment of the arrears of £40 per year granted her for life for her attendance on the royal children, her request was denied.

Makin found a kindred spirit in Anna Marie van Schurman, the most brilliant European female scholar of the day. It is possible that she heard of Schurman through her brother John Pell, who became a professor of mathematics at Amsterdam when the German girl was studying in Utrecht. Like Makin, Schurman was proficient in many languages, including Syriac, Arabic, Chaldee, and Ethiopic. Not only did she read Latin, Greek, and Hebrew, but she also spoke them with a fluency that amazed the university scholars. Her competence extended to geography, mathematics, philosophy, the sciences, and divinity. Among Schurman's *Opuscula* there are two letters written in Greek signed Bathsua Makin, but they are undated. The ability to communicate in Greek was a rare skill among women at that time.

No mention is made of Makin's husband in records perused to date, but a letter dated October 24, 1668, indicates she did have a son. Makin corresponded with her brother John from time to time, and from some of his letters to others, which are in the British Museum Library, it is evident that their relationship was not always harmonious. Pell wrote to his wife, Ithumaria, in 1657, "I could wish that you had made an end with your sister Makin. You know that she is a woman of great acquaintance and no small impatience. She will not strike to rail at me and you, where ever she comes. . . ." But there was also more amiable correspondence between Makin and Pell. John was apparently a brilliant mathematician (we know he introduced the division sign, ÷, in his work in algebra, and was one of the first persons to be elected Fellow of the Royal Society). An undated letter to him reveals Makin's interest in his work. She asks his opinion about the new comet and requests that he send her information "out of the papers you showed me, that were sent you from beyond the sea." She offers to copy the papers and return the originals to him if he cannot have them copied conveniently. Her postscript is amusing: "I send you some raisins which are the best breakfast you can eat, if you spit out the stones."

Sadly, John's penchant for numbers did not extend to finances, for he was constantly hard pressed for money in spite of his having been given the living of the church at Fobbing and two others, plus chaplainship to the Archbishop of Canterbury. He died in poverty in 1685 at the age of seventy-five. Although continually urged to publish his work, he never did.

Makin's other brother, Thomas Pell, went to America about 1635 where he settled in Fairfield, Connecticut. He later secured a large tract of land from the Indians in 1654, a great deal of which lies in what is now Westchester County. In 1666 a patent from the Duke of York converted the tract into the lordship and manor of Pelham, and it passed in 1669 to John Pell, the only surviving son of his brother. When this young man was drowned in 1702, his two sons inherited the lands; they became the ancestors of the American branch of the family.

We do not know what Makin did for financial support after the execution of Charles I; no doubt records of her marriage would throw some light on this. John Evelyn's *Diary* intimates that she might have been keeping a school for young gentlewomen in 1649, but definite information is lacking.

In 1646 Makin published *The Malady and Remedy*, a tract that presented a plea to Parliament to repeal the laws calling for imprisonment for debt, but her plea went unheeded. At one time her brother John was sent to debtor's prison, but, lacking dates, we cannot say that this experience inspired the publication. Until now, this tract has not been reprinted.

The poem to Lady Elizabeth Langham printed below has not been published before. Lady Elizabeth was the daughter of Ferdinando, Earl of Huntington; she became the wife of Sir James Langham in 1662. A well-educated woman, she excelled in languages. According to records, she died without issue, but Makin's poem mentions her as a mother: she was stepmother to Langham's children.

Makin's essay proposing a system of education for gentlewomen, extracts of which appear below, was unique in 1673. The author not only analyzes both the positive and negative aspects of her scheme, but also anticipates and systematically demolishes all objections that might arise to her proposal. Many of the ideas treated here are still current today.

BIBLIOGRAPHY

Manuscript

"Upon the much lamented death of the Right Honourable, the Lady Elizabeth Langham." Huntington Library Ms. H. A. 8799, San Marino, California. May 2, 1664.

Works

An Essay to Revive the Ancient Education of Gentlewomen. London: by J. D. to be sold by Tho. Parkhurst, 1673.
The Malady and . . . Remedy of Vexations and Unjust Arrests and Actions. London: n.p., September 24, 1646.

Related Readings

Ballard, George. *Memoirs of Several Ladies of Great Britain.* Oxford: Printed for the author by W. Jackson, 1752.
Granger, Rev. J. *Biographical History of England.* 5th ed. London: W. Baynes & Son, 1824.

✇

The Malady . . . and Remedy of Vexations and Unjust Arrests and Actions

BATHSUA MAKIN

[*London, September 24, 1646*]

It hath been observed, and by woeful experience found true, that the innovation and alteration of any fundamental point of the Common Law hath proved dangerous and destructive to the people's liberties; therefore it hath been the wisdom and care of our Grandees and wise Senators in former ages to provide for and look unto in the first place, to have the ancient laws and their liberties confirmed, which neither by intreaty or force of arms (though often essayed and attempted) the Commons of this Kingdom could ever be drawn or forced to forego or desert, but have against all oppression, overcoming all difficulties, constantly preserved in maintaining their laws and vindicating their liberties.

Duke William of Normandy after he had brought England under his obedience, attempted, and would have ruled by his own law, and began to govern all after the customs of Normandy; whereat the Nobility being much grieved, and the people therewith much sadded, and new troubles being ready to break forth, he upon the Commons' request and for quieting of the people by his Charter confirmed, which he twice before had by oath promised, and gave commandment to his Justiciars to see those Laws of King Edward, called the Confessor, to be inviolably observed, the great Charter of Liberties maintained throughout the whole Kingdom; being to the same effect, confirmed after by King Henry the first, who not only pleased his subjects in their relievements, but likewise in their sufferings, by punishing the chief ministers of their exactions; and the same was afterward ratified and made good by King John and Henry the third, and by many Parliaments since, by this present Parliament, and by the Petition of Right.

Now there is not any thing which more nearly concerneth, and which the Law more favoreth and regardeth, than the liberty and freedom of a man's person. And not without great reason, seeing a man's liberty is so precious and of that estimation that the same not undeservedly is valued above all other worldly and external blessings, and without which man can take little delight in what else he enjoyeth; for imprisonment of all other afflictions is one of the heaviest, oftentimes worse than death, for thereby a man is kept in lingering death, and is continually dying, so tender a care and due regard and provision therefore hath the Law ever had for the preservation of the people's liberties, and freeing men's persons from vexations of unjust actions, that by the Constitutions and fundamental Laws of this Kingdom no men were subject to imprisonment for debt, or other personal actions which were not criminal and capital, but only their goods were liable to be charged, yea, not their lands, but in some special cases.

Yet since by some late Statutes, made upon fair and specious pretences for the imprisoning men's bodies for debt, the liberty of the people hath been much encroached upon, and many thousands thereby made wretched and miserable, yea, and have starved in prison. It is not to be told what devices and feigned actions and causeless and unjust arrests, through the cunning dealing and crafty devices of Attorneys and Sollicitors are since daily framed and executed, to the grievous vexation and oppression of the people, whereby able and well minded men by such causeless arrests and groundless actions are utterly undone, especially merchants and tradesmen, who by such unjust attempts and wicked practices are causelessly cast into prison, and so deprived of their liberty, spoiled of their trade, and have lost their credit, whereby many of them are quite ruined and undone, being made a prey to Bailiffs and Sergeants, the caterpillers of the Commonwealth, and enslaved to the wills and lusts of hard hearted Jailers, when often the actions be either merely of malice or for vexation devised, or the debt but trivial and inconsiderable, if any at all.

Yet so high, and for so great sums be the same actions, as the parties imprisoned cannot (though men of considerable estates) procure bail for answering such actions, and so most injuriously still detained in prison, till either by death they be acquitted, or otherwise being deprived of all other means and hopes, constrained to submit and enslave themselves to the lusts and merciless cruelty of their adversaries. Now are not these doings, these practices, these kinds of men more dangerous, more destructive to the welfare and liberty of the people than open robberies, highway thieves, or burglaries?

For he that robs or steals from a man can take no more than what he finds in his present possession, or that he is able to carry away; whereas the other by such arrests and malicious (yea, for the most part groundless and causeless) actions siezes on a man's person, robs him of his liberty, spoils him of his trade, his credit, and all his means of subsistence and livelihood at once, his wife and children left desolate and forsaken, an oppression the more grievous and intolerable, the same being done by color of Law and countenance of Authority, which ought to be the refuge and sanctuary of the innocent and oppressed.

And while the party thus grieved and imprisoned strives to recover what he had so lost by such illegal oppressions, his misery is increased, the cure more dangerous than the disease, and by seeking to avoid one inconvenience, is hurried into a greater mischief, being driven to consume the remainder of his estate, if any be left him, by an endless and fruitless suit to the enriching of Attorneys and Solicitors, whose greatness and wealth rises from the ruins and spoiling of the people. For these men of Law and their confederates, as Under-Sheriffs, Bailiffs, Jailers, and their subordinate officers, the caterpillers of this Kingdom, who with their uncontrolled exactions and extortions, eat up the free-born people of this Nation, as if it were an act as lawful and necessary as to eat bread.

And as there is a near relation and correspondency between the druggist and apothecary, the clothier and the woolen-draper, the brazier and the tinker, so there is no less correspondency between these pettifoggers and officers of prisons, by which they abuse and inthrall the free-born people. By all which it is apparent, notwithstanding the many and often confirmed laws for the preservation of the people's just liberties, we only have the dead letter, show and shadow of the continuation thereof, being in truth utterly deprived of all benefit thereby, while we are thus subject to these kinds of arrests and imprisonments, from which no man can say he is free, save a few privileged persons, whose posterity and children are still under, and left unto the same vassalage and bondage.

Thus by these injurious, unjust and feigned actions and arrests, we that were and ever have been so accompted the most free people, are become the most enslaved people, yea, a Kingdom of slaves, whereof we have been for a long time regardless, till the same have insensibly overtaken us, and if the same be not speedily provided for and remedied, we shall never be able to recover and prevent this oppression and calamity, which I conceive the more to be minded, the same being so weighty a business, as nothing is of a more higher concernment, in regard we have no fitting provision for the prevention of this mischief and malady, till when and while the free-born people are subjected, and left open to such causeless and contentious actions and arrests; all your other laws that are or shall be made, though never so fair, spacious, or promising, are vain and fruitless, seeing they no ways secure men's persons, nor provide for their liberties.

So as though a man owe not anything, but have sufficiency for the discharge of his just debts and credits with an overplus for the comfortable subsistence of himself, his wife, and family, and whereby he may the better put himself forth for the preferment and advancement of his children; yet notwithstanding all this, he is subject, and both daily and hourly in danger, to be robbed and spoiled of all he hath, not by highwaymen and thieves, for these may be avoided or secured, if discovered aforehand, either by turning out of the way, or valor, or help of friends, neighbors, and country be rescued, not by pirates and sea-rovers; from these a man may by flight or fighting escape and gain a safe harbor. But by such as be the abjects of men, such as Job tells us, He disdained to "set with dogs of his flocks," by a company of Attorneys, Solicitors, Sergeants and Promoters, nay, by any one of these caterpillers, and earth-worms, who being set on mischief, or other displeasure causelessly conceived, or oftentimes wickedly hired thereunto, upon a pretended, feigned or forged action of an hundred pounds, a thousand pounds, or ten thousand pounds by addition or increase of a cypher; (though a man be not in the least liable to any such action) can take and seize upon his person, of what degree soever he be, (except a few privileged persons) and cast him into prison to his utter overthrow, and the destruction of his wife and children, no avoidance, no place nor sanctuary there is against these kind of men; whosoever comes under their power is in the way of destruction.

Wherefore, to free the Kingdom of this lamentable vassalage and bondage, and more easily to break this iron yoke of oppression, under which the whole land groaneth and waiteth with a longing expectation of deliverance, if the High Judicature and Court of Parliament do really intend and desire, as in all their protestations, declarations, and remonstrances they have professed and held forth to the world, to restore us to our native and pristine liberties, it much behoveth them to improve their interests, and by their wisdoms and power, for the freeing this people from this thralldom and oppression, speedily to provide some good and wholesome laws for the prevention and utter abolishing of all vexations and unjust actions and arrests for pretended debts, by which many thousand families are undone, and many able and well-minded men at this day are cast and lie in the devouring prisons under a miserable servitude and oppression, which by the frequentness and daily practice is common, and so insupportable, that the same is become one of the great burdens and grievances of the Kingdom, which is the rather to be minded by the Parliament for that this injustice and injurious dealing towards people is done and countenanced by and under the name and title of magisterial Authority, as a colorable pretext to those their unjust proceedings.

Therefore to neglect such an opportunity as this, which is now put into your hands (noble Senators and grave Consuls) to do good for the people for whom you are intrusted, were utterly a fault, and to pass by this mischief, in leaving us without hope, without comfort, prostitute to so great a destruction, would be no small blot and blemish to the proceedings of this honorable Senate, for to private men it is sufficient and commendable to abstain from wrong, but for you that be the Supreme Magistracy and Rulers of the people, to see and provide that none under you do wrong, for conniving at, or abetting the faults and miscarriages of their subordinate officers, superiors make them seem, and may truly be said to be their own.

Now for redress whereof I as a free commoner of England am bold to apply myself, and make my humble address unto you in the name and behalf of myself and many thousands free-born of this nation, spoiled of their birthright and liberty, now languishing in prisons by these kind of arrests and groundless vexatious actions, which our subtle and malicious adversaries have craftily brought us under. Our adversaries being the more encouraged thereunto, in regard they do us this injury *cum privilegio*, and under authority act this mischief, without fear, without charge, saving the disbursement of one four-pence for the arrest, though they lay a thousand pound action upon us, wherefrom to free and rescue ourselves, some of us have expended four thousand pounds, and have been worsted ten thousand pounds, yet never the nearer the recovery of our liberty, or unfettering ourselves from these our bonds and thralldom.

In consideration whereof, and for the saving us from a final and total overthrow, and preserving our posterity from such vassalage and future destruction, as is now fallen upon us, and threatening them, it is humbly

offered to the grave wisdom and consideration of the High Court of
Parliament, and for the relief and remedy in the premises, if so it seem fit
and agreeable with the Justice of that most honorable Court, that it may
by authority of Parliament be provided for the future:

I. That all such as are now imprisoned under any such arrest or action
may forthwith be enlarged, and full reparations made unto them for
their losses and sufferings.

II. That whosoever shall hereafter arrest and imprison, or procure to
be arrested and imprisoned any merchant or other free-born subject,
upon any action for debt, where the same is not really due and payable,
shall for the first offense in such case, pay to the party grieved and imprisoned double the sum wherewith he was unjustly and wrongfully
charged, over and above the debt truly due if any, the same to be levied
of the lands, goods, and chattels of the party so offending.

III. That whosoever shall hereafter arrest and imprison, or cause to be
arrested and imprisoned any merchant or free denison for any sum
whatsoever above a hundred pound, where there is no bond or spe-
cialty, shall first make affidavit before some judge of record, that such
sum or sums of money be truly due and unsatisfied, before the party
arrested, or to be arrested, be committed to any prison whatsoever for
the same.

IV. That whosoever shall offend in the like case for the second offense,
being lawfully convicted thereof, shall not only pay double the sum of
the action, but shall be likewise set upon the Pillory and stigmatized,
yea, and be disabled ever thereafter to sue or implead in any Court of
Record. And for the third offense, the same to be capital, being a crime
of such a high nature, and so punished as in other Commonwealths
and well governed States.

V. That if the party so offending have not goods and lands whereby to
answer such sum or sums of money, wherein he shall be condemned:
for his first offense, to be set upon the Pillory, and three months
imprisonment; for the second offense, to be set on the Pillory, and
stigmatized, and a year's imprisonment; and ever thereafter to be
disabled to sue or implead in any Court of Record.

VI. It is referred to your grave considerations, whether it be agreeable
to the Common Law and Magna Charta, which as to the people's
liberties by the Petition of Right and the Statute of the 17. *Carol.* made
for the abolishing the Star Chamber, and regulating the Council Board,
is confirmed; and to the defense and preservation whereof, you by oath

have bound yourselves, and so whether the same be convenient or legal to imprison men's bodies for debt and other faults not criminal, seeing yet the Sheriff may not seize and take the beasts of the plough upon any execution for debt, in favor and regard of tillage and husbandry, and so consequently, much less in all reason and equity the body of the man who is the master, owner, and guider of the beast, without whose skill and industry the beast of the plough is not only chargeable, but altogether unprofitable.

Lastly, we humbly conceive that the people ought not to be vexed with close and strict imprisonment from year to year in contempt of the writs and orders of the highest Courts of the Kingdom, especially when *re vera* [truth is concerned(?)], some of them are not justly indebted for the value of a penny; but for want of access to a full hearing of their causes, by means of the caterpillers aforesaid, have been turmoiled with eleven or twelve years' suits and imprisonments, even by those who are really indebted unto them, by which oppression some of us have been damnified divers thousands of pounds, and others quite ruined and undone.

Finis.

Upon the much lamented death of the Right Honourable, the Lady Elizabeth Langham

BATHSUA MAKIN

[*Huntington Library Ms. H.A. 8799. May 2, 1664*]

Pass not, but wonder, and amazed stand
At this sad tomb; for here enclosed lie

Such rare perfections that no tongue or hand
Can speak them or portray them to the eye;
Such was her body, such her soul divine!
Which now ascended, here hath left this shrine.
To tell her princely birth and high descent
And what by noble Huntingdon is meant,
Transcends the herald's art, beyond the rules
Of Or, or Argent, Azure, or of Gules;
To that nobility her birth had given
A second added was, derived from heaven;
Thence her habitual goodness, solid worth,
Her piety; her virtues blazon forth;
Her for a pattern unto after ages,
To be admired by all, expressed by sages,
Who when they write of her, will sadly sorrow
That she did not survive to see their morrow.
So good in all relations, so sweet
A daughter, such a loving wife, discreet
A mother; though not hers, not partial
She loved, as if they had been natural.
To th' Earl and Ladies she a sister rare,
A friend, where she professed, beyond compare.
Her hours were all precisely kept, and spent
In her devotions; and her studies meant
To share some for her languages, which she
In Latin, French, Italian happily
Advanced in with pleasure; what do I
Recount her parts? her memory speaks more
Than what can be, or hath been said before:
It asks a volume, rather than a verse,
Which is confined only to her hearse.
But now blessed soul, she is arriv'd at heaven,
Where with a crown of life to her is given
A new transcendent Name, to th' world unknowne,
Not writ in marble, but the saint's white stone:
Inthron'd above the stars, with glory crown'd,
Installed with bliss, and Hallelujahs sound.

ॐ

An Essay to Revive the
Ancient Education of Gentlewomen

BATHSUA MAKIN

[*London*, 1673]

To all ingenious and vertuous ladies, more especially to her Highness the
Lady Mary, eldest daughter to his Royal Highness the Duke of York.

Custom, when it is inveterate, hath a mighty influence: it hath the
force of Nature itself. The barbarous custom to breed women low is
grown general amongst us and hath prevailed so far that it is verily
believed (especially amongst a sort of debauched sots) that women are
not endued with such reason as men, nor capable of improvement by
education, as they are. It is looked upon as a monstrous thing, to pretend
the contrary. A learned woman is thought to be a comet, that bodes
mischief whenever it appears. To offer to the world the liberal education
of women is to deface the image of God in man; it will make women so
high and men so low; like fire in the house-top, it will set the whole world
in a flame.

These things are worse than these are commonly talked of and verily
believed by many who think themselves wise men; to contradict these is a
bold attempt, where the attempter must expect to meet with much
opposition. Therefore, Ladies, I beg the candid opinion of your sex,
whose interest I assert. More especially I implore the favor of your Royal
Highness, a person most eminent amongst them, whose patronage alone
will be a sufficient protection. What I have written is not out of humour to
show how much may be said of a trivial thing to little purpose. I verily
think, women were formerly educated in the knowledge of arts and
tongues, and by their education many did rise to a great height in
learning. Were women thus educated now, I am confident the advantage
would be very great: the women would have honor and pleasure, their
relations profit, and the whole nation advantage. I am very sensible it is
an ill time to set on foot this design, wherein not only learning but virtue

itself is scorned and neglected as pedantic things, fit only for the vulgar. I know no better way to reform these exorbitancies than to persuade women to scorn those toys and trifles they now spend their time about, and to attempt higher things, here offered: this will either reclaim the men, or make them ashamed to claim the sovereignty over such as are more wise and virtuous than themselves.

Were a competent number of schools erected to educate ladies ingenuously, methinks I see how ashamed men would be of their ignorance, and how industrious the next generation would be to wipe off their reproach.

I expect to meet with many scoffs and taunts from inconsiderate and illiterate men, that prize their own lusts and pleasure more than your profit and content. I shall be the less concerned at these, so long as I am in your favor; and this discourse may be a weapon in your hands to defend yourselves whilst you endeavour to polish your souls, that you may glorify God and answer the end of your creation, to be meet helps to your husbands. Let not your Ladyships be offended that I do not (as some have wittily done) plead for female preeminence. To ask too much is the way to be denied all. God hath made man the head; if you be educated and instructed as I propose, I am sure you will acknowledge it and be satisfied that you are helps, that your husbands do consult and advise with you (which if you be wise they will be glad of) and that your husbands have the casting voice in whose determinations you will acquiesce. That this may be the effect of this education in all ladies that shall attempt it, is the desire of

Your Servant.

Sir,

It should be the earnest endeavor of all men to employ their lives to those noble and excellent ends for which the omnipotent and all-wise Creator made them, which are: the glory of God, the eternal happiness of their immortal souls, and to be useful in their places. One generation passeth away and another cometh, but the earth, the theatre on which we act, abideth forever. All the works of the children of men do remain, not only in respect of the present and future emolument or detriment, caused by them, but also in reference to the influence they have as examples on succeeding ages. The harvest of bliss or woe will be according to the seed-time of this life. This life proceeds ordinarily as it begins,

Quo semel est imbuta recens servabit Odorem
   Testa diu—.
[A cask will long preserve the flavor with which, when new, it was once
impregnated.]

So great is the force of the first tincture anything takes, whether good
or bad. As plants in gardens excel those that grow wild, or as brutes, by
the management (witness the philosophers' dogs) are much altered, so
men, by liberal education, are much better as to intellectuals and morals.
All conclude great care ought to be taken of the males, but your doubt in
your letter is concerning the females. I think the greater care ought to be
taken of them, because evil seems to be begun here, as in Eve, and to be
propagated by her daughters. When the Sons of God took unto themselves the Daughters of Men, wickedness multiplied apace. It was the
cursed counsel of Balaam to debauch Israel by Balack's idolatrous
women. Wretched Jezebel excites Ahab to greater wickedness than he
could ever have thought of. God gave strict command to the Israelites not
to marry with heathenish women. When Solomon himself (the wisest of
men) did this, they soon drew his heart from God. Bad women, weak to
make resistance, are strong to tempt to evil: therefore without all doubt
great care ought to be taken, timely to season them with piety and virtue.

Your great question is, Whether to breed up women in arts and
tongues is not a mere new device, never before practised in the world.
This you doubt the more, because women are of low parts and not
capable of improvement by this education. If they could be improved,
you doubt whether it would benefit them. If it would benefit them, you
inquire where such education may be had, or whether they must go to
school with boys, to be made twice more impudent than learned. At last
you muster up a legion of objections.

I shall speak distinctly to your questions and then answer your
objections.

Women have formerly been educated in Arts and Tongues.

Little is recorded concerning the manner, how women were educated
formerly; you can expect my proof to be only topical and by circumstances.

It doth appear out of Sacred Writ, that women were employed in most
of the great transactions that happened in the world, even in reference to
religion. Miriam seems to be next to Moses and Aaron; she was a great

poet and philosopher, for both learning and religion were generally in former times wrapped up in verse.

The women met David, singing triumphant songs composed (it is like by themselves) a great specimen of liberal education.

Deborah, the deliverer of Israel, was without doubt a learned woman that understood the Law. Huldah the Prophetess dwelt in a college (we may suppose) where women were trained up in good literature. We may be sure she was a very wise woman, for King Josiah sends Hilkiah the Priest, and the nobles of his court, in a case of difficulty and danger, to consult with her. 2 Chron. 34:20–21 etc.

In the New Testament we find Anna a prophetess.

Paul, Rom. 16:1, commends unto them Phebe, who was not only a servant of Christ but a servant of the Church at Cencrea. Ver. 12. He tells us Triphena, Triphosa and Persis labored much in the Lord. Priscilla instructed Apollos.

. . . .

We may infer from the stories of the Muses that this way of education was very ancient. All conclude the heroes were men famous in their generation, therefore, canonized after their deaths. We may with like reason conclude, Minerva and the nine Muses were women famous for learning whilst they lived, and therefore thus adored when dead.

There is no question the Greeks and Romans, when most flourishing, did thus educate their daughters; in regard so many amongst them were famous for learning. As Sempronia, Cornelia, Lelia, Mutia, Cleobulina, Cassandra, Terentia, . . . and many others.

The Sybils could never have invented the heroic, nor Sappho the sapphic verses, had they been illiterate. Do you think Corinna could ever have thrice outdone Pindar, upon a solemn contest so excellent in his lyric verses that none else durst imitate him, had she not been instructed in the arts?

There was a contest between twenty Grecian and twenty Roman ladies, which were most excellent in learning. The Roman dames were the best orators, but the Grecian ladies the best philosophers. This plainly shows they both were instructed in all kind of good literature.

. . . .

Care ought to be taken by us to Educate Women in Learning.

That I may be more distinct in what I intend, I shall distinguish of women:

Women are of two sorts { Rich } Of good natural parts.
{ Poor } Of low parts.

I do not mean that it is necessary to the *esse* [being, or essential nature], to the subsistence, or to the salvation of women, to be thus educated. Those that are mean in the world have not an opportunity for this education; those that are of low parts, though they have opportunity, cannot reach this. . . . My meaning is, Persons that God hath blessed with the things of this world, that have competent natural parts, ought to be educated in knowledge; that is, it is much better they should spend the time of their youth to be competently instructed in those things usually taught to gentlewomen at schools, and the overplus of their time to be spent in gaining arts and tongues and useful knowledge, rather than to trifle away so many precious minutes merely to polish their hands and feet, to curl their locks, to dress and trim their bodies, and in the meantime to neglect their souls, and not at all, or very little, to endeavor to know God, Jesus Christ, themselves, and the things of nature, arts and tongues, subservient to these. I do not deny but women ought to be brought up to a comely and decent carriage, to their needle, to neatness, to understand all those things that do particularly belong to their sex. But when these things are competently cared for, and where there are endowments of nature and leisure, then higher things ought to be endeavored after. Merely to teach gentlewomen to frisk and dance, to paint their faces, to curl their hair, to put on a whisk, to wear gay clothes, is not truly to adorn, but to adulterate their bodies; yea, (what is worse) to defile their souls. This (like Circe's cup) turns them to beasts; whilst their belly is their god, they become swine; whilst lust, they become goats; and whilst pride is their god, they become very devils. Doubtless this under-breeding of women began amongst heathen and barbarous people; it continues with the Indians, where they make their women mere slaves and wear them out in drudgery. It is practiced amongst degenerate and apostate Christians, upon the same score, and now is part of their religion; it would therefore be a piece of Reformation to correct it, and it would notably countermine them who fight against us, as Satan against Adam, by seducing our women, who then easily seduce their husbands.

Had God intended women only as a finer sort of cattle, He would not have made them reasonable. Brutes, a few degrees higher than drils [baboons] or monkeys, (which the Indians use to do many offices) might have better fitted some men's lust, pride, and pleasure; especially those that desire to keep them ignorant to be tyrannized over.

God intended woman as a help-meet to man in his constant conversation and in the concerns of his family and estate, when he should most need, in sickness, weakness, absence, death, etc. Whilst we neglect to fit them for these things, we renounce God's blessing he hath appointed women for, are ungrateful to him, cruel to them, and injurious to ourselves.

I remember a discourse in Erasmus, between an abbot and a learned woman. She gives many good reasons why women should be learned, that they might know God, their Savior, understand his sacred Word, and admire him in his wonderful works; that they might also better administer their household affairs amongst a multitude of servants, who would have more reverence towards them because they were above them in understanding. Further, she found a great content in reading good authors at spare times. He gives her one answer to all this: That women would never be kept in subjection if they were learned—as he found by experience amongst his monks; of all things in the world he hated nothing so much as a learned monk who would always be contradicting his Superior, from the Decretals out of Peter and Paul. He cared not if all his monks were turned into swine, so long as they would be obedient, and not disturb him in his pleasures. Doubtless if that generation of sots (who deny more polite learning to women) would speak out, they would tell you: If women should be permitted the arts, they would be wiser than themselves (a thing not to be endured); then they would never be such tame fools and very slaves as now they make them; therefore it is a wicked mischievous thing to revive the ancient custom of educating them.

· · · ·

If any desire distinctly to know what they should be instructed in?

I answer: I cannot tell where to begin to admit women, nor from what part of learning to exclude them, in regard of their capacities. The whole encyclopaedia of learning may be useful some way or other to them. Respect indeed is to be had to the nature and dignity of each art and science, as they are more or less subservient to religion, and may be useful to them in their station. I would not deny them the knowledge of grammar and rhetoric, because they dispose to speak handsomely. Logic must be allowed, because it is the key to all sciences. Physic, especially visibles, as herbs, plants, shrubs, drugs, etc., must be studied because this will exceedingly please themselves, and fit them to be helpful to others. The tongues ought to be studied, especially the Greek and Hebrew; these will enable to the better understanding of the Scriptures.

The mathematics, more especially geography, will be useful: this puts life into history. Music, painting, poetry, etc., are a great ornament and pleasure. Some things that are more practical are not so material, because public employments in the field and courts are usually denied to women. Yet some have not been inferior to many men even in these things also. Witness Semiramis amongst the Babylonians; the Queen of Sheba in Arabia; Miriam and Deborah among the Israelites; Katherine de Medici in France; Queen Elizabeth in England.

· · · ·

In these late times there are several instances of women, when their husbands were serving their King and country, defended their houses and did all things as soldiers, with prudence and valor, like men.

They appeared before committees and pleaded their own causes with good success.

This kind of education will be very useful to women.

1. The profit will be to themselves. In the general they will be able to understand, read, write, and speak their mother-tongue, which they cannot well do without this. They will have something to exercise their thoughts about, which are busy and active. Their quality ties them at home; if learning be their companion, delight and pleasure will be their attendants, for there is no pleasure greater, nor more suitable to an ingenious mind, than what is founded in knowledge; it is the first fruits of heaven and a glimpse of that glory we afterwards expect. There is in all an innate desire of knowing, and the satisfying this is the greatest pleasure. Men are very cruel that give them leave to look at a distance, only to know they do not know; to make any thus to tantalize, is a great torment.

This will be a hedge against heresies. Men are furnished with arts and tongues for this purpose, that they may stop the mouths of their adversaries. And women ought to be learned, that they may stop their ears against seducers. . . . Heresiarchs creep into houses and lead silly women captive; then they lead their husbands, both their children; as the devil did Eve, she her husband, they their posterity.

· · · ·

We cannot be so stupid as to imagine that God give ladies great estates merely that they may eat, drink, sleep, and rise up to play. Doubtless they ought not to live thus. God, that will take an account for every idle thought, will certainly reckon with those persons that shall spend their whole lives in idle play and chat. Poor women will make but a lame excuse at the last day for their vain lives; it will be something to say, that they were educated no better. But what answer men will make, that do industriously deny them better improvement, lest they would be wiser than themselves, I cannot imagine.

More particularly, Women are $\begin{cases} \text{Unmarried.} \\ \text{Married.} \\ \text{Widows.} \end{cases}$

As for unmarried persons who are able to subsist without a dependance, they have a fairer opportunity than men, if they continue long in that estate, to improve the principles they have sucked in and to ripen the seeds of learning which have been sown in their minds in their tender years. Besides, this will be an honest and profitable diversion to possess their minds, to keep out worse thoughts. . . .

Married persons, by virtue of this education, may be very useful to their husbands in their trades, as the women are in Holland, and to their children, by timely instructing them before they are fit to be sent to school, as was the case of Caesar and the Lord Montague.

I need not show how any persons, thus brought up, if they happen to be widows, will be able to understand and manage their own affairs.

2. Women thus educated will be beneficial to their relations. It is a great blessing of God to a family, to provide a good wife for the head, if it be eminent; and a presage of ruin, when he sends a ranting Jezebel to a soft Ahab.

. . . . .

3. Women thus instructed will be beneficial to the nation. Look into all history, those nations ever were, now are, and always shall be, the worst of nations, where women are most undervalued; as in Russia, Ethiopia, and all the barbarous nations of the world. One great reason why our neighbors the Dutch have thriven to admiration, is the great care they take in the education of their women, from whence they are to be accounted more virtuous and to be sure more useful than any women in the world. . . .

The memory of Queen Elizabeth is yet fresh. By her learning she was fitted for government and swayed the scepter of this nation with as great honor as any man before her.

Our very reformation of religion seems to be begun and carried on by women.

Mrs. Anne Askew, a person famous for learning and piety, so seasoned the Queen and ladies at Court, by her precepts and examples, and after sealed her profession with her blood, that the seed of reformation seemed to be sowed by her hand.

. . . .

My intention is not to equalize women to men, much less to make them superior. They are the weaker sex, yet capable of impressions of great things, something like to the best of men.

. . . .

The inference I make from hence is, that women are not such silly giddy creatures as many proud ignorant men would make them, as if they were incapable of all improvement by learning, and unable to digest arts that require any solidity of judgment. Many men will tell you, they are so unstable and unconstant, borne down upon all occasions with such a torrent of fear, love, hatred, lust, pride, and all manner of exorbitant passions, that they are incapable to practice any virtues that require greatness of spirit, or firmness of resolution. Let such but look into history, they will find examples enough of illustrious women to confute them.

. . . .

Objection. If we bring up our daughters to learning, no persons will adventure to marry them.

Answer. 1. Many men, silly enough (God knows), think themselves wise, and will not dare marry a wise woman, lest they should be over-topped.

2. As some husbands, debauched themselves, desire their wives should be chaste and their children virtuous, so some men, sensible of their own want, (caused by their parents' neglect), will choose a learned woman in whom they may glory, and by whose prudence their defect may be supplied.

3. Learned men, to be sure, will choose such the rather, because they are suitable. Some men marrying wives of good natural parts, have improved themselves in arts and tongues, the more to fit them for their converse.

. . . .

Objection: . . . They will be proud, and not obey their husbands. To this I answer: what is said of Philosophy is true of knowledge; a little philosophy carries a man from God, but a great deal brings him back again; a little knowledge, like windy bladders, puffs up, but a good measure of true knowledge, like ballast in a ship, settles down and makes a person move more even in his station; 'tis not knowing too much, but too little that causes irregularity. This same argument may be turned upon men; whatever they answer for themselves, will defend woman. . . . Do not deny women their due, which is to be as well instructed as they can; but let men do their duty, to be wiser than they are. If this doth not please, let silly men let wise women alone; the rule is, All should be (as near as they can) equally yoked.

. . . .

Objection: Women do not desire learning.

Answer: Neither do many boys, (as schools are now ordered) yet I suppose you do not intend to lay fallow all children that will not bring forth fruit of themselves, to forbear to instruct those which at present do not thank you for it. . . .

Objection: Women are of low parts.

Answer. So are many men; we plead only for those which have competent parts. To be sure, some women are as capable of learning, and have attained to as great height in it as most men: witness those examples before produced.

If this be true, their parts generally are lower than men's, there is the more need they should by all convenient means be improved. Crutches are for infirm persons.

. . . .

Objection: It is against custom to educate gentlewomen thus; those that do attempt it will make themselves ridiculous.

Answer: This argument might have been used to the Irish; not to use traces at plow and cart, but to draw their horses by their tails, which was a general custom amongst them. Bad customs (when it is evident they are so) ought to be broken, or else good customs can never come into use. That this is a bad custom is evident, continued upon a bad ground. Let women be fools, and then you may easily make them slaves.

. . . .

Let a generous resolution possess your minds, seeing men in this age have invaded women's vices; in a noble revenge, reassume those virtues which men sometimes unjustly usurped to themselves, but ought to have left them in common to both sexes.

MARGARET CAVENDISH, DUCHESS OF NEWCASTLE

1623–1673

M ARGARET CAVENDISH was the daughter of Thomas Lucas of St. John's Abbey, Colchester, and Elizabeth Leighton, daughter of John Leighton, Gentleman, of London. After the dissolution of the monasteries under Henry VIII the abbey lands were parceled out to court favorites or sold to men of affluence. John Lucas, Thomas's grandfather, purchased the site of St. John's Abbey and part of its lands in 1548. The mansion built on the grounds remained the family seat for several generations.

Margaret's father was educated at Pembroke College, Cambridge, and then entered the legal profession and became interested in politics. In 1597 he fought a duel with Sir William Brooke, a relative of Lord Cobham, and killed him. A sentence of outlawry was declared against him and he fled to France, leaving Elizabeth, to whom he was betrothed, pregnant. Their son Thomas was born during his father's exile and declared illegitimate. In 1604 when Cobham was sent to the Tower as a prisoner for his alleged complicity in a plot to seat Arabella Stuart on the English throne, James I pardoned Lucas and allowed him to return home. He married Elizabeth at once, and their first legitimate son, John, was born in 1606. In all, eight children were born to the couple; the eighth, the fifth daughter, was Margaret, born in 1623. Two years later her father died.

Margaret's education was casual, if not haphazard. In her brief autobiography she described tutors who taught the sisters dancing, music, needlework, and French. Among the aristocracy at this time, the common attitude toward the education of women was that they should be taught only those things they could be expected to use in their married lives—reading, perhaps some mathematics, and French, plus the so-called "ornamental arts." Margaret once wrote, "I do not repent that I

136

spent not my time in learning, for I consider it is better to write wittily than learnedly." But later in life she longed for more instruction in poetry, history, philosophy, and mathematics. She wrote that women were fools, uneducated, and that by entrusting the care of each generation of women to the last, this foolishness was being perpetuated.

The Lucas family spent six months each year in London and six months in Colchester. When the children married, their families swelled the Lucas household. In London they engaged in all the popular pastimes—dancing, attending plays and musicals, riding in carriages in order to be seen, and participating in the amusements at court. Margaret became well known for her eccentricities of dress; when Samuel Pepys, John Evelyn, and others mocked her, she retorted that she preferred to set the mode rather than follow it. She dreamed that her husband would be a composite of Caesar "for his valor," Ovid "for his wit," and Shakespeare "for his comical and tragical humour."

The Lucas family were ardent Royalists. In 1642, when the Civil War was threatening all of England, Parliamentary troops attacked St. John's Abbey on the pretext that Sir John Lucas, who had been knighted by Charles I, had arms and horses there for the king's service. Most items of value, such as jewels, silver, and rare furnishings, were either destroyed or carried off; before long a good deal of their lands were sequestered, and much was never restored. Margaret never forgot or forgave this treatment of her family. She accompanied her sisters and their husbands to the Royalist stronghold at Oxford. Queen Henrietta Maria had left for the Continent, where she was attempting to raise support for Charles, and did not return to England until July 1643, when she joined the royal family at Oxford, housed at Merton College. When Margaret learned that she required attendants, she begged her mother to be allowed to serve as Maid of Honor. Although at first the family disapproved, she eventually had her way. Later when the queen fled to France Margaret accompanied her.

While in France, Margaret met Sir William Cavendish, Marquis (later Earl) of Newcastle, son of Sir Charles Cavendish and Katherine, daughter of Cuthbert, Lord Ogle. He had served as a leader in the Royalist army until he went into exile on the Continent with Prince Charles and other members of the royal family and nobility. Although essentially a military man, Sir William was patron to many poets and dramatists of the day, including Ben Jonson (said to have been his favorite), Richard Brome, John Ford, and James Shirley. To Margaret, Sir William possessed all the virtues of Caesar, Ovid, and Shakespeare, and she was at once romantically attracted. When the marriage was finally arranged, Newcastle courted her with poems and love gifts. They were married in December 1645. The couple settled in Antwerp but returned to England immediately after the Restoration in 1660.

The Duchess described herself as being of a melancholy temper rather than a merry one, more interested in writing than in the company of other people; her greatest pleasure was found in solitary pursuits. The happy, outgoing child had become an extremely shy person when not with her own family. The bibliography below will attest to her literary output, which was prodigious. She wrote plays that were never acted, philosophical studies too obscure to be taken seriously, poems and essays that were, according to her detractors, of insufficient literary value. Her biography of her husband, however, compares well with other seventeenth-century works in this genre.

At one point the Duchess was invited to attend a meeting of the Royal Society, whose membership was restricted to men. To the dismay of Samuel Pepys and John Evelyn, her arrival with at least six attendants threw the meeting into confusion for a time. Then she observed the experiments performed by Robert Boyle and Robert Hooke—the weighing of air, the dissolving of a piece of mutton in sulphuric acid, and others. Her interests were eclectic.

The Duchess knew that her literary works were not well received, although she was praised by Sir Kenelm Digby, Thomas Hobbes, Henry More, Thomas Shadwell, and others to whom she presented copies as they came from the press. She revised her books continually and saw several editions published during her lifetime. After her death in December 1673, her husband published the letters and poems that had been written in her praise, flattering letters and addresses from Cambridge University, Christian Huygens, Thomas Charleton, Joseph Glanville, Hobbes, Digby, Shadwell, and Clement Ellis. Newcastle himself wrote the epitaph that appears on the tomb in Westminster Abbey, where the two can be seen, lying in effigy side by side:

Here lyes the Loyall Duke of Newcastle and his Dutches, his second wife, by whome he had noe issue; her name was Margarett Lucas, youngest sister to the Lord Lucas of Colchester; a noble familie, for all the Brothers were Valiant and all the Sisters virtuous. This Dutches was a wise, wittie and learned Lady, which her many Bookes do well testifie; she was a most virtuous and a loving and careful wife, and was with her Lord all the time of his banishment and miseries, and when he came home never parted from him in his solitary retirements.

The *Works* of Margaret Cavendish, Duchess of Newcastle, have not been published in their entirety in this century. She had a penchant for accuracy, a great wit, shy manner, and delightful imagination. And she wrote to please herself.

BIBLIOGRAPHY

Works

The Description of a New World. London: By A. Maxwell, 1666, 1668.
Grounds of Natural Philosophy. London: By A. Maxwell, 1668.
Letters. London: By T. Newcomb, 1676.
Nature's Pictures. London: For J. Martin & J. Allestrye, 1656. Also, by A. Maxwell, 1671.
Observations upon Experimental Philosophy. London: By A. Maxwell, 1666, 1668.
Orations of Divers Sorts. London: n.p., 1662.
The Philosophical and Physical Opinions of Margaret Cavendish, Duchess of Newcastle. London: For J. Martin & J. Allestrye, 1655. Also, by William Wilson, 1663.
Philosophical Fancies. London: By Tho. Roycroft for J. Martin & J. Allestrye, 1653.
Philosophical Letters. London: n.p., 1664.
Playes Written. London: By A. Warren for John Martyn, James Allestrye, and Tho. Dicas, 1662.
Plays, never before printed. London: By A. Maxwell, 1668.
Poems and Fancies. London: By T. R. for J. Martin & J. Allestrye, 1653. Also by W. Wilson, 1664, and by A. Maxwell, 1668.
CCXI Sociable Letters. London: By Wm. Wilson, 1664.
CCXI Sociable Letters. Facsimile edition. Menston, England: Scolar Press, 1969.
The World's Olio. London: For J. Martin & J. Allestrye, 1655. Also by A. Maxwell, 1671.
Brydges, Sir Samuel Egerton, ed. *A True Relation of the Life of Margaret Cavendish, Duchess of Newcastle.* Lee Priory, Kent, England: n.p., 1814.
Firth, Sir C. H., ed. *Life of the Thrice Noble . . . Prince, William Cavendish.* London: J. C. Nimmo, 1886, 1903, 1906.
Goulding, Richard William, ed. *Letters of Margaret Lucas to her future Husband . . . 1645.* London: J. Murray, 1909.
Lower, Mark Antony, ed. *The Lives of William Cavendish, duke of Newcastle, and of his wife, Margaret, duchess of Newcastle.* London: J. R. Smith, 1872.

Related Readings

Costello, Louisa. *Memoirs of Eminent Englishwomen.* 4 vols. London: R. Bentley, 1844.

Granger, Rev. J. *Biographical History of England.* 5th ed. London: W. Baynes & Son, 1824.

Grant, Douglas. *Margaret the First.* London: Rupert Hart-Davis, 1957.

Selections from

Nature's Pictures,
Drawn by Fancies Pencil to the Life

MARGARET CAVENDISH, DUCHESS OF NEWCASTLE

[*London, 1656*]

TO THE READER

I must intreat my readers to understand that though my natural genius is to write fancy, yet in this work I have strove, as much as I can, to lay fancy by in some out-corner of my brain, for lively descriptions to take place; for descriptions are to imitate, and fancy to create; for fancy is not an imitation of nature, but a natural creation, which I take to be the true Poetry: so that there is as much difference between fancy, and imitation, as between a creature and a creator: but some poetical tales of discourses, both in verse and prose; but most in prose hath crowded in amongst the rest, I cannot say against my will, although my will was forced by my natural inclinations and affections to fancy, but otherwise I have endeavored to describe and imitate the several actions of life, and changes of fortune, as well as my little wit, weak observations, and less learning can compose into several discourses. Also I am to let my readers to understand that though my work is of comical, tragical, poetical, philosophical, romantical, historical and moral discourses, yet I could not place them so exactly into several books, or parts, as I would, but am forced to mix them one amongst another, but my readers will find them in the volume, if they please to take notice of them; if not, there is no harm done to my book, nor to me the authoress.

M. Newcastle.

AN EPISTLE TO MY READERS

Perchance my feigned stories are not so lively described as they might have been, for that my descriptions are not so lively expressed by the pen as Sir Anthony Van Dyke his pictures by the pencil, by reason I have not copied them from true originals, but just as fancy forms; for I have not read much history to inform me of the past ages; indeed I dare not examine the former times, for fear I should meet with such of my sex that have out-done all the glory I can aim at, or hope to attain; for I confess my ambition is restless, and not ordinary; because it would have an extraordinary fame. And since all heroic actions, public employments, powerful governments, and eloquent pleadings are denied our sex in this age, or at least would be condemned for want of custom, is the cause I write so much, for my ambition being restless, though rather busy than industrious, yet it hath made that little wit I have to run upon every subject I can think of, or is fit for me to write on; for after I have put out one book more that I am writing, I cannot tell what more to write, unless I should write of the like subjects again, which would be as tedious as endless.

M. Newcastle.

HER EXCELLENCIES TALES IN VERSE
from THE FIRST BOOK

Readers, I find the Works which I have wrote,
Are not so bad, as you can find much fault;
For if you could, I doubt you would not spare
Me in your censures, but their faults declare;
For I perceive the World is evil bent,
Judging the worst, although it good was meant;
And if a word to wantonness could wrest,
They'll be so pleased, and often at it jest;
When every foolish tongue can with words play,
And turn good sense, with words, an evil way:
But at my writings let them do their worst,
And for their pains with ignorance be curst.

In winter cold, a company was met
Both men and women by the fire set;
At last they did agree to pass the time,
That everyone should tell a tale in rhyme.
The women said, they could no number keep,
Or could they run on smooth and even feet.
Why, said the men, all women's tongues are free
To speak both out of time, and nonsensely.
And drawing lots, the chance fell on a man,
When he had spit and blowed his nose, began.

· · · ·

A *Description of Diverted Grief*

A man that had a young and a fair wife,
Whose virtue was unspotted all her life,
Her words were smooth from which her tongue did slide,
All her discourse was wittily applied;
Her actions modest, her behavior so,
As when she moved, the Graces seemed to go.
Whatever ill she chanced to hear or see,
Yet still her thoughts as pure as angels be.
Her husband's love seemed such, as no delight
Nor joy could take out of his dear wife's sight.
It chanced this virtuous wife fell sick to death,
Thus to her husband spake with dying breath.
    Farewell, my dearest husband, die I must,
Yet do not you forget me in the dust,
Because my spirit would grieve, if it should see
Another in my room thy Love to be;
My ghost would mourn, lament, that never dies,
Though bodies do pure loves eternalize.
You Gods, said he, that order Death and Life,
O strike me dead, unless you spare my wife.
If your decree is fixed, nor altered can,
But she must die, O miserable man!
Here do I vow, great Gods all witness be,
That I will have no other wife but thee;
No friendship will I make, converse with none,
But live an Anchoret myself alone;
Thy spirits sweet my thoughts shall entertain,

And in my mind thy memory remain.

Farewell, said she, for now my soul's at peace,
And all the blessings of the gods increase
Upon thy soul, yet wish you would not give
Away that love I had whilst I did live.
Turning her head, as if to sleep she lay,
In a soft sigh her spirits flew away.

When she was dead, great mourning he did make,
Would neither eat, nor drink, nor rest could take,
Kissing her cold pale lips, her cheeks, each eye,
Cursing his Fates he lives, and may not die.
Tears fell so fast, as if his sorrows meant
To lay her in a watery monument.
But when her corpse was laid upon the hearse,
No tongue can tell, nor his great grief express.
Thus did he pass his time a week or two,
In sad complaints, and melancholy woe;
At last he was persuaded for to take
Some air abroad, ev'n for his own health's sake.
But first, unto the grave he went to pray,
Kissing the earth wherein her body lay.
After a month or two, his grief to ease,
Some recreations seeks himself to please;
And calling for his horses and his hounds,
He means to hunt upon the Champain grounds:
By these pastimes his thoughts diverted are,
Goes by the grave, and never drops a tear.
At last he chanced a company to meet
Of virgins young and fresh as flowers sweet;
Their clothing fine, their humors pleasant gay,
And with each other they did sport and play:
Giving his eyes a liberty to view,
With interchanging looks in love he grew.
One maid amongst the rest, most fair and young,
Who had a ready wit, and pleasant tongue,
He courtship made to her, he did address,
Cast off his mourning, love for to express;
Rich clothes he made, and wondrous fine they were,
He barbed and curled and powdered sweet his hair;

Rich gifts unto his mistress did present,
And every day to visit her he went.
They like each one so well, they both agree
That in all haste they straight must married be.
To church they went, for joy the bells did ring,
When married were, he home the bride did bring.
But when he married was some half a year,
Then certain lectures from his wife did hear;
And whatso'er he did, she did dislike,
And all his kindness she with scorns did slight;
Cross every word she would that he did say,
Seemed very sick, complaining every day
Unless she went abroad, then she would be
In humor good in other company.
Then he would sigh, and call into his mind
His dear dead wife that was so wondrous kind;
He jealous grew, and was so discontent,
Soon of his later marriage did repent;
With melancholy thoughts fell sick and died;
His wife soon after was another's bride.
        When she had done, the men aloud did cry,
        Said, she had quit her tale most spitefully.

        Another man, to answer what she told,
        Began to tell, and did his tale unfold.

The Effeminate Description

A man awalking did a lady spy;
To her he went, and when he came hard by,
Fair Lady, said he, why walk you alone?
Because, said she, my thoughts are then my own;
For in a company my thoughts to throng,
And follow every foolish babbling tongue.
        Your thoughts, said he, were boldness for to ask.
To tell, said she, it were too great a task:
But yet to satisfy your mind, said she,
I'll tell you how our thoughts run commonly.
Sometimes they mount up to the heavens high,
Then straight fall down, and on the earth will lie;

Then circling runs to compass all they may,
And then sometimes they all in heaps do stay;
At other times they run from place to place,
As if they had eachother in a chase;
Sometimes they run as fancy doth them guide,
And then they swim as in a flowing tide:
But if the mind be discontent, they flow
Against the tide, their motion's dull and slow.
                    Said he,
    I travel now to satisfy my mind,
Whether I can a constant woman find.
    O sir, said she, it's labor without end,
We cannot constant be to any friend;
We seem to love to death, but 'tis not so,
Because our passion moveth to and fro;
They are not fixed, but do run all about;
Every new object thrusts the former out:
Yet we are fond, and for a time so kind,
As nothing in the world should change our mind:
But if misfortune come, we weary grow,
Then former fondness we away straight throw;
Although the object alter not, yet may
Time alter our fond minds another way;
We love, and like, and hate, and cry,
Without a cause, or reason why.
Wherefore go back, for you shall never find
Any woman to have a constant mind;
The best that is shall hold out for a time,
Wavering like wind, which women hold no crime.

HER EXCELLENCIES COMICAL TALES IN PROSE
from THE FIRST PART

The Tobacconist

There were two maids talking of husbands, for that the most part is the theme of their discourse, and the subject of their thoughts;

Said the one to the other, I would not marry a man that takes tobacco for anything.

Said the second, then it is likely you will have a fool for your husband, for tobacco is able to make a fool a wise man: for though it doth not always work to wise effects, by reason some fools are beyond all improvement, yet it never fails where any improvement is to be made.

Why, said the first, how doth it work such wise effects?

Said the second, it composes the mind, it busies the thoughts, it attracts all outward objects to the mind's view, it settles and retents the senses; it clears the understanding; strengthens the judgment, spies out errors; it evaporates follies, it heats ambition, it comforts sorrow, it abates passions, it excites to noble actions; it digests conceptions, it enlarges knowledge, it makes reason pleader, and truth judge in all disputes or controversies betwixt right and wrong.

Said the first, it makes the breath stink.

Said the second, you mistake; it will make a stinking breath sweet.

It is a beastly smell, said the first.

Said the second, Civet is a beastly smell, and that you will thrust your nose to, although it be an excrement, and for anything we know, so is ambergris, when tobacco is a sweet and pleasant, wholesome and medicinal herb.

from THE THIRD PART

The Marriage of Life and Death

Death went awooing to Life: but his grim and terrible aspect did so affright Life that she ran away, and would by no means hearken unto his suit.

Then Death sent Age and Weakness, as two ambassadors, to present his affection; but Life would not give them audience.

Whereupon Death sent Pain, who had such a persuasive power, or power of persuasion, that made Life yield to Death's embracements. And after they were agreed, the wedding-day was set, and guests invited.

Life invited the five Senses, and all the Passions and Affections; and Beauty, Pleasure, Youth, Wit, Prosperity; and also, Virtue, and the Graces.

But Health, Strength, Cordials, and Charms refused to come; which troubled Life much.

But none that Death invited refused to come, as being old Father Time, Weakness, Sickness, also all sorts of Pains, and all sorts of Diseases, and killing Instruments; besides, Sighs, Tears, and Groans, and Numbness and Paleness.

But when Life and Death met, Death took Life by the hand; then Peace married them, and the rest made their bed of oblivion, wherein Life lay in the cold arms of Death. Yet Death got numerous issues; and ever since, whatsoever is produced from Life, dies. Where, before this marriage, there was no such thing as dying, for Death and Life were single, Death being a bachelor, and Life a maid. But Life proved not so good a wife as Death a husband; for Death is sober, staid, grave, discreet, patient, dwelling silently and solitary, where Life is wild, various, unconstant, and runs about, shunning her husband Death's company.

But he, as a loving and fond husband, follows her; and when he embraces her, she grows big, and soon produces young Lives. But all the offspring of Death and Life are divided, half dwelling with Life, and half with Death.

But at this wedding, old Father Time, which looked the youngest although he was the oldest in the company, and danced the nimblest and best, making several changes in his dances; besides, he trod so gently, and moved so smoothly, that none could perceive how he did turn and wind and lead about. And being wiser than all the rest with long experience, he behaved himself so handsomely, insinuated so subtilly, courted so civilly, that he got all the ladies' affections; and being dextrous, got favors from every one of them, and some extraordinary ones; for he devirginated Youth, Beauty, Pleasure, Prosperity, and all the five Senses, but could not corrupt Wit, Virtue, nor the Graces.

But Nature, hearing of the abuse of her maids, was very angry, and forced him to marry them all. But they, although they were enamoured of him before they were married, yet now they do as most other wives do, not care for him; nay, they hate him, rail and exclaim against him; that what with his peevish, froward, and cross wives, and with the jealousy he hath of Sickness, Pains, and Mischances that often ravish them, he is become so full of wrinkles and his hair is turned all gray.

But Virtue and Wit, which are his sworn friends, and sweet companions, he recreates himself with their pleasant, free, honest, and honorable societies.

from THE TENTH BOOK

Heavens Library, which is Fames Palace
Purged from Errors and Vices

Jove and some of the other gods, being set in council, Pallas being
one, rose up and bowed to Jove, and thus spake: Great Jove, said she, I
ought in duty and love to inform you not only of the vices and errors,
which are numerous in the world, which in time may bring it to confusion, but those errors and vices are crept into your great Library, Fames
Palace, and if order be not taken to destroy them, they will devour all
your best and noblest records. Jove answers that vices were as serpents,
and errors as worms, bred in the bowels of Nature, of which she could
never be cured, for the gods had no medicine strong enough to purge
them out, and by reason they were from all eternity, they could not be
destroyed, for if any thing could be destroyed that is from all eternity,
then we ourselves might be destroyed; but, said Jove, we can cast them
out of our own mansions, though we cannot cast them out of Nature's
bowels; also we can hinder them from coming in, wherefore Fame is to be
reproved for suffering the Library to be so foul and full of filthy vermin.
Whereupon Mercury was sent to call Fame to appear before Jove and his
council. So when Fame came, Jove told her that gods and goddesses
ought to be just and upright, and to have their Palaces pure, and full of
Truth, which, said he, you nor your Palace hath not been, for you are
partial and your court full of faction, and my Library your Palace, foul
and full of wormy errors, which if it had been kept pure and clean, they
would never have entered, or if they had entered, you might have caused
them to have been swept out by Old Father Time. Fame answered that it
was not her fault, for Mars, Venus and Fortune had sent them in, and it is
not for me to oppose so great a god as Mars, or so great a goddess as
Venus, or so fit a judge to determine what was best to be flung out or what
to be placed therein, for none is fit to judge those causes but you, great
Jove, and your council. Jove approving what Fame said, told his council,
that after they had taken some repast, they would sit in council again, and
their only business should be to purge and cleanse their Library. So after
they had feasted with ambrosia and nectar, they returned to council,
where they did first decree:

That all those records as were to be cast forth should be heaped up
together, and then they would decree their disposals. After that they did

decree that all those records that were of usurpers, and invaders should be cast forth;

Next, that all fabulous and profitless records should be cast forth. Thirdly, all wanton and amorous records.

Fourthly, all records of useless laws and inhuman sacrifices.

Fifthly, all records of tedious speeches, or vain and factious oratory.

Sixthly, all obstructive controversy, as being destructive to Truth, should be cast out; also tedious disputes and sophistry; but Mars, Cupid and Mercury opposed it, as much as they could, saying,

That if all these records should be cast forth, the famous Library would be very empty.

Jove said, it was an infamous Library whilst they were kept therein, and that no records ought to be in Fames Library but of such acts as suppressed vice and advanc't virtue, and profitable for the life of man, and those of necessary inventions, but chiefly those that glorified the gods and sung their praises, declaring their power, wisdom, justice, and love; whose authors ought to have their memory recorded to everlasting Time: as for the works of natural Poets, said Jove, the fates have decreed them several places in the Library, wherefore it is not in our power to remove them, but those that are like false coin, that have only got by unjust means the stamp of the true figure, and not the worth of the metal, such as are dross or basely mixed, nor not pure and perfect pieces, we shall find out by their trial.

After they had decreed the generalities, they sat in council on the particularities, as which were unworthy to be kept or worthy to be cast out; first, they began with Moral and Natural Philosophers, Physicians, and Chemists, where Jove said, all but some few ought to be cast forth, for to what purpose should we stuff the Library with the repetitions and false commentaries, of which all modern records are for the most part but repetitions of the old, the alterations only in language.

As for the Philosophers, the first shall be Plato, his works shall be kept, all but his Commonwealth, and that shall be put out by reason it was so strict, it could never be put in use, nor come into practice. The rest, Pythagoras, Epicurus, Socrates, and Aristotle. As for Physicians, only Hippocrates and Galen and Paracelsus for his medicines, and Ramund Lully for the Philosopher's Stone, for although their records be lost in the rubbish of the Library, yet old Father Time shall be employed to find them out; and other records that are buried in the dust, which is worthy of perspicuous places; also Aristotle's Logic and Rhetoric was kept, and for Grammar, Lilly. The next they came to consider were Mathematical Records, whereof none was to be kept but Archimedes and Euclid. As for the records of Invention, all that are either necessary, profitable, or pleasant shall be enrolled; but all such invention as is hurtful, distrustful, obstructful, vain and useless shall be cast forth.

Then said one of the gods, Archimedes must be cast out, for he invented many engines of war. 'Tis true, said Jove, but by reason it was in the defense of the city he lived in, and was a native thereof, he shall be spared. The next were Astronomers, whereof four were kept, as Copernicus, Tichobrahe, Ptolemy, and Galileo. The next sort shall be Orators and Law Makers; there were Moses, Lycurgus, and Solon kept. For Orators only, Thucydides and Demosthenes; as for Tully, he was a vain boasting fellow, and Seneca a mere pedant and a dissembling pretending Philosopher, and therefore they shall out. For Politics only Achitophel and Machiavell. Then they came to Heroic records; Jove said that all the records that were out of the actions of those they call the Heroes, most of them ought to be cast out, being violators of Peace, and destroyers of Righteous Laws and Divine Ceremony, prophaners of our Temples, breaking down our altars and images, robbing us of our treasures, therein to maintain their ill-gotten power, or to get that power they have no right to, having no justice but strength to make their titles good; besides, they are the greatest troublers of Mankind, robbers and thieves, disposing the right of ancient possessions and defacing the Truth of ancient times. With that, Mars rose, and bowing to Jove, said, May it please your great godhead: there are your Priests that have made it good by divine laws, and many Lawyers that justify it by the Laws of every Kingdom, and by the Laws of Nations, and will you cast down that which your Priests and Lawyers preach and plead up? With that, Pallas rose up and spoke.

Great Jove, said she, wisdom knows that force makes the gown stoop, and Mercury knows that Orators' tongues are as often bribed for fear as reward, and those two professions plead always for the stronger side, and falsifies your text always for interest, and turns right to wrong, and makes the test and laws, such a nose of was, which will take any print, or else, how should such various disputes arise in that we hold sacred as Divinity, and every cause disputed pro and con, in all courts by opposite counsels. Wherefore, all-seeing Jove, your power will rectify it, and it will be justice to throw them out; wherefore let all the records of all those of the heroic acts and Heroes both of Greeks and Romans, that were invaders or usurpers, with their Heroes, as Alexander, Hannibal, Scipio, Caesar, and all the rest, and all other records and Heroes, of what nation soever, which is of that injurious, turbulent, ambitious and vainglorious nature, whereof there be thousands which ought to be cast into hell's dungeon, the place of infamy, there let their actions be recorded, and not usurp heaven's great and glorious Library as they did the earth's. Then said Mars, you must cast all the Heroic actions and worthies in Homer's works into that dungeon. That must not be, said Jove, for Homer was heaven's chronologer, and the records of the gods of heaven must not be cast into hell; besides, there was a just pretence for that war, for the Grecians had received a palpable injury, and the Trojans did but defend themselves, and though the injury done and the wrong received, were but by two single men, and the quarrel, but for a light inconstant woman, yet it was a riot, and the more faulty and less pardonable because it was a riot of our deputies on earth, for Kings are Gods and Deputies and Viceregents, and therefore sacred, and ought not to be injured; but when they are, their injurers are to be severely punished, and heaven forbid we should be so unjust, to cast out all Heroic action, and warring Heroes; no, we cast out only those that make war unjustly, vaingloriously, or covetously.

Then Mars asked if Tamberlain should be cast out?

Jove said yes, for he had no right to the Turks' Empire.

Then he asked if Scanderbeg should be thrown out?

Jove said no, for it is lawful for any to get their own, and to maintain their right by what force soever, and that Scanderbeg had reason to fight for and to maintain by force his own inheritance.

Then he asked if the records of the Jews' Heroes, and their Heroic actions in the Land of Canaan should be cast out?

Jove said no, for that Land was given them by the gods.

Then they came to Romances, where Jove said, All Romances should be cast out but Don Quixote, by reason he hath so wittily abused all other Romances, wherefore he shall be kept, and also have his books writ in golden letters.

Then Cupid spoke in their behalf, and intreated Jove, that they might not be cast out, for, said Cupid, Romances work as great effects upon the hearts of mortals, as my arrows tipped with gold doth; besides they are my Mother Venus's looking-glasses.

Jove said, they did corrupt mortals' thoughts, and made them neglect their divine worship, causing them to spend their time vainly, idly and sinfully.

Then Cupid desired Jove but to spare Amadis de Gaul, but Jove said that should be the first that should be cast out, by reason it was the original of all the rest. Likewise, said Jove, all Fables shall be cast out but Aesop's Fables, which profit mankind by his morals; also Lucian and Rabelais shall be kept, both for their huge wit and judgment, rectifying Scholars' understandings; and though some that are spiteful at their wit, calls them scoffers, yet they are not so, but teachers of truth in a pleasant style, and those that say they are prophaners, judge presumptuously and maliciously on them. At this sentence Mercury joyed.

At last they came to judge of Poets, where Homer, Pindar, and Anacreon were preferred as the three first.

Then one of the gods named Virgil as the fourth. Jove said, it was a question whether Virgil was a true Natural Poet or not, by reason he was rather an imitator of Homer than of Nature, and his praise was more for his language than either for fancy or natural description; wherefore, said Jove, he might be questioned for a true born Natural Poet; and since it may be doubted he is a bastard kind, I will prefer Horace before him, who certainly is a true begotten Poetical son of Nature. Said another of the gods, I should judge Ovid to be placed before either of them both, for the sweetness of his verse and fineness of his fancy, the curious intermixing and subtil interweaving of his several discourses, themes, arguments, or transmigrations. Jove said, for his part he was no friend to Ovid, for divulging his several amours, and if it were in my power, said Jove, to alter the decrees of fate, I would cast him forth, but by reason he is a right Natural Poet, I cannot; but yet I can place him in heaven's Library as I will, and therefore he shall not be before, neither Horace nor Virgil, but he shall stand in the sixth place; in the seventh place shall stand Martial.

Said Cupid, your god-head hath forgot Tibullus and his son.

No, said Jove, they ought to be put out, because their verses were wanton.

Said Cupid, your god-head cannot put them out because they are Natural Poets.

Then let them, said Jove, be placed in some out-corner of the Library. At which sentence Cupid frowned, knowing his mother Venus would grieve to have them disrespected. Then was placed the Comedian Terence, and Plautus, and the Tragedian Seneca; and after they had given their judgments of all the ancient Poets, which were more than could be numbered in this place, they tried the Moderns, whereof they could not find one true Natural Poet, not amongst five hundred, for though there is an infinite company of them, yet hardly one true one amongst them all; for most of the Moderns have been like a company of ravens, that live upon dead carcasses: so they upon old authors, and some have been like maggots, that have been bred in their dead flesh, which is the living works of dead authors; and some like hornets, and some like bees, but very few rightly begotten from Nature; indeed so few as I am loath to set them down; so most of the Moderns were cast out. Then after they had divided the records as what to be put out and what to be kept in, there rose a great dispute amongst the gods, how those that were cast out should be disposed of. At last Jove decided the case: those that were wicked, mischievous and base, should be put into hell, and those that were idle, vain, useless and foolish, should be drowned in the river of Styx; but they were forced to make new boats to waft some to hell, and to drown others in the river, for there was such an infinite company that Charon had not leisure, neither could one boat serve their turn; but then there rose another dispute about those that go to hell. For, said some of the gods, the records must not be in paper, nor parchment, nor in metal, nor stone, by reason there is a continual and eternal fire in hell which will burn the one and melt and moulder away the other. Whereupon Jove ordered that those that were to go into hell should be recorded in Salamander-stone, on which the fire hath no force; for the more it is burnt, the more it is purified. After they had decreed this, all the records of Tyrants, Usurpers, Invaders, Murderers, Thieves, Ravishers, Extortioners, Detractors, Licentious Mutiners, Factious, Prophane, and Rebellious Records, with evil inventions were cast into hell, a room being provided as a Library, and one of the Furies with a fiery trumpet sounded out their reproach; and all those records that were Vain, Useless, Idle, Amorous, and Wanton, with all those that were Sophisterious, Tedious, Obscure, Pedantical, and those that were only Repetitions and false Commentaries, also those of useless Inventions, and those that were mere Rhymers, were cast into the River of Styx, and so drowned in oblivion.

KATHERINE PHILIPS

1632–1664

K ATHERINE FOWLER PHILIPS was the daughter of John Fowler, a prominent merchant of Bucklersbury, and his wife Katherine, daughter of Daniel Oxenbridge, Doctor of Physic and Fellow of the Royal College of Physicians in London. Her father was a wealthy member of the Clothworkers Company, having entered by "redemption," or purchase, as his father had not belonged. Fowler died in 1642. Four years later his widow married Sir Richard Phillipps of Picton Castle, Bart., a rich landowner from Pembrokeshire. After only two years of marriage and the birth of their daughter Elizabeth, Sir Richard died, leaving Dame Katherine Phillipps of Picton Castle extremely wealthy. Her third husband was Philip Skippon, the Parliamentary Major-General under Cromwell; he died before the Restoration. His wife lived until 1678.

As a child, Katherine Fowler Philips was sent to Miss Salmon's school for girls in Hackney, where she probably studied a little French and Italian and was thoroughly drilled in the catechism of John Ball, the well-known Puritan schoolmaster. About 1646 she joined her mother at Picton Castle in Wales, and from that time on she was always associated with that country.

James Philips of Tregibby and the Priory, Cardigan, was related to Sir Richard Phillipps by blood and by law—both were descended from Sir Thomas Phillipps, and James's first wife was Sir Richard's daughter Frances. When James married Katherine Fowler in 1648, shortly after the death of Sir Richard, he was fifty-four and his bride, sixteen. They took up residence at the Priory in Cardigan. Presbyterian in religion, as was fitting for a loyal supporter of the Commonwealth, James rose to become one of the most important men of South Wales; his positions in Cromwell's government were financially rewarding as well as influential. He spent several months each year in London, where Katherine greatly augmented her circle of friends. In 1655, Katherine bore a son, Hector, who lived less than two months; in 1656 a daughter, Katherine, was born.

Katherine's verses first appeared in print in 1651, prefixed to the poems of Henry Vaughan and to the collected works of Thomas Cartwright published that same year. From then on, many of her poems circulated in manuscript. Her Society of Friendship was first mentioned in 1651, but by the time of the Restoration it had apparently petered out. This society was not a salon; in all probability it never met, but existed solely in the mind of its founder, whom its members called the Matchless Orinda. She assigned classical names to herself and her friends, and wrote letters and verses to and about them. Only women were included in the society, although her husband and several other men were given names appropriate for the group. Those celebrated in the poems printed below are identified as follows: James Philips, her husband—*Antenor*. Sir Charles Cotterell, Master of Ceremonies at the court of Charles II, to whom she wrote the now-famous letters—*Poliarchus*. Henry Lawes— *Prince of Musicians*. Mrs. Mary Aubrey, her oldest friend, from a Welsh Royalist family—*Rosania*. Mrs. Anne Owen, her closest friend from 1652 to 1660—*Lucasia*.

Katherine's family and her husband's associates were all of the Parliamentary party, but her friends were all Royalists. It is not surprising to find that after the Restoration she allowed her hitherto private feelings free rein. She rejoiced in the Church of England, leaving Presbyterianism, and was thrilled at the overthrow of the Commonwealth. Even before Charles II set foot in England after he had been summoned to return from the Continent, she wrote a poem to him, "On the numerous Access of the English to wait upon the King in Flanders," in which she urged him to return speedily, before England was "depeopled" owing to the great numbers who rushed to the Continent to meet him. She thoroughly enjoyed the festivities that accompanied the king's return to London and developed new friendships at this time with literary and courtly members of London society.

By 1661 the Society of Friendship had died out and its founder claimed that she was turning her "melancholy muse" to other things; she began to write panegyric verse, heroic poems, and translations. Her reputation as a writer was well established: when she sailed in 1662 to Ireland with Anne Owen, her Lucasia, she was royally received in Dublin. She remained there for about a year while she attempted to settle certain property claims for her husband. James was deeply depressed—he had been ousted from his seat in Parliament and was being threatened with reprisals owing to his role in the government of the Commonwealth. However, he was never fined or imprisoned, but remained in Cardigan in semi-retirement. In Dublin, Katherine saw her translation of Corneille's play *Pompey* produced with great success at the Smock-Alley Theatre; it was also to succeed in England. When her legal affairs were finally concluded, she returned to Cardigan. In addition to the *Pompey*, she had also translated Corneille's *l'Horace*, which, with Sir John Denham's fifth act, was performed at court by nobles and royalty. Abraham Cowley wrote extravagant praises of her wit and virtue; Jeremy Taylor praised her as a friend and wrote a treatise on friendship for her; John Aubrey described her religious exercises and interests with hearty approval; the Earls of Orrery and Roscommon wrote poems for her; her eulogist compared her favorably with Sappho; she was admired by John Dryden; and she delighted Charles II.

At Cardigan in 1663 Katherine was torn between her duty to her husband and her longing for her friends in London. At the end of the year she journeyed to London, where she eventually contracted smallpox, and died in June 1664. She was buried in the church of St. Benet Sherehog beside her grandfather, grandmother, father, and son. (This church was burned in the Great Fire of 1666 and never rebuilt.) The literary circles in London considered her death a great calamity and Nicholas Rowe, Cowley, and others wrote commemorative verses and tributes. Her poems, translations, and letters were published many times; the first collected edition of her plays and poems was edited by her Poliarchus, Sir Charles Cotterell, in 1667. There is no standard edition of her works.

Mrs. L. I. Guiney wrote in 1903, "The time is at hand when no one who would study the history of English intellectual development on the spindle side, or the intimate temper of the great century which altered England, will forbear some measure of acquaintance with 'Orinda,' queen of those virtuous poets who were among the public successes of the not-yet-understood Restoration."

BIBLIOGRAPHY

Works

Letters from Orinda to Poliarchus. London: Printed by W. B. for Bernard Lintott, 1705, 1729.
Poems. (Unauthorized.) London: By J. C. for Rich. Marriot, 1664.

Cotterell, Sir Charles ed., *Poems by Mrs. Katherine Philips, the Matchless Orinda, to which is added Corneille's Pompey and Horace.* London: By J. M. for H. Herringman, 1667, 1669, 1678, 1710. Also by T. N. for Henry Herringman, 1678.

Guiney, L. I., ed. *Selected Poems.* 2 vols. Cottingham near Hull, England: n.p., 1904–1905.

Saintsbury, George, ed. *Poems.* (1678 edition.) In *Minor Poets of the Caroline Period*, vol. 1, pp. 405–662. Oxford: Clarendon Press, 1905.

Tutin, J. R., ed. *The Orinda Booklets.* With appreciative note by L. I. Guiney. Cottingham near Hull, England: n.p., 1903.

Related Readings

Costello, Louisa S. *Memoirs of Eminent Englishwomen.* 4 vols. London: R. Bentley, 1844.

Elmen, P. "Some Manuscript Poems by the Matchless Orinda." *Philological Quarterly*, vol. 30, 1951.

Roberts, W. Saint-Amant. "Orinda and Dryden's Miscellany." *English Language Notes*, vol. 1, 1964.

———. "The Dating of Orinda's French Translations." *Philological Quarterly*, vol. 49, 1970.

Souers, Philip Webster. *The Matchless Orinda.* Cambridge, Mass.: Harvard University Press, 1931.

To Rosania and Lucasia, Articles of Friendship

KATHERINE PHILIPS

[*H. E. Huntington Ms. HM 183, No. 17a (unpublished)*]

The souls which vertue hath made fit
Do of themselves incline to knit;
Yet wedlock having priests, allow
That I be friendship's Flamen* now.

* a priest devoted to the service of a particular deity.

For I can best perform the rite
Who of the Goddess had a sight;
To me her oracles she gave,
And did inspire me in her cave.

And 'tis my glory that I may
My faults redeemed, my debts repay,
No more my useless self I loath,
Since I can now oblige you both.

First then, the love you bear each other,
You must no more in silence smother,
Nor ceremoniously take pains,
To put your friendship into chains.

Formal addresses then disclaim,
And never must ye Madam name.
She gains most, who first condescends
For y'are more noble being friends.

Estrangements thus once voted down,
And all Punctilios of the town,
No time nor place believe unfit
Which will each other's sight admit.

Though friendship greatest service dares,
Its life consists in little cares,
These frequent tendernesses which
Make a concerned heart so rich.

You both must wear an open heart,
And freely your concerns impart.
By this your pleasure you will double,
And it will lessen all your trouble.

All distance may this hour destroy,
Confirm your love, begin your joy!
O how much kindness does afford—
That pleasant, and that mighty word!

If you these sounds do disapprove,
Ye cannot, or ye will not love,
But if ye like these lovely bands,
With them join hearts, and lips, and hands!
                    Orinda.

Selections from

Poems

BY THE MOST DESERVEDLY ADMIRED
MRS. KATHERINE PHILIPS, THE MATCHLESS ORINDA

[*London, 1667*]

Worthy Poliarchus,

It is very well that you chid me so much for endeavoring to express a part of the sense I have of your obligations; for while you go on in conferring them beyond all possibility of acknowledgment, it is convenient for me to be forbidden to attempt it. Your last generous concern for me, in vindicating me from the unworthy usage I have received at London from the press, doth as much transcend all your former favors, as the injury done me by that publisher and printer exceeds all the troubles that I remember I ever had. All I can say to you for it is, that though you assert an unhappy, it is yet a very innocent person, and that it is impossible for malice itself to have printed these rhymes (you tell me are gotten abroad so impudently) with so much abuse to the things, as the very publication of them at all though they had been never so correct, had been to me; to me (Sir) who never writ any line in my life with an intention to have it printed, and who am of my Lord Falkland's mind, that said,

He danger feared than censure less,
Nor could he dread a breach like to a Press.

And who (I think you know) am sufficiently distrustful of all, that my

own want of company and better employment, or others' commands
have seduced me to write, to endeavor rather that they should never be
seen at all, than that they should be exposed to the world with such
effrontery as now they most unhappily are. But is there no retreat from
the malice of this world? I thought a rock and a mountain might have
hidden me, and that it had been free for all to spend their solitude in what
reveries they please, and that our rivers (though they are babbling) would
not have betrayed the follies of impertinent thoughts upon their banks;
but 'tis only I who am that unfortunate person that cannot so much as
think in private, that must have my imaginations rifled and exposed to
play the mountebanks, and dance upon the ropes to entertain all the
rabble; to undergo all the railery of the Wits, and all the severity of the
Wise, and to be the sport of some that can, and some that cannot read a
verse. This is a most cruel accident, and hath made so proportionate an
impression upon me that really it hath cost me a sharp fit of sickness since
I heard it, and I believe would be more fatal but that I know what a
champion I have in you, and that I am sure your credit in the world will
gain me a belief from all that are knowing and civil, that I am so innocent
of that wretched artifice of a secret consent (nor which I am, I fear,
suspected) that whoever would have brought me those copies corrected
and amended, and a thousand pounds to have bought my permission for
their being printed, should not have obtained it. But though there are
many things, I believe, in this wicked impression of those fancies, which
the ignorance of what occasioned them, and the falseness of the copies
may represent very ridiculous and extravagant, yet I could give some
account of them to the severest Cato, and I am sure they must be more
abused than I think is possible (for I have not seen the book, nor can
imagine what's in't) before they can be rendered otherwise than Sir
Edward Deering says in his Epilogue to *Pompey*:

> —No bolder thought can tax
> Those rhymes of blemish to the blushing sex,
> As chaste the lines, as harmless is the sense,
> As the first smiles of infant innocence.

So that I hope there will be no need of justifying them to Virtue and
Honor; and I am so little concerned for the reputation of writing sense,
that provided the world would believe me innocent of any manner of
knowledge, much less connivance at this publication, I shall willingly
compound never to trouble them with the true copies, as you advise me to

do: which if you still should judge absolutely necessary to the reparation of this misfortune, and to the general satisfaction; and that, as you tell me, all the rest of my friends will press me to it, I should yield to it with the same reluctancy as I would cut off a limb to save my life. However I hope you will satisfy all your acquaintance of my aversion to it, and did they know me as well as you do, that apology were very needless, for I am so far from expecting applause for anything I scribble, that I can hardly expect pardon; and sometimes I think that employment so far above my reach, and unfit for my sex, that I am going to resolve against it forever; and could I have recovered those fugitive papers that have escaped my hands, I had long since made a sacrifice of them all. The truth is, I have an incorrigible inclination to that folly of rhyming, and intending the effects of that humor, only for my own amusement in a retired life, I did not so much resist it as a wiser woman would have done; but some of my dearest friends having found my ballads, (for they deserve no better name) they made me so much believe they did not dislike them, that I was betrayed to permit some copies for their divertisement; but this, with so little concern for them, that I have lost most of the originals, and that I suppose to be the cause of my present misfortune; for some infernal Spirits or other have catched those rags of paper, and what the careless blotted writing kept them from understanding, they have supplied by conjecture, till they put them into the shape wherein you saw them, or else I know not which way it is possible for them to be collected, or so abominably transcribed as I hear they are. I believe also there are some among them that are not mine, but every way I have so much injury, and the worthy persons that had the ill luck of my converse, and so their names exposed in this impression without their leave, and that few things in the power of Fortune could have given me so great a torment as this most afflictive accident. I know you, Sir, so much my friend, that I need not ask your pardon for making this tedious complaint; but methinks it is a great injustice to revenge myself upon you by this harangue for the wrongs I have received from others; therefore I will only tell you that the sole advantage I have by this cruel news is that it has given me an experiment, That no adversity can shake the constancy of your friendship, and that in the worse humor that ever I was in, I am still,

Worthy Poliarchus,

Cardigan,   Your most faithful, most obliged

Jan. 29, 1663/4   Friend, and most humble Servant,

Orinda

TO MR. HENRY LAWES

Nature, which is the vast creation's soul,
That steady curious agent in the whole,
The art of heaven, the order of this frame,
Is only number in another name.
For as some King conquering what was his own,
Hath choice of several titles to his crown,
So harmony on this score now, that then,
Yet still is all that takes and governs men.
Beauty is but composure, and we find
Content is but the concord of the mind,
Friendship the unison of well-tuned hearts,
Honor the chorus of the noblest parts,
And all the world on which we can reflect
Music to th'ear, or to the intellect.
If then each man a little world must be,
How many worlds are copied out in thee,
Who art so richly formed, so compleat
T'epitomize all that is good and great;
Whose stars this brave advantage did impart,
Thy nature's as harmonious as thy art?
Thou dost above the poets' praises live,
Who fetch from thee th'eternity they give.
And as true reason triumphs over sense,
Yet is subjected to intelligence:
So poets on the lower world look down,
But Lawes on them; his height is all his own.
For, like divinity itself, his lyre
Rewards the wit it did at first inspire.
And thus by double right poets allow
His and their laurel should adorn his brow.
Live then, great Soul of Nature, to assuage
The savage dullness of this sullen age.
Charm us to sense; for though experience fail
And reason too, thy numbers may prevail.
Then, like those ancients, strike, and so command
All nature to obey thy gen'rous hand.
None will resist but such who needs will be

More stupid than a stone, a fish, a tree.
Be it thy care our age to new-create:
What built a World may sure repair a State.

TO MR. HENRY VAUGHAN, SILURIST, ON HIS POEMS

Had I adored the multitude, and thence
Got an antipathy to Wit and Sense,
And hugged that fate in hope the world would grant
'Twas good affection to be ignorant;
Yet the least ray of thy bright fancy seen,
I had converted, or excuseless been;
For each birth of thy Muse to after-times
Shall expiate for all this age's crimes.
First shines thy Amoret, twice crowned by thee,
Once by thy love, next by thy poetry:
Where thou the best of unions dost dispence,
Truth clothed in Wit, and Love in Innocence.
So that the muddiest lovers may learn here,
No fountains can be sweet that are not clear.
There Juvenal revived by thee declares
How flat man's joys are, and how mean his cares;
And generously upbraids the world that they
Should such a value for their ruin pay.
But when thy sacred Muse diverts her quill,
The landscape to design of Leon's hill;
As nothing else was worthy her or thee,
So we admire almost t'idolatry.
What savage breast would not be raped to find
Such jewels in such cabinets enshrined?
Thou (filled with joys too great to see or count)
Descend'st from thence like Moses from the Mount,
And with a candid, yet unquestioned awe,
Restor'st the Golden Age when Verse was Law.
Instructing us thou so secur'st thy fame,
That nothing can disturb it by my name;
Nay I have hopes that standing so near thine
'Twill lose its dross, and by degrees refine.

Live till the disabused world consent,
All truths of use, or strength, or ornament,
Are with such harmony by thee display'd
As the whole world was first by number made;
    And from the charming rigour thy Muse brings,
    Learn, there's no pleasure but in serious things.

APHRA BEHN

1640(?)–1689

APHRA BEHN is still an enigma. Claims that she was born in Canterbury or in Wye, Kent, have not been proved, nor do we know when or into what family she was born. Reportedly, the family went to Surinam in 1663, when her father was appointed colonial governor there, but he died en route and they were forced to return to England the following year. Some brief biographical details appear in her novel *Oroonoko*, but nothing else is known of her early life. Scholars have speculated that she married a Mr. Behn, an English merchant of Dutch ancestry, in 1664 and that he died in 1665, but hard evidence is still lacking.

She must have had some connections at court, however, for it is documented that in 1666 the powerful Lord Arlington sent her to Holland as a spy, an unusual occupation for a woman. In two years at Antwerp, she was very successful and obtained considerable information, but the £125 she received did not cover her expenses. She returned to England at her own expense, where, unable to repay money she borrowed, she was soon in debtors' prison. Presumably friends obtained her release, but it was painfully obvious that she needed some kind of independent means in order to survive. Most women in her position looked for husbands or lovers; Behn chose independence. As assets, she had an inventive imagination, a command of words, a sense of the dramatic, and some connections in the theater. In September 1670 her first play, *The Forced Marriage*, opened successfully at Lincolns-Inn-Fields, with Thomas Betterton in the leading role.

For Behn it was the beginning of a long career. She wrote or translated more than twenty plays, most of which were highly applauded. Besides *The Forced Marriage*, she wrote one other tragicomedy, *The Amorous Prince* (1671), and one tragedy, *Abdelazar* (1676), but her best work was in comedy, for which she showed a distinct flair. *The Rover* (1677) and *The Emperor of the Moon* (1687) were still popular in the mid-eighteenth century, as was *The False Count* (1681), later sentimentalized into *The Merry Counterfeit*.

In her own time, she was a pioneer. Only a few women before her had been serious writers; Behn was the first to become a professional and earn her living by her pen. Perhaps her arrival on the scene was fortuitous; in 1670 the theaters were avidly searching for new plays, and a writer with originality and skill was welcomed, even if female. Within a few years her male contemporaries grudgingly accepted her as a strong contender in the fiercely competitive theatrical world.

This is not to suggest that she was given total equality, that the prejudice against "female scribblers" was not intense, or that Behn did not receive criticism more severe than just. She gave her enemies ammunition by refusing to accept attacks with modesty, tears, or admissions of inferiority; instead she fought back, and her prefaces are often sharp counterattacks against slander and libel.

Writing plays sustained her for over a decade, but by 1684 theatrical tastes were beginning to change. Behn turned from drama to poetry with the publication of *Poems upon several Occasions*, and to fiction with *Love Letters between a Nobleman and his Sister*. She continued to publish both poetry and stories for the next five years, working hard from necessity, for she was never free from debt. Literature did not provide a large income; although male writers could build a reputation and expect posts in government, such avenues were not open to women.

In 1688, ill and destitute, sensing that death was near, she displayed an astonishing creative vitality: in that year she published two poems honoring James II and his queen, one celebrating Queen Mary after the Glorious Revolution had deposed James, and several minor poems. Other works that year included translations of *Agnes de Castro* (Mlle. de Brillac), *The History of Oracles* (Fontenelle) and *Lycidus* (Paul Tallemant), as well as fiction, *The Fair Jilt*, and her most famous story, *Oroonoko*. The last shows the evils of slavery and gives a picture of the "noble savage" that antedates Rousseau by a century. After Behn's death, Thomas Southerne dramatized the story into one of the most frequently performed tragedies of the early eighteenth century.

Her comedies are witty and still amuse, her light verse reveals a frank delight in sex that conflicts with the popular Restoration image of the passive woman, and her prose fiction displays both narrative skill and psychological perception. Yet during her lifetime, she was ridiculed and reviled. For using the same language that in male playwrights was considered wit, she was charged with bawdiness. With no solid foundation in fact, a reputation for indecency clung to her name for two centuries, and Pope's couplet in the *Epistle to AUGUSTUS*:

> The stage how loosely does Astraea tread,
> Who fairly puts all characters to bed

was quoted by those who never saw or read her work. The Victorians, who regarded the Restoration as an age of immorality, looked upon Behn as a particularly vicious example, and during the nineteenth century her work was not published at all. A brief sketch by the anonymous friend who wrote an introduction to her collected stories suggests that to some of her contemporaries at least, such a reputation was considerably exaggerated:

> She was of a generous and open temper, something passionate, very serviceable to her Friends in all that was in her Power, and could sooner forgive an Injury than do one. She had Wit, Honour, Good-humour, and Judgment. . . . For my part, I knew her intimately, and never saw aught unbecoming the just Modesty of our Sex, though more gay and free than the Folly of the Precise will allow. She was, I'm satisfied, a greater Honour to our Sex than all the Canting Tribe of Dissemblers that die with the false Reputation of Saints.

BIBLIOGRAPHY

Collections

Plays. 2 vols. London: Jacob Tonson and R. Wellington, 1702.
The Plays, Histories and Novels of the ingenious Mrs. A. Behn. 6 vols. London: John Pearson. 1871.
Two Tales. The Royal Slave and The Fair Jilt. London: Folio Society, 1953.
Baker, Ernest, ed. *The Novels of Mrs. Aphra Behn.* London: Routledge, 1905.
Gildon, Charles, ed. *The Histories and Novels of the late Ingenious Mrs. Behn.* London: S. Briscoe, 1696.
———. *Histories, Novels and Translations, written by the most ingenious Mrs. Behn.* London: W[illiam] O[nley] for S[amuel] B[riscoe], 1700.
Phelps, Robert, ed. *Selected Writings of the Ingenious Mrs. Aphra Behn.* New York: Grove, 1950. (Evergreen Books, no. 3)
Summers, Montague, ed. *Works of Mrs. Aphra Behn.* 6 vols. London: William Heinemann, 1915.

Works

Abdelazar; or, The Moor's Revenge. London: J. Magnes and R. Bentley, 1677.
The Amorous Prince, or, The Curious Husband. London: J. M. for Thomas Dring, 1671.
The City-Heiress; or, Sir Tomothy Treat-All. London: D. Brown, 1682.
The Dutch Lover. London: Thomas Dring, 1673.
The Emperor of the Moon. London: R. Holt for J. Knight and F. Saunders, 1687.
The Fair Jilt: or, The History of Prince Tarquin and Miranda. London: R. Holt for W. Canning, 1688.
The False Count; or, A New Way to play an Old Game. London: M. Flasher for Jacob Tonson, 1682.
The Feign'd Courtizans, or, a Night's Intrigue. London: Jacob Tonson, 1679.
The History of the Nun: or, the Fair Vow-breaker. London: A. Baskerville, 1689.
The Lady's Looking-Glass, to dress herself by: or, the Whole Art of Charming. London: W. Onley for S. Briscoe, 1697.
Love Letters between a Nobleman and his Sister. 3 vols. London: J. Hindewarsh and J. Tonson, 1693. Reprinted in The Novel in Letters, ed. N. Wuerzbach. Miami, Fla.: University of Miami Press, 1969.
The Lucky Chance, or, an Alderman's Bargain. London: R. H. for W. Canning, 1687.
The Lucky Mistake. London: R. Bentley, 1689.
La [sic] Montre: or, the Lover's Watch. London: R. H. for W. Canning, 1686.
Oroonoko; or, the Royal Slave. London: R. H. for W. Canning, 1688.
Poems upon Several Occasions: with a Voyage to the Island of Love. 2 vols. London: R. Tonson and J. Tonson, 1684.
The Roundheads; or, The Good Old Cause. London: D. Browne, 1682.
The Rover; or, the Banish't Cavaliers. London: John Amery, 1677.
The Rover. Edited by Frederick M. Link. London: Edward Arnold, 1967. (Regents Restoration Drama Series).
Sir Patrick Fancy. London: E. Flesher for R. Tonson, 1687.
The Town-Fopp; or, Sir Timothy Tawdrey. London: T. N. for J. Magnes and R. Bentley, 1677.
The Widow Ranter, or, the History of Bacon in Virginia. London: James Knapton, 1690.
The Young King: or, the Mistake. London: D. Browne, 1683.
The Younger Brother: or, The Amorous Jilt. Edited by Gildon Charles. London: J. Harris, 1696.

Related Readings

Cameron, William J. New Light on Aphra Behn. Monograph no. 5. Auckland, N. Z.: Univ. of Auckland, 1961.
Link, Frederick M. Aphra Behn. Twayne English Authors Series, no. 63. New York: Twayne Publishers, 1968. Good criticism of the works.
Sackville-West, Hon. V. M. S. Aphra Behn, the Incomparable Astrea. London: Gerald Howe, 1927.

Woodcock, George. *The Incomparable Aphra*. London: T. V. Boardman, 1948. Good biography.

☙

The Unfortunate Bride, or the Blind Lady a Beauty

APHRA BEHN

[*London, 1698*]

Frankwit and Wildvill were two young gentlemen of very considerable fortunes, born in Staffordshire, and during their minority, both educated together, by which opportunity they contracted a very inviolable friendship, a friendship which grew up with them; and though it was remarkably known to everybody else, they knew it not themselves; they never made profession of it in words, but actions; so true a warmth their fires could boast, as needed not the effusion of their breath to make it live. Wildvill was of the richest family, but Frankwit of the noblest; Wildvill was admired for outward qualifications, as strength and manly proportions, Frankwit for a much softer beauty, for his inward endowments, pleasing in his conversation, of a free and moving air, humble in his behavior, and if he had any pride, it was but just enough to show that he did not affect humility, his mind bowed with a motion as unconstrained as his body, nor did he force this virtue in the least, but he allowed it only; so amiable he was, that every virgin that had eyes knew too she had a heart, and knew as surely she should lose it. His Cupid could not be reputed blind; he never shot for him but he was sure to wound. As every other nymph admired him, so he was dear to all the Tuneful Sisters, the Muses were fired with him as much as their own radiant god Apollo; not their loved springs and fountains were so grateful to their eyes as he, him they esteemed their Helicon and Parnassus too; in short, whenever he pleased, he could enjoy them all. Thus he enamored the whole female sex, but amongst all the sighing captives of his eyes, Belvira only boasted charms to move him; her parents lived near his, and even from their childhood they felt mutual love, as if their eyes at their first meeting had struck out such glances as had kindled into amorous flame. And now Belvira, in her fourteenth year (when the fresh spring of young virginity began to cast more lively bloomings in her cheeks, and softer longings in her eyes) by her indulgent father's care was sent to London to a friend, her mother being lately dead. When, as if fortune ordered it so, Frankwit's father took a journey to the other World, to let his son the better enjoy the pleasures and delights of this. The young lover now with all imaginable haste interred his father, nor did he shed so many tears for his loss as might in the least quench the fires which he received from his Belvira's eyes, but (master of seventeen hundred pounds a year, which his father left him) with all the wings of love he flies to London, and sollicits Belvira with such fervency that it might be thought he meant Death's torch should kindle Hymen's; and now as soon as he arrives at his journey's end, he goes to pay a visit to the fair mistress of his soul, and assures her that though he was absent from her, yet she was still with him; and that all the road he traveled, her beauteous image danced before him, and like the ravished Prophet, he saw his Deity in every bush; in short, he paid her constant visits; the sun ne'er rose or set but still he saw it in her company, and every minute of the day he counted by his sighs; so incessantly he importuned her that she could no longer hold out, and was pleased in the surrender of her heart, since it was he was conqueror, and therefore felt a triumph in her yielding; their flames now joined, grew more and more, glowed in their cheeks, and lightened in their glances; eager they looked, as there were pulses beating in their eyes; and all endearing, at last she vowed that Frankwit living she would ne'er be any other man's; thus they passed on some time, while every day rolled over fair, Heaven showed an aspect all serene, and the sun seemed to smile at what was done; he still caressed his charmer with an innocence becoming his sincerity, he lived upon her tender breath, and basked in the bright lustre of her eyes, with pride and secret joy.

He saw his rivals languish for that bliss, those charms, those rapturous and ecstatic transports which he engrossed alone. But now some eighteen months (some ages in a lover's calendar) winged with delights, and fair Belvira now grown fit for riper joys, knows hardly how she can deny her pressing lover and herself to crown their vows and join their hands as well as hearts. All this while the young gallant washed himself clean of that shining dirt, gold; he fancied little of Heaven dwelt in his yellow angels, but let them fly away as it were on their own golden wings; he only valued the smiling babies in Belvira's eyes. His generosity was boundless as his love, for no man ever truly loved that was not generous. He thought his estate like his passion was a sort of a Pontick Ocean, it could never know any ebb; but now he found it could be fathomed, and that the tide was turning: therefore he sollicits with more impatience the consumation of their joys, that both might go like martyrs from their flames immediately to Heaven; and now at last it was agreed between them that they should both be one, but not without some reluctancy on the female side, for 'tis the humor of our sex to deny most eagerly those grants to lovers for which most tenderly we sigh: so contradictory are we to ourselves, as if the Deity had made us with a seeming reluctancy to his own designs, placing as much discords in our minds as there is harmony in our faces. We are a sort of airy clouds, whose lightning flash out one way, and the thunder another. Our words and thoughts can ne'er agree. So, this young charming lady thought her desires could live in their own longings, like misers, wealth-devouring eyes; and e'er she consented to her lover, prepared him first with speaking looks, and then with a fore-running sigh, applied to the dear charmer thus:

"Frankwit, I am afraid to venture the matrimonial bondage; it may make you think yourself too much confined, in being only free to one."

"Ah! my dear Belvira," he replied, "that one, like manna, has the taste of all; why should I be displeased to be confined to Paradise, when it was the curse of our forefathers to be set at large, though they had the whole world to roam in. You have, my love, ubiquitary charms, and you are all in all, in every part."

"Ay but," replied Belvira, "we are all like perfumes, and too continual smelling makes us seem to have lost our sweets. I'll be judged by my cousin Celesia here, if it be not better to live still in mutual love, without the last enjoyment."

(I had forgot to tell my reader that Celesia was an heiress, the only child of a rich Turkey merchant who when he died left her fifty thousand pound in money, and some estate in land; but, poor creature, she was blind to all these riches, having been born without the use of sight, though in all other respects charming to a wonder.)

"Indeed," says Celesia, (for she saw clearly in her mind), "I admire you should ask my judgment in such a case, where I have never had the least experience; but I believe it is but a sickly soul which cannot nourish its offspring of desires without preying upon the body."

"Believe me," replied Frankwit, "I bewail your want of sight, and I could almost wish you my own eyes for a moment to view your charming cousin, where you would see such beauties as are too dazzling to be long beheld; and if too daringly you gazed, you would feel the misfortune of the loss of sight much greater than the want on't; and you would acknowledge that in too presumptuously seeing, you would be blinder then than now unhappily you are."

"Ah! I must confess," replied Belvira, "my poor dear cousin is blind, for I fancy she bears too great an esteem for Frankwit, and only longs for sight to look on him."

"Indeed," replied Celesia, "I would be glad to see Frankwit, for I fancy he's as dazzling as he but now described his mistress, and if I fancy I see him, sure I do see him, for sight is fancy, is it not? Or do you feel my cousin with your eyes?"

"This is indeed a charming blindness," replied Frankwit, "and the fancy of your sight excels the certainty of ours; strange! that there should be such glances even in blindness? You, fair maid, require not eyes to conquer; if your night has such stars, what sunshine would your day of sight have, if ever you should see?"

"I fear those stars you talk of," said Belvira, "have some influence on you, and by the compass you sail by now, I guess you are steering to my cousin. She is indeed charming enough to have been another offspring of bright Venus, blind like her brother Cupid."

"That Cupid," replied Celesia, "I am afraid has shot me, for methinks I would not have you marry Frankwit, but rather live as you do without the least enjoyment, for methinks if he were married he would be more out of my sight than he already is."

"Ah! Madam," returned Frankwit, "love is no chameleon: it cannot feed on air alone."

"No but," rejoined Celesia, "you lovers that are not blind like love itself, have amorous looks to feed on."

"Ah! believe it," said Belvira, "'tis better, Frankwit, not to lose Paradise by too much knowledge; marriage-enjoyment does but wake you from your sweet golden dreams. Pleasure is but a dream, dear Frankwit, but a dream, and to be wakened."

"Ah! dearest but unkind Belvira," answered Frankwit, "sure there's no waking from delight, in being lulled on those soft breasts of thine."

"Alas!" replied the bride-to-be, "it is that very lulling wake you;

women enjoyed are like romances read, or raree-shows once seen, mere tricks of the sleight of hand which, when found out, you only wonder at yourselves for wondering so before at them. 'Tis expectation endears the blessing; heaven would not be heaven, could we tell what 'tis. When the plot's out you have done with the play, and when the last act's done, you see the curtain drawn with great indifferency."

"O my Belvira," answered Frankwit, "that expectation were indeed a monster which enjoyment could not satisfy; I should take no pleasure," he rejoined, "running from hill to hill, like children chasing that sun which I could never catch."

"O thou shalt have it then, that Sun of Love," replied Belvira, fired by this complaint and gently rushed into his arms, rejoicing, so Phoebus rushes radiant and unsullied into a gilded cloud.

"Well then, my dear Belvira," answered Frankwit, "be assured I shall be ever yours, as you are mine; fear not you shall never draw bills of love upon me so fast as I shall wait in readiness to pay them; but now I talk of bills, I must retire into Cambridgeshire, where I have a small concern as yet unmortgaged; I will return thence with a brace of thousand pounds within a week at farthest, with which our nuptials by their celebration shall be worthy of our love. And then, my life, my soul, we shall be joined, never to part again."

This tender expression moved Belvira to shed some few tears, and poor Celesia thought herself most unhappy that she had not eyes to weep with too; but if she had, such was the greatness of her grief that sure she would have soon grown blind with weeping. In short: after a great many soft vows and promises of an inviolable faith, they parted with a pompous sort of pleasing woe; their concern was of such a mixture of joy and sadness, as the weather seems when it both rains and shines. And now the last, the very last adieus was over, for the farewells of lovers hardly ever end, and Frankwit (the time being summer) reached Cambridge that night, about nine o'clock; (strange! that he should have made such haste to fly from what so much he loved!) and now, tired with the fatigue of his journey, he thought fit to refresh himself by writing some few lines to his beloved Belvira; for a little verse after the dull prose company of his servant was as great an ease to him, (from whom it flowed as naturally and unartificially as his love or his breath) as a pace or hand-gallop, after a hard, uncouth and rugged trot. He therefore, finding his Pegasus was no way tired with his land travel, takes a short journey through the air, and writes as follows:

My dearest dear Belvira,
You know my soul, you knew it yours before,
I told it all, and now can tell no more;
Your presence never wants fresh charms to move,
But now more strange and unknown power you prove,
For now your very absence 'tis I love.
Something there is which strikes my wandering view,
And still before my eyes I fancy you!
Charming you seem, all charming, heavenly fair,
Bright as a goddess does my love appear,
You seem, Belvira, what indeed you are.
Like angelic offspring of the skies,
With beatific glories in your eyes.
Sparkling with radiant lustre all divine,
Angels, and Gods! O heavens! how bright they shine!
Are you Belvira? can I think you mine!
Beyond ev'n thought, I do thy beauties see,
Can such a heaven of heavens be kept for me!
O be assured, I shall be ever true,
I must————
For if I would, I can't be false to you.
Oh! how I wish I might no longer stay,
Though I resolve I will no time delay,
One tedious week, and then I'll fleet away.
Though love be blind, he shall conduct my road,
Winged with almighty love to your abode.
I'll fly, and grow immortal as a God,
Short is my stay, yet my impatience strong,
Short though it is, alas! I think it long.
I'll come, my life, new blessings to pursue,
Love then shall fly a flight, he never flew,
I'll stretch his balmy wings; I'm yours, ————
                              Adieu.
                        Frankwit.

This letter Belvira received with unspeakable joy, and laid it up safely in her bosom, laid it where the dear author of it lay before, and wonderfully pleased with his humor of writing in verse, resolved not to be at all behind-hand with him, and so writ as follows:

You knew before what power your love could boast,
But now your constant faith confirms me most.
Absent sincerity the best assures,
Love may do much, but faith much more allures,

For now your constancy has bound me yours.
I find, methinks, in verse some pleasure too,
I cannot want a Muse, who write to you.
Ah! soon return, return, my charming dear,
Heaven knows how much we mourn your absence here:
My poor Celesia now would charm your soul,
Her eyes, once blind, do now divinely roll.
An aged Matron has by charms unknown,
Given her clear sight as perfect as thy own.
And yet, beyond her eyes, she values thee,
'Tis for thy sake alone she's glad to see.
She begged me, pray remember her to you,
That is a task which now I gladly do.
Gladly, since so I only recommend
A dear relation, and a dearer friend,
Ne'er shall my love—but here my note must end.
                    Your ever true Belvira.

When this letter was written it was straight shown to Celesia, who looked upon anything that belonged to Frankwit with rejoicing glances; so eagerly she perused it that her tender eyes beginning to water, she cried out (fancying she saw the words dance before her view), "Ah! cousin, cousin, your letter is running away, sure it cannot go itself to Frankwit?" A great deal of other pleasing innocent things she said, but still her eyes flowed more bright with lustrous beams, as if they were to shine out now all that glancing radiancy which had been so long kept secret, and as if, as soon as the cloud of blindness once was broke, nothing but lightnings were to flash forever after. Thus in mutual discourse they spent their hours, while Frankwit was now ravished with the receipt of this charming answer of Belvira's, and blessed his own eyes which discovered to him the much welcome news of fair Celesia's. Often he reads the letter o'er and o'er, but there his fate lay hid, for 'twas that very fondness proved his ruin. He lodged at a cousin's house of his, and there (it being a private family) lodged likewise a Blackamoor lady, then a widow. A whimsical knight had taken a fancy to enjoy her; enjoy her, did I say? enjoy the Devil in the flesh at once? I know not how it was, but he would fain have been abed with her, but she not consenting on unlawful terms (but sure all terms are with her unlawful) the knight soon married her, as if there were not hell enough in matrimony, but he must wed the Devil too. The knight a little after died, and left this lady of his (whom I shall call Moorea) an estate of six thousand pounds per annum. Now this Moorea observed this joyous Frankwit with an eager look; her eyes seemed like stars of the first magnitude glaring in the night; she greatly importuned him to discover the occasion of his transport, but he denying it, (as 'tis the humor of our sex) made her the more inquisitive; and being jealous that it was from a mistress, employed her maid to steal it, and if she found it such to bring it her. Accordingly it succeeded, for Frankwit having drank hard with some of the gentlemen of that shire, found himself indisposed, and soon went to bed, having put the letter in his pocket. The maid therefore to Moorea contrived that all the other servants should be out of the way, that she might plausibly officiate in the warming the bed of the indisposed lover, but likely, had it not been so, she had warmed it by his intreaties in a more natural manner; he being in bed in an inner room, she slips out the letter from his pocket, carries it to her mistress to read, and so restores it whence she had it; in the morning the poor lover wakened in a violent fever, burning with a fire more hot than that of love. In short, he continued sick a considerable while, all which time the Lady Moorea constantly visited him, and he as unwillingly saw her (poor gentleman) as he would have seen a Parson; for as the latter would have persuaded, so the former scared him to repentance. In the meanwhile, during his sickness, several letters were sent to him by his dear Belvira, and Celesia too, (then learning to write) had made a shift to give him a line or two in postscript with her cousin, but all was intercepted by the jealousy of the black Moorea, black in her mind and dark, as well as in her body. Frankwit too writ several letters as he was able, complaining of her unkindness; those likewise were all stopped by the same Blackmoor Devil. At last it happened that Wildvill, (who I told my reader was Frankwit's friend) came to London, his father likewise dead, and now master of a very plentiful fortune, he resolves to marry, and paying a visit to Belvira, enquires of her concerning Frankwit; she all in mourning for the loss, told him his friend was dead.

"Ah! Wildvill, he is dead," said she, "and died not mine, a Blackmoor Lady had bewitched him from me; I received a letter lately which informed me all; there was no name subscribed to it, but it intimated that it was written at the request of dying Frankwit."

"Oh! I am sorry at my soul," said Wildvill, "for I loved him with the best, the dearest friendship; no doubt then," rejoined he, "'tis witchcraft indeed that could make him false to you. What delight could he take in a Blackmoor Lady, though she had received him at once with a soul as open as her longing arms, and with her petticoat put off her modesty. Gods! How could he change the whole Field Argent into downright Sables."

"'Twas done," returned Celesia, "with no small blot, I fancy, to the Female Scutcheon."

In short, after some more discourse, but very sorrowful, Wildvill takes his leave, extremely taken with the fair Belvira, more beauteous in her cloud of woe. He paid her afterwards frequent visits, and found her wonder for the odd inconstancy of Frankwit greater than her sorrow, since he died so unworthy of her. Wildvill attacked her with all the force of vigorous love, and she (as she thought) fully convinced of Frankwit's death, urged by the fury and impatience of her new ardent lover, soon surrendered, and the day of their nuptials new arrived, their hands were joined. In the meantime Frankwit, (for he still lived) knew nothing of the injury the base Moorea practiced, knew not that 'twas through her private order that the fore-mentioned account of his falsehood and his death was sent; but impatient to see his dear Belvira, though yet extremely weak, rode post to London, and that very day arrived there, immediately after the nuptials of his mistress and his friend were celebrated. I was at this time in Cambridge, and having some small acquaintance with this Blackmoor Lady, and sitting in her room that evening after Frankwit's departure thence, in Moorea's absence, saw inadvertently a bundle of papers which she had gathered up, as I suppose, to burn, since now they grew but useless, she having no further hopes of him. I fancied I knew the hand, and thence my curiosity only led me to see the name, and finding *Belvira* subscribed, I began to guess there was some foul play in hand, Belvira being my particularly intimate acquaintance. I read one of them, and finding the contents, conveyed them all secretly out with me, as I thought, in point of justice I was bound, and sent them to Belvira by that night's post, so that they came to her hands soon after the minute of her marriage, with an account how and by what means I came to light on them. No doubt but they exceedingly surprised her; but Oh! much more she grew amazed immediately after, to see the poor, now unhappy Frankwit, who privately had enquired for her below, being received as a stranger who said he had some urgent business with her in a back chamber below stairs. What tongue, what pen can express the mournful sorrow of this scene! At first they both stood dumb, and almost senseless; she took him for the ghost of Frankwit; he looked so pale, new risen from his sickness, he (for he had heard at his entrance in the house that his Belvira married Wildvill) stood in amaze, and like a ghost indeed, wanted the power to speak, till spoken to the first. At last, he draws his sword, designing there to fall upon it in her presence; she then imagining it his ghost too sure, and come to kill her, shrieks out and swoons; he ran immediately to her, and catched her in his arms, and while he strove to revive and bring her to herself, though that he thought could never now be done, since she was married, Wildvill, missing his bride and hearing the loud shriek, came running down, and entering the room, sees his bride lie clapt in Frankwit's arms, "Ha! Traitor!" he cries out, drawing his sword with an impatient fury, "have you kept that strumpet all this while, cursed Frankwit, and now think fit to put your damned cast mistress upon me? Could you not forbear her, neither even on my wedding day? Abominable wretch!" Thus saying, he made a full pass at Frankwit, and run him through the left arm, and quite through the body of poor Belvira. That thrust immediately made her start, though Frankwit's endeavors all before were useless. Strange! that her death revived her! for Ah! she felt that now she only lived to die! striving through wild amazement to run from such a scene of horror, as her apprehensions showed her, down she dropped, and Frankwit seeing her fall, (all friendship disannulled by such a chain of injuries) draws, fights with, and stabs his own loved Wildvill. Ah! Who can express the horror and distraction of this fatal misunderstanding! The house was alarmed, and in came poor Celesia, running in confusion, just as Frankwit was offering to kill himself, to die with a false friend and perjured mistress, for he supposed them such. Poor Celesia now bemoaned her unhappiness of sight, and wished she again were blind. Wildvill died immediately, and Belvira only survived him long enough to unfold all their most unhappy fate, desiring Frankwit with her dying breath, if he ever loved her, (and now she said that she deserved his love, since she had convinced him that she was not false) to marry her poor dear Celesia, and love her tenderly for her, Belvira's, sake, leaving her, being her nearest relation, all her fortune, and he, much dearer than it all, to be added to her own. So joining his and Celesia's hands, she poured her last breath upon his lips and said, "Dear Frankwit, Frankwit, I die yours."

With tears and wondrous sorrow he promised to obey her will, and in some months after her interrment, he performed his promise.

[MARY] DELARIVIERE MANLEY
1667(?)–1724

D ELARIVIERE MANLEY, who never used the name Mary, was born between 1667 and 1672, either on the island of Jersey or at sea between Jersey and Guernsey, the daughter of Sir Roger Manley, then Lieutenant Governor of Jersey. The second of three daughters, she was named after her mother and reared with her sisters and brother Francis in the atmosphere of a military garrison. The family was old Cavalier stock, and Sir Roger was in good favor with the Stuarts. Under normal circumstances, Delariviere could expect to be presented at court, marry into the gentry, and lead the protected life of a lady, but when her father died in 1687, leaving his small estate and his two unmarried younger daughters to the care of a cousin, John Manley, the bright future vanished. The cousin soon deceived Delariviere into a false marriage, then abandoned her with her infant son, and any hope of respectability was irretrievably lost.

Her training had been sketchy; the library of a literary-minded father and three months with a minister who taught her French had given her the education of a lady, none of which was marketable. Luck, or perhaps the reverse, brought her to the attention of Barbara Villiers, Duchess of Cleveland, former mistress of Charles II. The once-powerful, still-haughty, aging duchess, deciding that the young woman brought her luck at the gaming table, hired her as a companion. The arrangement lasted six months before the inevitable clash, and Manley again faced an uncertain future.

She retired to Exeter, where she could live more cheaply than in London, and spent the next two years writing plays "for her amusement," she said, though she probably had a more practical end in view. In 1696, armed with a comedy, a tragedy, and the protection of a lover, she again tried her fortune in London. Her lover was well-chosen—Sir Thomas Skipwith, one of the principal theatrical shareholders—and very shortly *The Lost Lover* opened at Drury Lane. It was not a success, but her

179

tragedy, *The Royal Mischief*, which opened two months later at Lincolns-Inn-Fields, brought both recognition and a handsome profit to its author.

The theater was not a secure world, and when the affair with Skipwith ended, Manley, never prudent with finances, was again penniless. She soon turned to John Tilly, deputy warden of the Fleet Prison, with whom she lived until 1702, when she left him after arranging for him to marry a rich widow. Once more it was necessary to make her way, and once more she turned to her pen. Flamboyant, imaginative, and verbal, she had gained entrance to London literary society during her years with Tilly, and her friends came to her assistance. In 1705 she published her satirical *Secret History of Queen Zarah and the Zarazians*, an attack on Sarah, Duchess of Marlborough, and the Whigs, and the following year her tragedy *Almyna* was produced at Sir John Vanbrugh's new theater in the Haymarket. In spite of this, her extravagance very nearly brought her into debtor's prison in 1707, and she began writing in earnest to keep away the bailiffs.

Her birth, combined with her extroverted nature, gave her opportunities to view upper-class society from a fairly close range, and she took full advantage of the position to write *Secret memoirs and manners of several persons of quality of both sexes, from the New Atlantis, an island in the Mediterranean* (1707). It was immediately popular, and everyone from the highest to the lowest read it avidly, trying to guess the identities of the characters so sharply etched with her acid ridicule. Shortly after, she began *The Female Tatler*, a satiric political journal that landed her in prison for a brief time. When discharged, she assisted Jonathan Swift in writing Tory pamphlets, succeeding him as the editor of *The Examiner*.

The death of Queen Anne in 1714 was the end of the Tory regime. Manley's political views were anathema to the Whigs, and now, vulnerable to the attacks of enemies, she needed a new mode of expression. She found it in *The Adventures of Rivella* (1714). Written to forestall a suspected attack by Charles Gildon, it was a highly romanticized biography cast in novel form, structured after the events of her own life and interlaced with spicy gossip. In it she drew a picture of herself as a young woman "who had the Misfortune to be Born with an indifferent Beauty," but who "was the Wittiest Girl in the World," with "a bewitching Air of Sincerity and Manners," along with "sparkling Wit and easy Gaiety."

She was growing older now, her health was declining, and she was afflicted with dropsy. As early as 1712, Swift, who had come to a grudging admiration of her, remarked, "I am heartily sorry for her; she has very generous principles for one of her sort, and a great deal of good sense and invention; she is about forty, very homely, and very fat" (28 January 1711/2). In 1720, the year she wrote *The Power of Love* in seven novels, she found another protector in John Barber, a successful printer. Reputedly, he treated her with great cruelty, but she stayed with him for the rest of her life and died at his house on 11 July 1724. She is buried at St. Benet's, Paul's Wharf, London.

Delariviere Manley was ridiculed during her lifetime, and even Swift disliked her style, "as if she had about two thousand epithets and fine words packed up in a bag, and that she pulled them out by handfuls, and strewed them on her paper, where about once in five hundred times they happen to be right" (22 August 1710). Nevertheless, her "novels," while lacking Augustan elegance, have a vigorous power and present an acerbic commentary on contemporary attitudes. Her sense of drama may violate eighteenth-century decorum: the story included in this anthology is not only modern in concept but in its energetic style. Manley's objective awareness of Violenta's psychological motivation reveals a hostility to the condition of women that is surprising for a time when they are popularly supposed to have accepted meekly whatever fate brought them. As a relatively uneducated woman competing with university-polished wits, she wrote with desperation, managing to support herself in an antagonistic society. Her achievement in the development of early narrative prose is worthy of serious critical appraisal.

BIBLIOGRAPHY

Works

Almyna; or, The Arabian Vow. London: William Turner, 1707.
The Adventures of Rivella. London: no publisher, 1714. Sometimes listed as *Memoirs of the Life of Mrs. Manley.*
Bath Intrigues. London: J. Roberts, 1725.
Court Intrigues in a Collection of Original Letters from the Island of the New Atlantis. London: John Morphew, 1711.
Letters Written by Mrs. Manley. London: R. Bentley, 1696.
The Lost Lover; or, The Jealous Husband. London: R. Bentley, 1696.
Lucius, the first Christian King of Britain. London: J. Barber, 1717.
A modest enquiry into the Reasons of the Joy expressed by a Certain Sett of People upon the Spreading of the Report of Her Majesty's Death. London: J. Morphew, 1714.

The Power of Love: In Seven Novels. London: John Barber, 1720.
The Royal Mischief. London: R. Bentley, 1696.
The Secret History of Queen Zarah, and the Zarazians. [London: n.p.], 1705.
Secret Memoirs and Manners of several Persons of Quality . . . from the New Atlantis. London: J. Morphew, 1709.
Memoirs of Europe. 2 vols. London: John Morphew, 1710.
A True Relation of the several Facts and Circumstances Of the intended Riot and Tumult on Queen Elizabeth's Birthday. London: J. Morphew, 1711.
Kostle, Patricia, ed. *The Novels of Mary Delariviere Manley.* Gainesville, Florida: Scholars' Facsimiles and Reprints, 1971.

The Wife's Resentment

DELARIVIERE MANLEY

[*from* The Power of Love, *1720*]

When the Duke of Calabria, Son to Frederick King of Arragon, was Vice-Roy of the Kingdom of Valentia, he kept his Court in the City of Valentia, which was then the chief and only Rampart of that Part of Spain, esteemed as the Seat of Justice, Faith and Humanity. Among its other Ornaments, the Beauty of their Women was deservedly thought the greatest; to which was joyned the Reputation of Understanding, and such a keenness of Wit, that it grew into a Proverb, *When a Fellow was dull and thought a Block-head, that he must go to Valentia.* In the time of this Vice-Roy, lived Seignior Roderigo, Knight of Valentia, descended of the ancient, illustrious and rich Family of the Ventimiglia. This noble Lord was devoted to his Pleasures, and besides a handsom Person, had an Address and Behaviour that was pleasing to every Body. He did not love his Studies; and there being no War at that time to employ an active Mind, for want of better Business, according to the Custom of Spain, he walked up and down the City, wasting his Youth in Trifles, Musick, Masquerades, courting of Ladies, a Form of Devotion which was very common, and fit for such Pilgrims, designing only to conquer, not to be conquered; for as yet all Women were equally indifferent to him, he had no more Esteem or Tenderness for one than another; his Business was meer Gallantry, he knew not what it was to love; provided he could but triumph, he valued not the Conquest. The whole City rang of his Inconstancy, and yet he was so handsome, so rich, and of such eminent Quality, that he still found a favourable Reception amongst the Ladies; each one imagining that her Charms were sufficient to make a Convert of him. His Youth, good Meen, gay Temper and Generosity, introduced him everywhere. Some aspired to gain him for a Husband, the already married for a Gallant, and they succeeded the best. Thus he never thought of the Injury he did others, but led a Life of Pleasure, unthinking and without Principles. His Conversation did not lie in the Road of such Persons who either could or cared to teach him. One must love People a good deal whom one takes Pains to convince or instruct. Thus Roderigo daily made the Tour of the City of Valentia, to the Ruin of many an easy Damsel; but that was none of his Concern, for amongst all the Vertues, he was yet wholly unacquainted with that of Remorse.

Seignior Roderigo was ranging the City one Holy-day, That being the time the Ladies shew themselves at their Doors or Windows, when he beheld a Face that was entirely new to him; neither had he, 'till then, seen any thing so handsom in Valentia. This young Maid suddenly cast her Eyes upon the Count; his Garb was very rich and distinguishing. She met his Looks in such a manner, that he thought a Pistol had been discharged at his Heart; he felt as hot and fatal a Fire, and which he had never been sensible of before. This fair Creature had the greatest Lustre, the finest Water, as we may call it, in her Eyes, that was ever seen; her Air was modest; her height, inclining rather to tall; her taper Waist and exact Simmetry well deserved Consideration; She was in a Habit rather neat than fine, but there was a *Je ne scay quoy* that might very well arrest the Curiosity of those that passed along: Tho', her Eyes excepted, there was none of her other Features so glorious, unless her Complexion, which was varnished by Nature with a Gloss shining like polish'd Marble, and whiter than Imagination, an uncommon Charm in Spain, and would, even in England, be looked upon as a very extraordinary Beauty.

Roderigo, disarmed by the Flashes of her Eyes, staid some time to gaze on her that had wounded him to so dangerous a degree. The Maid, perceiving how intent the Count was in beholding her, with a modest Blush, retired into the House. He pass'd and repass'd before the Door several times in hopes of seeing her again, perceiving that she purposely avoided him; and by that means lost the Diversion of gazing on the Holy-day Folks, he absconded behind a Corner of the Street. After some time That ravishing Beauty, having no longer seen the Person that had by his Admiration caused her to withdraw, returned to the Door to entertain her self innocently with looking on the Passengers, which on Sundays and Holy-days is almost the only Liberty allowed to the Spanish Women, and those too of an inferior degree. Roderigo having watch'd her every Motion, returned to the Attack. Finding her again at the Door, by which he again encountered the full Lustre of her lovely Eyes, he made a Stop before her, and bow'd thrice with that Submission and Languishment, as was able, in a less intelligent Country than Spain, where Persons from their Infancy speak with their Eyes and Fingers, to convince her, that That Cavalier was surpriz'd by her Beauty. The young Creature, named Violenta, who had more Wit than all the Women of Valentia besides, considering her Years, beheld with Delight the extraordinary Mien and Application of that Stranger; from a fatal Presentiment she felt something within that made her wish to engage him. She answer'd his Salute in so graceful and peculiar a manner, that he was more and more confirm'd her Slave. What was now become of that Indifferency, with which he had triumphed over the Foible of the greatest Ladies in Valentia? He, whose Business had hitherto been to give Love, rather than take it, was in a moment reduc'd to be one of the Order of Lovers; to wish, sigh, and desire, in return of those Sighs and Desires he had caus'd in others.

Violenta having done enough to engage Roderigo, and shew her native Civility, once more withdrew. The Night coming on, there was no Prospect of her returning again that Evening, which caus'd the Count also to depart; but not without taking full Notice of the House, the Street, and the Ways that led to it. When he came home, he sent for one of his Agents in Amour, who knew all the Persons in Valentia, to enquire of him, by Description, of the Name and Quality of such a young Maiden, living in such a Street, situated at the Corner of such a Square, near such a Church, opposite to such a Palace; by which particular Account the Engine quickly found how it went with the Count; and that he must have made more than ordinary Observation, to be able to give him such a true Chart of the Coast. This Person shook his Head, and told the Don, 'He knew the Maiden very well, but fear'd she was not for his Lordship's Turn, for that no Virgin in Valentia had so fair and honest a Report; that her Wit was more commended than her Beauty, for she could both read and write, in which she took extreme Delight.' An Accomplishment which, in those

Days, few Ladies aim'd at, since they believed all inferior Knowledge, as
well as the Sciences, was reserv'd for the other Sex. This Procurator
added, 'That her Name was Violenta, a poor Orphan, kept by her
Mother, who had been some Years a Widow, her Husband no better than
a Goldsmith; that he had also left two Sons, who follow'd his Trade in
great Obscurity; that Violenta had the Reputation of being extream
modest; and tho' she was sought by many, yet was she defam'd for none.'

Count Roderigo was so far gone in Love, and his first Love too, that if
his Intelligencer had brought him the most disadvantageous Character in
the World, it could not have cur'd him. This favourable Report did
certainly inflame his Passion the more; he resolv'd to send her a Declara-
tion of Love, which he did in Form, but the Maid return'd him no
Answer. However, as the Letter had been receiv'd and read by her, he did
not absolutely despair. The next Day he sent her another, more passionate than the former, letting her know the Name and Quality of her Lover,
together with the Present of a Pair of Bracelets, valu'd at Five hundred
gold Ducats. She return'd the Bracelets, and with it this Letter:

To Count Roderigo di Ventigmelia, Knight of Valentia
My Lord,

Your Person is handsom, you present very well, you Letter is witty
and extraordinary well writ; but what are all these Accomplishments to a
Virgin that values nothing but Vertue? That which Courage is to your
Sex, Chastity is to ours; and indeed more, since the greatest Cowardice is
retrieveable by one Act of Valour, but Modesty is rarely or never to be
regain'd. Neither my Eyes nor my Vanity shall be entertain'd at so vast a
Hazard: Yet, that your Lordship may not think me altogether stupid, I do
confess, that your Addresses have flatter'd both; my Sight, by your
Person, my Pride by the Offer you make me of your Heart. But, illustrious
Cavalier, 'tis neither by the one nor the other that a Maid must conduct
her self, who knows the true Estimation of Vertue, and who would die in
the Defence of it. This from the humblest of your Servants,

Violenta

Roderigo saw the gaining the Heart of this fair Person must be a Work
of Time; but as he was prodigiously in earnest, and was so far from
having any other Affair of the Heart, that this was the first time his was
ever touch'd; he pursu'd her with such Assiduity, that she durst no longer
appear either at her Windows or Door; From thence he trac'd her to
Church, where, to be near her, he committed a Thousand Indecencies.
She chang'd every Day the Place and Hour of her Devotions; yet he every

where found her out, and still it was all the same Story, he must perish without her Pity, and nothing but her Love could preserve him. When he had urg'd this to her in a Letter, with the Tautology and true Impertinence of a real Lover (for when they are really affected, those Creatures fly certainly beyond all common Sense) she return'd him this Answer:

To Count Roderigo di Ventigmilia, Knight of Valentia
My Lord,

You very eloquently tell me you shall die if I continue unkind; but I very plainly tell your Lordship, that I must perish if I prove otherwise: Since I know it will be impossible for me to live after the loss of my Honour. I conjur you to leave me in Repose, lest I be oblig'd to shut my self up in a Cloister to avoid your Pursuit. I may justly complain of that Moment when first I saw you, for if it has made your Lordship unhappy, I am not less miserable; if it has taught you what it is to Love, it has not left me insensible; but I neither must nor will indulge either my Heart or Eyes! I have a Mind truly intrepid in the Cause of Vertue, which neither the Preservation of your precious Life, nor that of my Mother, Brothers, or of my own, can ever induce me to forsake: I would see the whole World in a Conflagration, and myself in the middle of it, before I could be brought to do any thing contrary to the Rules of Modesty. Wonder not, that a Maid so meanly born and educated, should have such exalted Ideas of Vertue: I have study'd her well, all her Ways are lovely, Peace and Honour attend her Votaries in this Life, a fragrant Report when they are dead, and a Crown of Glory hereafter! How despicable are those Advantages which you offer me in exchange? Consider of it and farewell.

This Pursuit lasted six Months. At length, all that the Count could obtain, was a Confession that she lov'd him within the Degrees of Honour, but not a Jot beyond it. Yet as much in love as Roderigo was, during all that Time, he never once thought of marrying her: The Disparity between them was so great he had no Notion of Wedlock. In Spain they have other Maxims than in England; here a Person enobles his Wife, there, 'tis a Reproach for a Man of Quality and to his Descendants, if he chance to mingle with the People. However, Violenta, as her Heart was too haughty to speak first of that Union, so she resolv'd he should never have Favours of her without it. One Day, he had so well order'd his Intelligence, that he had Notice of a Visit she had design'd to make to a Maiden of the same Rank. Roderigo, by the Force of Presents, got leave of that Person to conceal himself in her Closet 'till Violenta came; soon after he surpriz'd her with his Sight. Being left together, he said to her, with some Coldness, 'Considering, Madam, the small Regard you have given either to my Letters or Presents, I may compare your Subtilty to that of a Serpent, who is said to close his Ears, for fear of hearing the Voice of the Charmer; which has made me forbear writing or sending to you; and I wish I had the same Power to desist from seeing you, since my mortal Enemy could not more cruelly torment me. If Love were not involuntary, I could never submit to such Usage. What Objection have you to the truest Lover, to the most passionate Adorer that ever was? Were it possible for you to look into my Heart and know what I suffer, you could not persist in your Tyranny! I die for you! but you will not pity me!'

'My Lord,' answer'd the discreet Maid, 'I do more than pity you, I simpathize with you in every thing; I feel all your Pains, I sigh as much, I lament as much, and perhaps I love as much, but with this difference, which makes me more wretched than you can be, that you have your Redress in your own Power, which, alas! is not in mine; you may be cur'd whenever you please, but it is quite otherwise with me! I am ready to be commanded by you, but you will not obey me; you think me too far beneath your Quality, whilst I wish you were not so much above mine. But since there is no descending for you, nor any Exaltation for me, leave me in repose from this moment, and content your self with having the first Place in my Heart, which no other shall ever possess; but for the Favours your Lordship expects, they are not mine to bestow. I have devoted my self to Vertue, all my Thoughts, Words and Actions, are dedicated to that Goddess! I cannot take the smallest Part from her without an immortal Offence; therefore do not be displeas'd if I never see you more!' Here she brake from his Arms that would have retain'd her; and coming home, she made a Vow to make no Visit, and to go no where, unless to Church, 'till she were releas'd of Roderigo's Persecutions for fear of meeting him, as she had done that Day.

The Count very well understood what Violenta aim'd at in her Discourse; but he could not bring himself, notwithstanding the Extremity of his Love, to debase his Blood so far as to mingle by Marriage with one of her low Degree. Observing the small Progress that he had made in fifteen Months Courtship, and that there was no Probability of advancing farther, he resolv'd to do all that was in his Power towards curing himself of so infamous and uneasy a Passion. He began to return to his old Practice of Gallantry; gave Balls, Treats, Musick and Entertainments to the Ladies, who had very much lamented that alteration in his Temper, tho' they knew not the Cause; they did all that was possible to keep up his good Humour and engage him amongst them, but in vain; he carry'd within his Breast that which poison'd all his Delights. A Lover who is not yet in the Rank of the Happy, reserves his Heart wholly, without any Division, for the cruel Person to whom Destiny has made a Present of it. All the Favours upon Earth, from the greatest Beauties could have no Taste for Roderigo. Satisfy'd of this cruel Circumstance, he found it impossible for him to live any longer in a State of Rebellion against his Sovereign Mistress; wherefore he return'd to her with all the Contrition imaginable, full of Penitence, for having dar'd to attempt so impossible a thing, as breaking the Chains she had impos'd upon him. That cruel Tyrant of the Heart, brought him once again to sue, with all the humble Arts of Flattery, for the least contemptible Favour; but that prudent Maid told him, There was none such in Love, the smallest being of equal Value to the greatest: As in a Ladder of Stairs, the lowest Step is as necessary as the highest, tho' the last lands you at the Place where you desire to be, and where you could never have arriv'd but by those Degrees. Which Rule well observ'd, a Virgin ought never to permit her Lover the smallest Favour, not the Freedom of her Hand or Lip, for the Lover's Touch, nay, his very Breath, sullies and takes from Modesty its native Lustre, and destroys the Merit of being wholly innocent.

Poor Roderigo was not like to make any great Progress amidst these exalted Notions; at length he bethought him of another Expedient: He resolv'd to change his Battery, and knowing they were pretty poor, he made Donna Camilla a Visit, Violenta's Mother, in which he confess'd his Passion for her Daughter, and complain'd of the ineffectual eighteen Months Courtship he had paid her. The old Gentlewoman, to whom this was no great News, tho' she affected to be ignorant, answer'd that Violenta was highly honour'd by those Marks of his Respect, but that she was a Maid unskill'd in Courts, rude of Fashion, and not us'd to the Conversation of Persons of his Quality. In the End, he presented her with a thousand Ducats, towards her Occasions, and told her, he would assign her Daughter a handsom Dowry, if she could find any honest Man for her Husband, where she might be well dispos'd of, provided she would have some small Consideration of his Suffering, and afford him a little Ease from that intollerable Rack he endur'd! Donna Camilla, whose Sense of Honour was not inferior to Violenta's, let him know, with all Regard to his Quality, that she was offended at his Proposal; that her House was no place to purchase Vertue in, whose Price was inestimable! The Count carry'd back his Ducats, which he could not get the good Gentlewoman to touch; and fell to debate farther with himself, what was next to be done. He could not abandon the Maid, That he had in vain essay'd; he could not by Diversion drive her out of his Thoughts, that was a fruitless Project; he could not corrupt her, nor could he live without her! He found he had but lost time in all his Enterprizes, and prolong'd his own Torment, which daily augmented: Therefore he at last resolv'd to marry her. And tho' she was neither of such Birth or Fortune as his Quality deserv'd, yet her Vertue and Accomplishments, her Beauty and Discretion deserv'd greater Advancement! This Resolution once taken, he found he was much more at his Ease, and even wondred at himself for not coming to the Point before. Now he felt Mercy and Compassion for the Maid intrude into his Breast, where only Self-love had dwelt before. He own'd, that it was pity so fair an Example of Vertue should be cast away; that 'twas hard, a Life so faultless should be attended with Infamy and Ruin! and was therefore pleas'd looking upon himself as a Person destin'd to reward her Chastity, raise her abject Fortune, and draw forth of Obscurity, a bright Example, which the Virgins of the Age might imitate. Thus compos'd, he fell into a Slumber, where he thought Violenta appear'd to his Sight, with her Hair flowing! her Dress infinitely disorder'd! her Face sully'd with Tears! and her Breast bruis'd with the Blows she had given her self! She struck a Dagger to his Heart, and told him, That was the Reward of Treachery and Inconstancy! The Blow pain'd him so much, by Imagination, that he awakened in a horrible Fright, and giving a great Shriek, he found himself upon the Floor, where he had fall'n in his Agony: But having no Opinion at all of Dreams, he apply'd this to his restless Mind, which always carry'd Violenta's Idea. The next Morning, he determin'd to make her a Visit in form, and propose to her the Accomplishment, as he hop'd of both their Desires. He found her at her Needle, for she was always employ'd, according to an Inscription at the Villa Benediti:

Donna virtuosa, non sa star otiosa.
A vertuous Lady can never be idle.

Violenta flush'd red as Scarlet at seeing Don Roderigo enter, then turn'd pale as Ashes, with such an universal Trembling, that she was unable to support herself without sitting. 'Is this Aversion, fair Creature, or some kinder Passion?' said the Count, 'that you are always thus disordered when I see you?'

'Say rather,' answered the Maid, 'it is my better Angel that warns, and makes me shudder and shrink from you as my evil Genius, as the Persecutor of Vertue, as a Tyrant, that would force from me the only Treasure I possess! As one that must either leave me in repose, or take away my Life. Something whispers my Soul that your Passion will be fatal to me; I would fly you as an Abhorrence to Nature, as a Destroyer of Chastity.'

'As the Man you love, fair Violenta,' interrupted the Count with a Smile, 'your Disorder and Invectives are more glorious for me than the Favours of others; you could not be thus affected for a Person indifferent to you; since in so soft a Creature, Hatred could never have so great an Ascendant, or work you to such a Degree; it must be the kinder Passion from which I expect advantagious Effects.'

'If that were true, my Lord,' answered the constant Maid, 'as I will not pretend to convince you of the contrary, I would starve and die a Martyr to my Desires, rather than gratify the smallest Wish, at the expence of my Virtue! Yes, Count Roderigo, I do love, and have loved you for a long time. I will not presume to say that I retained my Indifferency a Minute after I first beheld you; and from that inauspicious Moment I felt other Sentiments for your Lordship, than I had ever done for any of your Sex. When you had abandoned me, to renew the vitious Pursuits of your former Gallantries, you left a Fury in my Breast to supply your Place, or a worse Tormentor; a Fiend, that amidst all your Sufferings you have been a Stranger to. Jealousy, that cruel Tyrant! allowed me not a moment's Repose; Thus, since I have dared to demonstrate, that my Pains rather exceed yours, and that I am not at all in Debt to you for what you have endured; let us make a drawn Battel of it, Both call off our Forces at once, and no more trouble one another with our mutual Follies; let us try to cure ourselves as well as we can. As to my Part, I have determined to do something but what, I cannot yet resolve; neither ought I to tell your Lordship, lest it should look like threatning, or a Desire of being retained; but certainly, my Lord, this is the last time I will ever allow my self the Liberty to converse with you. I beseech your Lordship not to be displeased, when you are refused the Door; you shall suddenly hear that I have either taken the Veil, or have abandoned my Mother, Brothers, Country, and wander'd far from Valentia to seek my Bread in a foreign Clime, distant from your Lordships cruel Persecution.' She ended this Discourse with a Shower of Tears. Roderigo, unable to stand the Torment, fell at her Feet, and confess'd to her the Design that brought him thither, and the Resolution that he had taken to marry her.

As we have often beheld the Sun break out with sudden Glory, in the midst of Clouds and Rain, so darted from Violenta's Eyes, Rays of Light which restored to every Charm its native Grace; Then the Count discovered how truly lovely she was. She gave loose to Joy, and spoke such transporting Things, full of Gratitude and Passion, that Roderigo confess'd the greatest Pleasure was in pleasing, and how far the transport of vertuous Love exceeded the sophisticated Pleasures of the Vicious. Violenta telling him that though he exceeded her in all other Advantages, yet she could not be outdone in Love; that she would be Emulous to please him, and hoped by her Obedience to make him one Day confess he would not exchange her for the noblest Lady. At which he thanked her for her good Intentions, and pluck'd a Diamond-Ring from his Finger of great Value, which he gave her as a Pledge of their Marriage; and then, and not 'till then, had he ever presumed to kiss her; so sacred and inviolable had that chast Maid preserved herself, amidst the Flames of Love that had surrounded her from the Count's Passion without, and from her own Fires within. A Pattern worthy the Imitation of young Virgins, who, though perhaps vertuous in what they call the Main, yet prostitute their Modesty too far in suffering the Touches of the Hand, the Neck, and the Kisses of Men. They may assure themselves, that they lose a great degree of their Value, by such unwarrantable Freedoms; as the Lustre wears off the richest Silks by handling, and the inimitable Blue from the Plum, which when once lost, can never be restored. A great many Things more might be said against so vile a Custom; besides the Habit and Air of Lightness that it gives a Virgin, by which she is with much greater Facility brought to suffer further Liberties, and very often loses her Character for those she has granted, under the Notion that they are but innocent Freedoms, inwardly satisfied with being, what they call essentially vertuous.

After the Count and Violenta had interchanged their mutual Vows, Roderigo beg'd her to conceal his Happiness for some time, because of the inequality of their Condition, 'till he had taken Care to inform his Relations and Friends gradually of their Marriage; however, he permitted her to discover it to her Mother, and her Brothers, bidding her invite them to be therein the Evening, and he would bring a Priest out of the Country, who knew them not, with the first Valet of his Chamber whom he could trust, that her Maid who was brought up by Donna Camilla from her Youth might also be admitted, to make up the Number of Witnesses Six, which was sufficient to attest a Marriage, if ever it should come by any unforeseen chance to be disputed. You need not ask whether Violenta were very diligent and careful to put all Things in order; she dress'd up the Nuptial Chamber and Bed, with all the Decency the Time and her Circumstances allowed her. At length, the long look'd-for Hour approached, the Bridegroom came, and brought along with him a Priest, and his Gentleman. They were married in the Presence of Violenta's Mother and her two Brothers, Ianthe the Maid, and the Count's Valet, without either Pomp or Preparation, of any Expence requisite for the Nuptials of a Man of his Extraction and great Possessions.

Roderigo vouchsafed to sit down to Eat with the Mother and Brothers of his new Bride, whom he acknowledged and caressed by those Appellations. They had prepared a very handsome Supper, and were as happy in their own Opinions, as Persons suddenly raised from Poverty to Wealth, or from a mean Degree to an exalted State of Honour. They conducted the new-married Pair to the Bride-Chamber, and then took their leave, recommending them to the Mercy of Love, and Favour of the Night: Which I shall no otherways describe, Than by a Person long labouring under the extremity of Thirst, who at length arrives to a Place, where he can quench that violent Distress, where he quaffs at liberty in flowing Bowls, and unstinted Draughts of Pleasure.

In the Morning, Violenta, without assuming the Airs of a Countess, begg'd her Lord, since he was now in possession of what he had so long and vehemently desired, that he would prescribe Rules to her Conduct, assuring him, that she should be as diligent to observe his Orders, and as ambitious to please him in whatever he desired, as the poorest Slave, who was most faithful, most dutiful, and affectionate to his Master. Roderigo said, 'Sweet, charming Wife, I beg you to use none of those affected Airs of Humility to me; I am burthened with them, I beseech you let me hear no more of that; you are now my Wife, and so you must conduct your self; I have no less Value for you, than if you were descended from the noblest Family in Spain. Hereafter you will be convinced of this Truth; but 'till I have taken Order for my Affairs, I require you by the Obedience of which you boast your self, to conceal our Marriage; and pray be not displeased, if I am often from you in the Day-time, but every Night shall be yours. As soon as I go home I will send you two thousand Ducats, not to buy your Wedding-Cloaths, it is not yet time for that. When we publish our Marriage, I will my self take care to provide you what in all Respects shall be fit for my Bride: But Women need Trifles as well as Essentials, and

I would not have my dear Violenta want any Thing within my Power to grant.

˙ Seignior Roderigo departed thus from his Lady's House, who entertained him with such passionate Love and Sweetness, that for a Years time he never thought himself happy but when he was in the Arms of his dear Violenta; omitting not one Night from embracing and sleeping with her; which could not be carried so privately, notwithstanding all the Caution he used, but the Neighbours discovered his Resort to Donna Camilla's House, and were prodigiously scandaliz'd at it. They imagined that Violenta was kept by the Count; some of the well-meaning Part (as to the others they tattled abroad and at home, and were very glad that they had got a Piece of Scandal to entertain the Town with) reproached Donna Camilla and her Sons for tolerating that Abuse: They even reprimanded Violenta, lamenting her Misfortune, whose Reputation had flourished twenty Years in Honour, and been a fair Example to all the Virgins of Valentia, that she should now fall by the Gripes of Poverty, involving her Mother and Brothers in her Sin, a Prey to Shame and Dishonesty; deploring those happy Days in which she was thought not only the fairest but chastest Maid in all that Part of Spain; but now degenerating from her accustomed Vertue, her Behaviour was esteemed light, abandoned to lascivious Love, one who was contented, by the Price of Sin, to support herself and her Mother in Ease and Plenty. Poor Violenta, whose Conscience acquitted her from these slanderous Reproaches, took less Care of their spreading, because she knew her own Innocence; yet could not help being very uneasy at the Difference she found in the Behaviour of her Friends, the open Scoffs and Fleers of some of the boldest of them; and which was more sensible, the cold Civilities and freezing Looks of the better manner'd and most Charitable: Yet assuring herself that she had an Antidote in reserve against all their Poyson, and that when her Marriage was publish'd, it would serve as an excellent Moral against the Malice of such who were forward to condemn only upon Appearances and false Opinion: But when those Reproaches were most cutting, Though her Husband were *the Lord of her Idolatry*, and whom she would much rather die than displease, she could not forbear telling him her Sufferings, and begg'd him very earnestly to take her home to his House, since it was as much to the Injury of His Reputation, that such infamous Reports should be spread of a Woman, whom they would one Day find had the Honour to be his Wife.

Count Roderigo knew very well how to delay Violenta's Request, having found the great Secret of her Passion, that she dreaded nothing so much as his Displeasure; he could cunningly give her Cause to apprehend the Effects of it, since she had rather have offended the whole World together, than in the smallest Matter displease her Lord. Her humble manner of Education had not yet given Place to a desire of Rank or Greatness; she knew no Ambition but that of retaining Roderigo by her Charms and Goodness; and whereas she had been slow to receive the Fire of Love, so much the fiercer and surer it burnt in her Heart, which had not the least Taste of Delight, but in the enjoyment of Roderigo, an eager Thirst of Virtue being the only Thing that could ever rival her Lord in her Esteem. The Count's Observation soon rendered him Master of this Secret; and seeing there was nothing new for his Desires; that he had even surfeited with the delicious Banquet; that it was all but a Repetition of the same Delight; he first began to wonder how he could so eagerly pursue a common Pleasure; and then enquired of his Memory, which was but too faithful, whether he had ever done so or no? And when by melancholy Proof he was too well convinced of the State of his Affairs, he grew from Cool to more Cold, from Frost to Ice, from Ice to Aversion, and a Hatred of his own Folly for so unworthily matching himself with the Lees of the People. In this Fluctuation of his Thoughts, he often forbore her Bed; which, when he approached, it was rather like a Sinner than a Husband, to gratify the Call of Nature, and in which a common Strumpet might as easily have assisted, than from the first Motive of generous Love and Husbandly Tenderness and Affection.

Violenta's Duty and Sense of Gratitude, had so far enslaved her Will to his Pleasure, that she durst not even complain of his Neglect; and when, after several Days absence, she presumed to send a Letter to him to his Palace, to enquire of his Health, and the Cause why she did not see him, he acted the Tyrant to the Life; and at their next meeting gave her to understand, that if she any more presumed to enquire into his Recesses, he would never forgive, nor own her for his Wife. This was as a Dagger to pierce the Heart of the miserable Violenta. Her Complaints rather wearied, than softened him; he look'd upon her as a despicable Creature, whose Reputation being lost, not one of any Figure would appear in her Defence, or imagine her to be married to him, especially if they should see him married to another. There are many Vices which are not believed, because of their Magnitude, Such Roderigo thought would be his double Marriage, forgetting that he had ever heard of Religion; forgetting the

Call of his own Conscience; for certainly there must be a Remorse for betraying so vertuous a Creature. He took up his old Haunts of Gallantry and Luxury, which terminated in a violent Passion for a fair young Creature called Aurelia, the sole Daughter and Heiress of Don Ramires, one of the chiefest Knights, and most honourable Families in all Valentia.

Count Roderigo was considerable for Estate and Quality, without any allay but a Flirt of youthful Pleasure which was imagined would pass away with his Youth, if not sooner, should he once marry and settle; and who was incomparably the most advantageous Match in the City. Don Ramires quickly came to an Accommodation with his Proposals, offering a very large Dowry with his Daughter in Present, and the rest of his Estate in Reversion, after the Death of himself and his Wife. Count Roderigo settl'd all Things to their Satisfaction, and the Marriage was solemnized to the Pleasure of all Persons concerned, and the good Will of those, who having no immediate Interest in those Nuptials, were delighted with any publick Occasion of Mirth and Joy.

The Marriage done and ended, the Bride and Bridegroom continued at Don Ramires's House, where they lived in all the Pleasures of the Happy; such as new married Persons of high Rank and prosperous Fortunes enjoy, without any Remorse for what Violenta might suffer, when she should hear the News of his Inconstancy. He look'd upon her as an idle Girl, a Creature of low Degree, the Favourite of an Hour, a little Mistress with whom he had condescended to squander away some superfluous Hours of Youth but unworthy his Regard when in cooler Thoughts, or to expect the Continuance of his noble Name and Family from. In short, he forgot that ever she had been of any Consequence to his Happiness! He forgot he had married her; and hearing so many People talk of her as a Mistress he kept, he imagined it was so, and no more; never fearing, from her excessive Love and humble Behaviour, that he needed to apprehend any Thing from her Resentment; more especially from those Mechanicks her Brothers, who indeed had no Part of their Sister's Spirit or Understanding; and who dreamt of no other Notions of Honour but what they expected to find in their Customers. Donna Camilla, her Mother, he looked upon as a Piece of old Household-Stuff quite out of Date; poor and independent as she was, he knew it would be very difficult for her, at that time of day, to find any one to espouse her Interests against his in Valentia.

Thus Seignior Roderigo, fearless of the Reproaches of Violenta, publickly espoused Donna Aurelia in the Face of the Sun, in the great

Church of Valentia; immediately the Report of such a fine Wedding was
carried to all Parts of the City. Violenta's Brothers were first informed of
it, they ran to their Mother to let her know the Disaster; yet without that
honourable Resentment which is always found in the Well-born. According to the Custom of Spain, they should immediately have made the
Villain's Blood attone for the Injury he had done their Sister, and to which
they were Witnesses; but their Souls were of a Piece with their Profession,
they did not dream of Honour and Revenge, provided they could Sell
their Plate; nay they were so sordid as to comply with the Orders
Roderigo had given his Intendant to go to such Persons, meaning Violenta's Brothers, and bespeak from them all the necessary Vessels, and
Utensils, whether of Silver, Silver-gilt, or Gold Plate, that was necessary
for his Degree, to furnish his House and Table upon his Nuptials with a
Person of Aurelia's Quality and Fortune.

Donna Camilla indeed resented the Abuse, not only as a Person of a
high Heart, but as one who wept drops of Blood for the Dishonour of her
Daughter; she sent for her Sons, reproaching them with the Pitifulness of
their Spirit, to take Employment from the Man they should much sooner
destroy. They protested to her that they knew not when the Plate was
bespoke, but that it was for the Publication of their Sister's Marriage; and
afterwards could not go back from their Word, the Gentleman only
designing to oblige them for their Sister's sake. Camilla seeing them to be
such Stocks, and Stones sent them away and was contented to mourn
alone. This wretched Dame lived in great Anguish, because she durst not
make her Complaint to any, and was ignorant of the Name of the Priest
who had married her Daughter; neither would she impart her Sorrow to
Violenta, imagining she would too soon hear of the fatal Disaster that
was befallen her.

And indeed, this vertuous Lady, only tantalized with the Hopes of
Greatness, with the mock Scene or airy Idea of Grandeur, which like a
golden Bough hung far out of her reach, was the last in knowing what
was now stale News in Valentia. A Person of her Penetration, however
blinded she was by Love and Roderigo's continual Pretences, thought
there must be something extraordinary to make him absent himself so
frequently as he did. At first she used to write him the kindest Letters to
enquire of his Health; but the Airs he took to himself, as we have before
related, soon gave her enough of presuming to enquire after him. He had
carry'd all things with a high Hand; her humble Spirit durst not dispute
the Pleasure of so great a Man. He might lie away as long as he thought

fit, the Joy she had when he came again made her forget the Pain she had suffered by his Absence. She always receiv'd him with Smiles, and never with cold Looks or Reproaches. Having lately used her to stay away several Nights together, she did not wonder at it now; but she was not left long in Ignorance. Her next Neighbours, meerly to insult her, asked what she would do for a Sweet-heart now her Lord was marry'd? how came it that she was not at the Wedding? especially since it was so publick, and the finest that was ever seen in Valentia? Donna Aúrelia was a charming Bride!

Violenta having very well examined these Reports, for she at first regarded them as Stories design'd by malicious Persons only to insult her, when she grew confirm'd in the Truth, her Heart was immediately open to Wrath, Indignation, Madness and Revenge. All the Furies of Hell enterd like a Torrent into her Breast, and in a moment expell'd her native Softness; Love hid his Face and would be seen no more; he took wing with all his Train and Dependants, and flew for ever away from that hospitable Heart where he had been so fondled and tenderly entertain'd. The Sense of Honour lost, of her Vertue demolish'd, her Chastity over-thrown, her ruin'd Reputation swell'd her to an Extremity of Resent-ment; she tore her Ornaments, her Dress, her Hair; she stamp'd, and travers'd her Apartment like a raging Bacchanal; like Medea, furious in her Revenge; like the Fiends with fatal Torches in their Hands, to set the World on Fire: She was more than all these, she was herself, That is to say, most miserable and most outragious. She could not weep, that Distress was too soft for her obdurate Grief; she could not in a long time speak, even the Relief of Words were deny'd her; she could only beat her Breast, groan, and puff her Breath out, as if Flames had come at every Blast. At length, Nature, unable longer to maintain so cruel a War against itself, suffered this wretched Creature to sink down on the Carpet for an interval of time, that she might recover Strength enough to renew the Conflict; essaying several times to rise, she sunk again, and with Groans pour'd forth this Torrent of Complaints.

'Alas! alas! what inexpressible Torture does my poor Heart endure without the least Prospect of Relief? No one Creature on the whole Earth can give me Ease! what Ruin do I suffer for no Offence of mine? ah Fortune! Fortune! Thou art so totally my Enemy, that thou hast not left me so much as the Prospect of a Friend to revenge my Injury. Oh Blood! Blood! a Villain's Blood! too small an Expiation for ruin'd Chastity! Oh cruel Husband! Do not my Groans Echo in thy Ears? Dost thou not hear my Voice crying aloud for Vengeance? Canst thou regard any other Object but thy first, thy lawful Wife? dishonour'd by thy Cruelty, and suffering a thousand furious Martyrdoms for thy Adulterous Crime! Ah Ungrateful! Is this, thou monstrous Wretch, all the Return that thy base Heart can make for excessive Love, unshaken Fidelity and obedient Humility? Since this is all that thou canst bestow upon me, I will pay my self, be sure I will. Thy Blood shall be the Atonement, that I may die with Joy, insensible of Pain.'

Donna Camilla and her Sons, with Ianthe, hearing her Voice so outragious, talking loudly to herself like a Tempest or a Whirlwind, went up to her Chamber, where they found her so deform'd with Rage and Fury, that she was almost out of their Knowledge; they fear'd she would run Mad, and said whatever they could to reduce her from those violent Pangs; but their Endeavours increas'd rather than allayed the Storm. Reason was utterly lost upon her, she was insensible to all things but Revenge, which she insatiably thirsted after; Then, as she said, she should be at rest. Finding they could make no Impression upon her obdurate Mind, Donna Camilla and her Sons withdrew, leaving the old Maid Ianthe, whom Violenta lov'd more than any other, to take care she did herself no hurt. This poor Creature had from her Childhood, when she was first made a Slave, been bred up by Donna Camilla. The Slave had brought up Violenta, and so tenderly lov'd her, that she would have done anything for her Relief. After she had flatter'd and humour'd her Rage a-while, she told her Lady, That if she would suspend her Fury for a little time, she would go herself and seek out Count Roderigo and hear what he had to say, and she doubted not but to order the Matter so well, that she would bring him along with her, where, if he did not give her the Satisfaction she desired, she might do with him as she pleased, and wreak upon him her just Revenge.

'No! no, Ianthe!' said Violenta, 'those are light and small Offences that we can be reasoned out of the Sense of; what Roderigo had committed against me, Reason it self supports me in my Desire of Vengeance! And should my Heart give way to any other Thoughts, I would with my own Hands divide it from this wretched Body! nothing but his Life alone can satisfy me! God caused me to be born his Instrument of Wrath to punish the Injury done my Honour; what Reputation remains to me but that of an abominable Whore? Shall he live who has bestow'd so vile a Quality upon me? Shall he breathe in Pleasure whilst I hourly pine away in Infamy? That base Seducer, that Wretch without Principles or Honour, who used laughingly to say, as I then thought in jest, but the Villain was too much in earnest, That Maids of my base Birth had no Pretensions to Honour, what had we to do with such fantastick Notions? Vertue and Chastity were pretty Names indeed for Boors to play with! As if Courage were only appropriated to Men of Quality, or Modesty to Noble Women. Yes, Roderigo, thou shalt know that my Sentiments were worthy the most exalted Birth! Thou shalt feel it by the Ardour of thy Wife's Resentment! by that height of Vengeance with which I will appease and vindicate my Honour! and if thou, Ianthe, dost deny to assist me, I will do the Work alone. Thou art a Stranger born, and leadest the Life of a poor wretched Slave, condemn'd all thy Days to Drudgery; I have here two thousand Ducats, and several Jewels which that false Traytor gave me; they are destin'd by Heaven to reward that Person who shall assist me in my Revenge. I will now put that Treasure in thy Hands, I will give all to thee, if thou wilt help me to sacrifice Roderigo to my injur'd Honour. Too well I know there is but little Redress for so mean a Person as I am, to expect by Law, against two the most potent Families in Valentia. When the Question is, which shall be prov'd the Wife, and which the Whore! most certain, Don Ramirez's Daughter must have the honourable and I the infamous Appellation. Justice waits upon the Great, Interest holds the Scale, and Riches turns the Ballance. Besides, I know not even the Priest who marry'd us, perhaps he was not a Priest, and my Ruin was originally design'd; or if he be, Roderigo will take care to keep him far from my Knowledge. Wherefore, my dear Ianthe, if from my Youth thou didst ever love me, or that thou wert ever sensible of the Love I had for thee, shew me the Effects now, when thy Help is most necessary. If thou dost deny me, I will execute my Purpose alone; the first time I ever behold him, with these enrag'd, accurs'd Eyes, I will strike him dead, or murder him with these two trembling Hands, without any other Assistance.'

Ianthe hearing what Violenta said, and well knowing her undaunted Resolution and Heroick Spirit; after she had revolv'd and debated several things in her Mind, resolv'd at length to devote her self wholly to her Mistress's infernal Commands, potently mov'd at her being defam'd and dishonour'd by the presence of Marriage; and partly prompted by Covetousness and the desire of Liberty, by which she should gain so great a Reward; with which she meant to fly away to her own Land, and seek her Kindred and Parents, if they were yet alive or to be found. When she was thoroughly resolv'd, she embraced Violenta and said to her, 'Madam, here I plight my Faith and Hand to you. Your poor Ianthe shall follow your Commands in Life and Death! I have as great an Appetite to revenge your Dishonour as your self can desire; but that we may be sure to effect it, you must disguise your Rage, and put on you the Habit of Dissimulation. You shall write the Count a Letter, as you well can do, to invite him hither; as if you only griev'd at the Loss of his Heart, and did not dispute Aurelia's Title to his Bed. Leave the rest to my Management. When we have him here fast, we will send him to Rest in a more assur'd Place, where he shall everlastingly continue, to curse the time whenever he betrayed poor Virgins by the sacred Pretence of Marriage.'

Violenta hearkned to her as the Oracle that was to resolve her Destiny, and feed her bloody and cruel Vengeance. That fair Prospect, which stood before her, of Revenge, caused her, like Ebbing Seas after the Workings of a mighty Storm, to sink appeas'd, tho' within she stood collected and ready to execute what the most cruel Hatred can inspire. She gave her self so much Respite as to write him a Letter; which fully express'd all she suffered, and what more she was like to suffer; and then she rose into distant Threatenings of what a Lover forsaken might attempt; yet soon sunk again into the more humble Necessities of a Lover, who could not live without the Sight of the Person beloved; which as a Reward of all her Sufferings she beseeched him to grant her; in an indirect Manner, seeming to give up her Title to Marriage, if she could hope to preserve what she much more valued, that which once she had to his Heart.

'Take there, Ianthe,' says the afflicted Violenta, 'thy Passport to Roderigo; if thou can'st play thy Part as well as I have done mine, we may then assure our selves, that my Vengeance will be compleat. I may rest satisfied my date of Life shall not be long, since Life is more insupportable to me than a Thousand Deaths, and yet I cannot die unrevenged.'

Ianthe having the Letter, rose early the next Morning, and rendered herself with great Diligence at the House of Don Ramirez, where she waited obsequiously 'till she could speak with some Person belonging to the Count, which was not long after. Ianthe seeing that Gentleman who was present at Roderigo's first Marriage, he blush'd, and would have avoided her, pretending to go about Affairs for his Master. The old Slave, who was not to learn her Business at that time of day, bore up briskly to him, whispering him in the Ear, ask'd how the Count did! and if she might be admitted to the Honour of speaking with him alone, for her Business required Privacy? Don Roderigo being soon advertised of this by his Servant, came forth, and pointed her towards the Street, where he presently followed her; to whom smilingly, she said, having made him a feigned Courtesy, and presented him the Letter, 'I am a poor Slave, my Lord, and can neither write nor read, yet I dare lay my Life, there is humble Suit made to you in that Paper for the Sight of your sweet Person; and to say the Truth, my poor Mistress has been very much injured by you (not in the Point of Marriage, for I never thought Madam Violenta, a beggarly Tradesman's Daughter, was a fit Wife for the great Count Roderigo) but that you will not vouchsafe to visit her, that she may not be miserable all at once; you take no Care to cure her Dishonour, by providing her a Husband in some other Place, which would prevent the Infamy she will meet with from being a forsaken Mistress. She loves you in a lost manner, she is ready to die, and no longer than last Night, said to me, Dear Ianthe, I cannot possibly live without the Sight of him; though I must not pretend, after his Marriage with the Lady Aurelia, to have him for my Husband; I wish he would still regard me as his Friend, and provide for me that I fall not into Poverty, and would set apart but one Day in the Week, or rather Night, for fear of the Neighbours, that I might be happy in his Love: And sure my Lord,' added the old Impertinent, 'you cannot do a better Thing, if it were but for the Pleasure of telling your self that you have the fairest Wife, and most beautiful Mistress of any Nobleman in all Spain.'

Roderigo list'ning with profound Attention to what the Slave said, as gathering from thence the Pacifick Sentiments of her Mistress, took and opened the Letter, which when he had read, he fell to consider what it contained. The warring Passions rose in his Breast, as Heat and Cold meet and jostle together, pent up in the same Cloud; Love and Hatred, Compassion and Disdain, combated in his Heart, and vex'd him with Contrarieties: Then pausing upon an Answer, he thought it necessary to flatter her Despair, 'till he could see her to take his Measures, that she might not by her offensive Fondness give any disturbance to his new Enjoyments. 'My dear Friend, Ianthe,' said the dissembling Count, recommend me to the good Grace and Favour of thy charming Mistress; for this time I will write her no Answer, but to Morrow Night at Eight a Clock I will be sure to wait upon her, and give her an Account of this ugly Matter, and of what has happened since I had the Happiness of seeing her last; when I shall have told her the Necessity that urged me to what I have done, she will certainly pity rather than condemn me.'

Ianthe posted away with her good News to Violenta. They quickly set themselves to prepare all Things for Roderigo's Reception; whilst he told his new Bride he was call'd away by certain Affairs to his Villa, where he was obliged to remain a whole Night, but he would return the Morning after. Then ordering his Gentleman of the Chamber, who was the Confidant of all his Amours, he bad him command two Horses to be got ready, upon which they rode forth out of the City 'till it was duskish; then the Count fetch'd a Compass, and entered Valentia by another Gate; he ordered his Servant to put up the Horses in a strange Inn, and stay for him there 'till he returned from Violenta in the Morning. When he came to the House, he found Ianthe, with great Devotion, waiting his Arrival, with a settled Purpose to use him according to his Deserts. She conveyed him to the Chamber of her expecting Mistress; their meeting was such as might be well supposed between two Persons that had once desperately loved, and now as perfectly hated one another, but who yet with cold and dissembled Flattery now sought to deceive each other. Violenta represented to him her Despair when she heard of his Marriage, the Sorrow that she endured, having neither been able to eat nor sleep since the fatal Tidings of her Dishonour, and the loss of his Heart. Roderigo took her in his Arms, and protested to her he was still the same, but that the late Count his Father had left so vast a Debt upon the Estate, which was all mortgaged to Don Ramirez, that if it had not been in Consideration of this Marriage with his Daughter he would have seized upon his whole Inheritance, and then he must have been a Beggar, and unable to assist her whom he valued more than his Life; for though he were wedded to Aurelia, he loved none but Violenta, assuring her, that after a little time he meant to poyson his new Wife, and return to end his Days with her in Love and Happiness. He concluded this Discourse, which was only fram'd to appease her, with Protestations of his Love, and ten Thousand Vows of Constancy, which are easily sworn by those who intend only to deceive. Doubtless, if this miserable Woman had credited his Words and Oaths, and from thence have whispered Peace to her deluded Heart, he would have changed his Mind, and not thought himself ty'd to the Performance of his Vows, since he could so manifestly break that which he had made in the Sight of Heaven, when in the sacred Bands of Wedlock he had plighted his Faith indissolubly to hers.

The Count was very well satisfied that he found Violenta so well appeased; he thought he need not give himself much Trouble about that little Maid, a Creature of no Consequence, whom he might use as he pleased. She was careful not to mention any thing of her own Marriage, nor a Word of Revenge for her Dishonour. Her Complaints were wholly directed to her Fears of losing his Heart, which he could sooth without much Difficulty, since it was her Business to believe. After Supper, the Count not having taken much Rest for several Nights before, grew sleepy, and ordered his Bed to be made ready. We need not enquire whether Violenta and Ianthe obeyed his Commands with Diligence, in which consisted the good or evil Fortune of their Enterprize.

Violenta, to shew her self most affectionate, went first to Bed; as soon as they were laid, Ianthe drew the Curtains, and took away the Count's Sword, his Dagger she laid upon a Stool by her Mistress' Bedside; for though they had provided a large Knife for that Purpose, the Slave thought the Justice would be more remarkable if he fell by his own Weapon, but to make sure Work, she placed them both together; then taking away the Candles, she feigned to go out of the Chamber, but returned again, and lock'd the Door on the Inside, as if she had been gone away, and rested her self against the Door, waiting for the cruel Minute when her Mistress whould want her Assistance. The destin'd Count thinking himself alone in the Chamber with Violenta, began to embrace and kiss her; but she begg'd him to desist, 'till she awoke again, for having never rested since the News of his fatal Marriage, her Heart being now somewhat more at Ease, she found her self so sleepy she was not able to speak; and then she turned her self away from him to her Repose. Roderigo, who had had as little Sleep as possible, and perhaps stood more in need of Rest, very gladly comply'd with her Request, his designed Caresses were more in the prospect of pleasing her than himself; soon after he fell into a profound Sleep, which they were very well assured of, by the manner of taking his Breath. Violenta reached the Dagger, and feeling softly for the Place where she could most commodiously strike, raising her self in the Bed, and transported with Wrath, struck the Poniard into his Throat: Ianthe hearing him groan, leap'd briskly upon the Bed, and getting upon him with her Knees and Hands kept him down; He struggled, but Violenta, like another Medea, mad with Rage and Fury, redoubled her Stroke, and thrust the Point of the Dagger with such Force into his Throat, that she pierced it through on the other Side. The Wretched Count, thinking to make some Resistance against his cruel Destiny, received another Wound; being held down by Ianthe he could not use Hand nor Foot. Through the excessive Violence of his Pain, he had not Power to cry out or speak a Word. After he had received ten or twelve mortal Wounds, his Soul flew away from his martyr'd Body, in all probability to a dreadful Audit, since he was taken away in the Fulness of his Sins, without a Moment's Space for Repentance.

Violenta having finished this cruel Enterprize, commanded Ianthe to light a Candle. She approached with it near the Count's Face, and saw that he was without Life. 'Ah Traitor!' said she, 'thou oughtest to have been Years a dying, if I had enjoy'd Power sufficient thou certainly should'st; yet some Comfort it is to me to think, though I could not devote thy Body to suffer such Torments as thou did'st deserve, thy immortal Soul is fled without a Moment's warning to deprecate the Divine Vengeance!' Not able to quench her Hate, nor satisfy the furious Rage that burnt in her Breast, with the Point of the Dagger she tore the Eyes out of his Head, speaking to them with a hideous Voice, as if they were still alive, 'Ah trayterous Eyes, the Interpreters of a villainous Mind! come out of your shameful Seat for ever! the Spring of your false Tears is now exhausted and dried up, so that ye shall weep no more! no more deceive chast Virgins with your feign'd and falling Showers.' Her Rage rather increased than abated, she seized upon his Tongue, which, with her bloody Hands she pluck'd from the Root; and beholding it with an unrelenting Eye, said, as she was tearing it out, 'Oh perjured and abominable Tongue! false and cruel as thou wert, how many Lies didst thou tell, before with the Chain-short of this cursed Member, thou could'st make a Breach to overthrow my Honour? Of which being robb'd by thy Traiterous Means, I must devote my self to Death, to which I have now shewn Thee the Way.' Then, insatiable of Cruelty (like a Wolf fleshed upon his Prey, irritated the more by the Taste of Blood) with the Knife she violently ripp'd up his Stomach; then launching her daring Hands upon his Heart tore it from the Seat, and gash'd it with a thousand Wounds, cry'd, 'Ah vile Heart, more obdurate and harder than Adamant! upon this cruel Anvil was forged the Chains that bound up my unlucky Destiny! What did I mean by wreaking my Vengeance upon the Eyes and Tongue of this insatiable Monster? The Heart! This infamous Heart of thine was the original of all my Misery! It was by this the Traitor was taught to flatter and betray! Oh that I could erst have discovered thy base Imaginations, as now I do thy material Substance, I might then have preserved my self from thy abominable Treason and Infidelity! yet shall not the Hand only have Reason to complain that it made no part of my Revenge, when it had so great a one in my Ruin! Take, cursed Instrument,' said she, dismembering his Right-Hand from his Body, 'Take thy Reward for the Faith thou didst dare to plight to me in the Face of Heaven! Extream Provocations must have extream Punishment, my only Grief is that thou art dead and cannot feel the Torture.' When she had mangled the Body all over, with an infinite number of Gashes, she cry'd out, 'Oh infected Carrion, once the Organ and Instrument of a most vile and traiterous Mind, now thou are repaid as thy Merits did deserve.'

Ianthe, with Horror and exceeding Terror, had immovably beheld her Butchery, but when she said to her, 'Ianthe, now I am at ease! my poor labouring Heart is light'ned of its Burthen! Come Death when thou wilt, thou shalt find me able to bear thy strongest Assaults! I have daily proved thy Torture, lest I should not bring my full Revenge to the desired Period! Help me then to drag this unworthy Wretch out of my Father's House, where I was first dishonoured, where the Odour of my chast Name was exchanged for Poysonous Infamy! Since my Vertue is traduced abroad, my Revenge shall be as manifest, and this Carcass be exposed as publickly as was my Reputation.'

Violenta and Ianthe dragg'd the Body to a Chamber Window, and threw it out upon the Pavement in the Street, with the several Parts that she had cut off. That done, she said to Ianthe, 'Take this Casket, there is in it all my Jewels and two thousand Ducats in Gold, which I promised thee; ship thy self at the next Port thou shalt come at, get thee over into Africa to save thy Life as speedily as thou canst, and never return into these Parts again, nor to any other where thou art known.' Which Ianthe purposed to have done though Violenta had not counsell'd her to it. The poor Slave, being just ready to depart, embrac'd and kiss'd her Mistress; she took her leave with a doleful Farewell, and went in Search of better Fortune; and from that Time was never heard no more. All the Pursuit that was made after her prov'd ineffectual, since no Creature in Valentia could ever recover the least Knowledge of the Way she had taken.

Soon as Day appeared, the first that pass'd through the Street discover'd the dead Body; one told another of the strange Spectacle that lay there to be seen, but no Man knew who it was, because the Eyes were pick'd out, and the other Members mutilated and deformed. By that time it came to be Eight a-Clock, there was such a multitude of People assembled that it was almost impossible to come near the Body. The generality thought Thieves had murder'd and stript the Dead Person, because he was found in his Shirt; Others were of a contrary Opinion. Violenta, who was at her Window, hearing them give their several Judgments, came down and with a firm Voice said to the Multitude,

'Gentlemen, you dispute about a Thing which if I were examined by the lawful Magistrate, I could give undoubted Evidence of. This Murder cannot be discovered by any other than by me, without great Difficulty.' Which Words her Neighbour easily believed, thinking this was a Person slain by some of her Lovers that were jealous of her; for poor Violenta had lost her former good Reputation since the Report that Count Roderigo kept her.

These Words were carried to the Magistrates, who, with their Officers of Justice, soon came to the Place, where they found Violenta more undaunted than any of the Spectators! They enquir'd of her immediately, 'What Account she could give of that Murder?' Without Fear of Hesitation she reily answered, 'My Lords, He that you see here dead is Count Roderigo di Ventimiglia: And because many Persons are concern'd in his Death; as, his Father in Law Don Ramirez, his new Wife Donna Aurelia, and all his own Relations; if your Lordships please, I would, in their Presence, before our most noble Vice-Roy the Duke of Calabria, freely declare what I know of this unhappy Affair.'

The Magistrates, amaz'd to see so great a Man as Roderigo lie there, inhumanly slain and butcher'd, took Violenta into Custody 'till the Vice-Roy's Pleasure was known; who being urged by his own Curiosity, and the Importunity of Don Ramirez, Donna Aurelia his Daughter, and the Kindred of the Deceas'd; commanded, after Dinner, she should be brought to her Examination in the great Hall of the Palace; where the Vice-Roy, the Judges, the Evidence and all Persons being met, there was so great a Crowd, that it was not possible to thrust in another Creature. Violenta, as if she were conscious of well doing, and glow'd with the Pride of some worthy Action performed, in the Presence of them all, with a loud and clear Voice, without either Rage or Passion, first recounted the chast Love between Count Roderigo and her self during the space of Eighteen Months, tho' without receiving the Returns he expected: That within a while after, quite vanquish'd with Love, he marry'd her secretly in her own House: That the Nuptials were solemnized by a Priest unknown, in the Presence of her Mother, Brothers, and two Servants, whereof one of them was the Count's Gentleman, and still in his Service: That she had been more than a Year his most obedient Wife, without the least Offence given on her Part. Then she repeated to them his second Marriage with Donna Aurelia, there present. Adding, that as he had depriv'd her of her Reputation of Honour, she had sought Means to deprive him of his Life; which she had effected by the Assistance of her

Maid Ianthe, who, being filled with Remorse, had drowned her self in the Sea. 'Think not, most noble Duke,' added she, 'that I have given you this plain Relation to move your Pity and prolong my Life; I could for ever have escaped your Justice, if I had so intended! my Purpose was to have my Honour as publickly cleared as it was aspersed; for a Terror to all young Virgins, how they receive the Addresses of Persons so greatly above them; and to warn them how they consent to a clandestine Marriage, as I have done, by which I am this Day brought to Ruin. I hold my self unworthy to live, after being stained with Blood; tho' that Blood was shed to wash away my Stain. So far am I from desiring Life that I cannot endure to live. I beg Death of your Justice, lest in saving my Body you condemn my Soul, and force me with my own Hands to commit the most unpardonable Sin, that of Self-Murder!'

The Duke, the Magistrates, and all the Spectators were amazed at the Courage and Magnanimity of the Maid; and that One of so little Rank should have so great a Sense of her Dishonour. The People were so far moved with Pity that they wept with lukewarm Tears, to think so fair and chast a Creature should meet with such great Misfortunes. Detesting the Memory of Count Roderigo, they thought his Death too small an Expiation for a Wretch, who, under the pretence of sacred Marriage, could enjoy her Love, and then traiterously wed himself to another. The Vice-Roy resolving not to give too hasty a Judgment, remitted back Violenta to Prison; and gave Orders for the dead Count to be Interr'd as obscurely as his Crime deserved; taking from Violenta all Weapons by which she might do her self an Injury. They used such Diligence, that the Priest who marry'd them was sought out and found. The Count's Gentleman also deposed what he knew of the Nuptials, and his Lord's design'd Visit to Violenta the Night before the Murder was committed. All Things were so fully proved, that nothing could be more plain, unless they could have had the Confession of the dead Lord himself. Violenta, notwithstanding the Pity of the People, the Intercession of the Ladies, and the Applause her Chastity and Magnanimity deserved, was condemned to be Beheaded; not only for that she had presumed to punish the Count's Offence by her own Hand, without the help of Justice, but for the unexampled Cruelty committed afterwards upon the dead Body.

Thus the fair and vertuous Violenta ended her Life; her Mother and Brothers being acquitted. She dy'd with the same Spirit and Resolution with which she had defended her Chastity; and was Executed in the Presence of the Duke of Calabria, who caused this History to be registered, with other Things worthy Remembrance, that happen'd at Valentia in his Vice-Royalty. Bandwell reports that Ianthe was put to Death with her Mistress, but Paludanus, a noble Spaniard, alive at that Time, who wrote an excellent History in Latin, positively declares that she was never apprehended; which Opinion I have followed, as that which seemed to be the most probable.

SUSANNAH CENTLIVRE

1667(?)–1723

T HE INFORMATION WE HAVE about Susannah Centlivre's early life is
even less certain than what we know about Delariviere Manley.
The most reliable account says that her father was a Mr. Freeman of
Holbeach, Lincolnshire, a Dissenter whose estate was confiscated at the
Restoration and who then retreated to Ireland with his wife. Whether
Susannah was born in Ireland or in England is unclear, but it is probable
that her father died when she was three years old, her mother when
Susannah was twelve. One parent evidently remarried, and all stories of
her early years agree that she left home when she was about fifteen in
order to escape a harsh step-parent.

Though her childhood was unhappy, it seems clear that she had at
least been taught to read and write, and that somehow on her own she
accumulated a haphazard store of knowledge that included a fluency in
French and a certain amount of literary background. It was not a practical education in terms of earning a living, and exactly what she did and
where she went between the time she left home and her first appearance in
London in 1700 is as vague as her earlier history. One popular but
unproved story is that, disguised as "cousin Jack," she spent a year with
Anthony Hammond at Cambridge, where she was not only his mistress
but his fellow-student, learning grammar, logic, rhetoric and ethics along
with him. Another version suggests a one-year marriage with Stephen
Fox's nephew, but neither story has been substantiated.

In any case, she eventually became a strolling player, because, according to William Rufus Chetwood, a wen on her left eyelid "gave her a
masculine air." Her portrait does not agree with this description, but it is
true that as an actress she did specialize in "breeches parts" (male roles).
At some time in the late 1690s, she married Carroll, an army officer, and
she probably retired from the stage for a while, but when he was killed in
a duel some months after their wedding, she returned to her only means
of livelihood once more. The theater was a difficult and uncertain profes-

sion; players were paid only for actual performances, not by the week, and most barely subsisted on their wages.

She began to increase her income by writing. Although she occasionally published letters and poems, most of her literary work consisted of adaptations of plays from earlier authors. *The Perjur'd Husband*, produced at Drury Lane in 1700, was the first of nineteen plays written between then and 1723. For the next few years she continued to act, but in 1706, when she was playing Alexander the Great in a company of strollers at Windsor, she met and married Joseph Centlivre, "yeoman of the mouth" to Queen Anne. His title was a respectable one, indicating that he was one of the principal chefs for the Court, but her enemies used it against her and referred to her contemptuously as "the cook's wife."

Marriage meant not only respectability but security, and she ceased acting, although she continued to write and was soon recognized by the literary and theatrical circles of London. Among her friends she counted Delariviere Manley, Poet Laureate Nicholas Rowe, playwrights George Farquhar and Richard Steele, and a large number of actors and actresses. In her prefaces and plays she was outspoken in her resentment of the common prejudice against female authors, and with reason, for several of her works held the stage for almost two centuries, and a number were translated into French and German; Lessing's *Miss Sara Sampson* shows clear evidence of her influence. Among her most successful and long-lasting plays were *The Basset Table* (1705), *The Busy Body* (1709), *The Wonder* (1714), still popular in 1776 when David Garrick chose it for his farewell appearance, and *A Bold Stroke for a Wife* (1718).

Although, like all women of the time, she was disfranchised, she took an intense interest in politics. A passionate Whig, she was devoted to the Hanovers, and after the accession of George I in 1715 she gave her political views full rein, arousing the antagonism of the Tory satirists Alexander Pope and Jonathan Swift, both of whom attacked her savagely. Their satires are in part responsible for the reputation for immorality assigned to her by later generations, for however irregular her youghful years had been, her life with Joseph Centlivre was both conventional and decorous.

Despite the political bias, her plays were—and still are—excellent theater. Her one original work, written in collaboration with John Mottley, the compiler of *Joe Miller's Joke Book*, was *A Bold Stroke for a Wife*. It provided a virtuoso role for Robert Wilks, leading man at Drury

Lane, and introduced the term "Simon Pure" into the language, the name of the hypocritical Puritan in the play. She stopped writing about 1720, apparently because of a serious illness, and she died 1 December 1723 at her home in Spring Gardens, a prosperous area of eighteenth-century London.

Her plays display a thorough and practical knowledge of the theater; her prefaces, though rarely as caustic as those of her predecessor, Aphra Behn, are often sharp defenses of her position as a playwright. Her dedications are no more fulsome than those of others, and frequently give an insight to the genesis of the work or the circumstances of production. The plays themselves are lively and amusing and present a view of life that still appeals to audiences.

BIBLIOGRAPHY

Collections

The Dramatic Works of the celebrated Mrs. Centlivre. 3 vols. London: John Pearson, 1872.
Works of the celebrated Mrs. Centlivre. 3 vols. London: J. Knapton, 1761.

Works

The Artifice. London: T. Payne, 1723.
The Basset-Table. London: Jonas Browne, S. Chapman, 1706.
The Beau's Duel: or, a Soldier for the Ladies. London: D. Browne, N. Cox, 1702.
A Bickerstaff's Burying; or, Work for the Upholders. London: B. Lintot, 1710.
A Bold Stroke for a Wife. London: W. Meres and F. Clay, 1724 (2d ed.).
The Busie Body. London: B. Lintot, 1732.
Mar-plot; or, the Second Part of The Busie Body. London: Jacob Tonson, 1711.
The Cruel Gift. London: A. Bettesworth, 1717.
The Gamester. London: William Turner, William Davis, 1705.
The Gotham Election. London: S. Keimer, 1715.
Love at a Venture. London: John Chantry, 1706.
The Man's Bewitch'd; or, the Devil to do about her. London: Bernard Lintott, 1710.
The Perjur'd Husband: or, the Adventures of Venice. London: Bennet Banbury, 1700.
The Perplex'd Lovers. London: Owen Lloyd, 1712.
The Platonick Lady. London: n.p., 1707.
The Stolen Heiress, or, the Salamanca Doctor outplotted. London: n.p., 1703.
A Wife Well Manag'd. London: n.p., 1715.
The Wonder: a Woman keeps a Secret. London: A. Bettesworth, 1714.

Related Readings

Bowyer, John Wilson. *The Celebrated Mrs. Centlivre.* Durham, N. C.: Durham
University Press, 1952.

꿎

The Perjur'd Husband

SUSANNAH CENTLIVRE

[*1700*]

TO THE READER

I should not trouble my Reader with a Preface, if Mr *Collier*[1] had
taught Manners to *Masks*, Sense to *Beaux*, and Good Nature to *Criticks*,
as well as Morality to the Stage; the first are sure to envy what they can't
equal, and condemn what they don't understand; the Beaux usually take
a greater liberty with our sex than they would with their own, because
there's no fear of drawing a Duel upon their hands; the latter are a sort of
rude splenatick Men, that seldom commend any thing but that they have
a hand in. These Snarling Sparks were pleas'd to carp at one or two
Expressions, which were spoken in an Aside by one of the Inferiour
Characters in the Drama; and without considering the Reputation of the
persons in whose mouths the language is put, condemn it strait for loose
and obscure: Now (with submission to better Judges) I cannot believe
that a Prayer-Book shou'd be put into the hands of a woman, whose
Innate Vertue won't secure her Reputation; nor is it reasonable to expect
a person, whose Inclinations are always forming projects to the dishonour of her Husband, shou'd deliver her Commands to her Confidant in
the words of a Psalm. I heartily wish that those that find fault with the
liberty of my stile, wou'd be pleas'd to set a Pattern to the Town, by
Retrenching some of their Debaucheries, for Modesty thrives best by
Example. Modest Language from the truly Vertuous is expected, I mean
such as will neither act ill, nor suffer ill to be acted: It is not enough that
Lucy says she's honest, in having denied the Brutal part; who ever thinks

Vertue centers in that, has a wrong notion of it; no, Vertue is a tender Plant, which cannot live in tainted ground; Vertue is what the air of Flattery cannot blast, nor the vile sordid dross of Gain poyson; and she that can withstand these two shocks may be stil'd truly vertuous. I ask my Reader's pardon for my bluntness, but I hope none of my Sex so qualified will condemn me for exposing the Vices of the seeming Religious.

I fear there is but too many hit by the Character of Signora Pizalta; I wish for the sake of the reverse party there were fewer, or they were better known, since the malicious world are so apt to judge of peoples Inclinations by the company they keep; which is sometimes Authentick, but not always an Infallible Rule. I shall say little in Justification of the Play, only desire the Reader to judge me impartially, and not condemn it by the shortness of its Life, since the season of the year ne're promis'd much better success. It went off with general Applause; and 'tis the opinion of some of our best Judges, that it only wanted the Addition of good Actors, and a full Town, to have brought me a sixth night,[2] there having been worse Plays within this twelvemonth approv'd of.

Love's Contrivance; or,
Le Médecin Malgré Lui

SUSANNAH CENTLIVRE

[*1703*]

PREFACE

Writing is a kind of Lottery in this fickle Age, and Dependence on the Stage as the Cast of a Die; the Chance may turn up, and a Man may write to please the Town, but 'tis uncertain, since we see our best Authors sometimes fail. The Criticks cavil most about Decorums, and crie up *Aristotle*'s Rules as the most essential part of the Play: I own they are in the right of it, yet I dare venture a Wager they'll never persuade the Town to be of their Opinion, which relishes nothing so well as Humour lightly tost up with Wit, and drest with Modesty and Air. And I believe Mr. *Rich* will own, he got more by the *Trip to the Jubilee*,[3] with all its Irregularities, than by the most uniform Piece the Stage cou'd boast of e'er since. I do not say this by way of condemning the Unity of Time, Place, and Action; quite contrary, for I think them the greatest Beauties of a Dramatick Poem; but since the other way of writing pleases full as well, and gives the Poet a larger Scope of Fancy, and with less Trouble, Care, and Pains, serves his and the Players End, why shou'd a Man torture, and wrack his Brain for what will be no Advantage to him. This I dare engage, that the Town will ne'er be entertain'd with Plays according to the Method of the Ancients, till they exclude this Innovation of Wit and Humour, which yet I see no likelihood of doing. The following Poem I think has nothing can disoblige the nicest Ear; and tho' I did not observe the Rules of *Drama*, I took peculiar Care to dress my Thoughts in such a modest Stile, that it might not give Offence to any. Some Scenes I confess are partly taken from *Molier*, and I dare be bold to say it has not suffer'd in the Translation: I thought 'em pretty in the French, and cou'd not help believing they might divert in an English Dress. The French have that light Airiness in their Temper, that the least Glimps of Wit sets them a laughing, when 'twou'd not make us so much as smile; so that where I found the Stile too poor, I endeavour'd to give it a Turn; for who e'er borrows from them, must take care to touch the Colours with an English Pencil, and form the Piece according to our Manners. When first I took those Scenes of *Molier*'s, I design'd but three Acts; for that reason I chose such as suited best with Farce, which indeed are all of that sort you'll find in it; for what I added to 'em, I believe my Reader will allow to be a different Stile, at least some very good Judges thought so, and in spight of me divided it into five Acts, believing it might pass amongst the Comedies of these Times. And indeed I have no reason to complain, for I confess it met a Reception beyond my Expectations:[4] I must own my self infinitely oblig'd to the Players, and in a great Measure the Success was owing to them, especially Mr. *Wilks*,[5] who extended his Faculties to such a Pitch, that one may almost say he out-play'd himself; and the Town must confess they never saw three different Characters by one Man acted so well before, and I think my self extremely indebted to him, likewise to Mr. *Johnson*[6] who in his way I think the best Comedian of the Age.

The Platonick Lady

SUSANNAH CENTLIVRE

[1707] [7]

Dedication

"To all the Generous Encouragers of *Female Ingenuity* this Play is Humbly Dedicated."

Gentlemen and Ladies:

My Muse chose to make this Universal Address, hoping, among the numerous Crowd, to find some Souls Great enough to protect her against the Carping Malice of the Vulgar World; who think it a proof of their Sense, to dislike every thing that is writ by Women. I was the more induc'd to this General Application, from the Usage I have met on all sides.

A Play secretly introduc'd to the House, whilst the Author remains unknown, is approv'd by every Body: The Actors cry it up, and are in expectation of a great Run; the Bookseller of a Second Edition, and the Scribler of a Sixth Night: But if by chance the Plot's discover'd, and the Brat found Fatherless, immediately it flags in the Opinion of those that extoll'd it before, and the Bookseller falls in his Price, with this Reason only, *It is a Woman's.* Thus they alter their Judgment, by the Esteem they have for the Author, tho' the Play is still the same. They ne'er reflect, that we have had some Male Productions of this kind, void of Plot and Wit, and full as insipid as ever a Woman's of us all.

I can't forbear inserting a Story which my Bookseller, that printed my *Gamester*, told me, of a Spark that had seen my *Gamester* three or four times, and lik'd it extremely: Having bought one of the Books, ask'd who the Author was; and being told, a Woman, threw down the Book, and put up his Money, saying, he had spent too much after it already, and was sure if the Town had known that, it wou'd never have run ten days. No doubt this was a Wit in his own Eyes. It is such as these that rob us of that which inspires the Poet, Praise. And it is such as these made him that Printed my Comedy call'd, *Love's Contrivance; or, Medicine Malgre lui,* put two Letters of a wrong Name to it, which tho' it was the height of Injustice to me, yet his imposing on the Town turn'd to account with him; and thus passing for a Man's, it has been play'd at least a hundred times.

And why this Wrath against the Womens Works? Perhaps you'll answer, because they meddle with things out of their Sphere; But I say, no; for since the Poet is born, why not a Woman as well as a Man? Not that I wou'd derogate from those great Men who have a Genius, and Learning to improve that Genius: I only object against those ill-natur'd Criticks, who wanting both, think they have a sufficient claim to Sense, by railing at what they don't understand. Some have arm'd themselves with resolution not to like the Play they are paid to see; and if in spite of Spleen they have been pleas'd against their Will, have maliciously reported it was none of mine, but given me by some Gentleman: Nay, even my own Sex, which shou'd assert our Prerogative against such Detractors, are often backward to encourage a Female Pen.

Wou'd these profest Enemies but consider what Examples we have had of Women that excell'd in all Arts; in Musick, Painting, Poetry; also in War; Nay, to our immortal Praise, what Empresses and Queens have fill'd the World? What cannot *England* boast from Women? The mighty *Romans* felt the Power of *Boadicea's* Arm: *Eliza* made *Spain* tremble; but ANNE, the greatest of the Three, has shook the Man that aim'd at Universal Sway. After naming this Miracle, the Glory of our Sex, sure none will spitefully cavil at the following Scenes, purely because a Woman writ 'em. This I dare venture to say in their behalf, there is a Plot and Story in them, I hope will entertain the Reader; which is the utmost Ambition of,

Gentlemen and Ladies
Your most obedient humble Servant,
Susannah Centlivre

ᵉᵍ

A Bickerstaff's Burying

SUSANNAH CENTLIVRE

[1710]

Dedication
"To the Magnificent Company of UPHOLDERS"[8]

Custom has made some Things absolutely necessary, and three Sheets
without a Dedication, or a Preface, by way of Excuse, would be an
unpardonable Indecency: To avoid which, I was considering at whose
Feet to lay these following Scenes. First I thought of offering it to all those
young Wives who had sold themselves for Money, and been interr'd with
Misery, from the first Day of their Marriage; but supposing their chief
Pleasure to consist in Pride, and that they had rather gratifie their Ambition in the Arms of a Fool, or Fourscore, than wed a Man of Sense of
narrower Fortunes, I concluded 'em unworthy of my Notice.

Then the Race of Old Men presented themselves in my Mind, who,
despising Women of their own Years, marry Girls of fifteen, by which
they keep open House for all the young Fellows in Town, in order to
encrease their Families, and make their Tables flourish like the Vine: But
my Aversion to Fools of all Kinds, made me decline them too.

At last, casting my Eyes upon the Title of the Farce, I found it could
justly belong to none but the Magnificent Company of *Upholders*, whom
the judicious Censor of *Great Britain* has so often condescended to
mention; to you then, worthy Sirs, whose solemn Train keeps up the
pompous State of Beauty, beyond the Limits of a Gasp of Breath, and
draws the gazing World to admire, even after Death; to you this Piece I
Dedicate; 'tis but Reason that you should receive some Tribute from us
Living, who so truly mourn us dead. What does not Mankind owe to
you? All Ranks and Conditions are obliged to you; the Aged and the
Young, the Generous and the Miser, the well-descended and the baser
born. The Escutcheons garnish out the Hearse, the Streamers and Wax
Lights, let us into the Name of a Man, which, all his Life had been hid in

Obscurity; and many a Right Honourable would fall unlamented, were it not for your decent Cloaks, and dismal Faces, that look as sorrowfully as the Creditors they leave unpaid. What an immense Sum might be rais'd from your Art to carry on the War, would you, like true *Britons*, exert your Power? The People being fond of Sights, what might not be gather'd at a Funeral, when the Rooms are clad in Sable, the Body dress'd out with all your skilful Care, the Tapers burning in their Silver Sockets, the weeping Virgins fixt like Statues round, and aromatic Gums perfume the Chambers, I think it preferable to the Puppet show, and a Peny a Head for all the Curious, would, I dare be positive, amount to more than the Candle-Wax; and so make Death subservient to the Living.

But this, Gentlemen, I leave to your superior Judgment in Politick Principles; and only beg leave to remind you, that in this crowded Town, there are a Prodigious Number of Mr. *Bickerstaff's* Dead Men,[9] that swarm about Streets; therefore, for the Sakes of the most ingenious Part of Mankind, you ought to take Care to interr them out of the Way, since he that does no Good in his Generation, should not be reckon'd among the Living.

And now to conclude, Gentlemen, I hope you'll pardon this Liberty I have taken, and accept this as a Token of the Respect I bear your noble Society: I honour you tho' I have no Desire of falling into your Hands, but I think we Poets are in no Danger of that, since our real Estate lies in the Brain, and our personal consists in two or three loose Scenes, a few Couplets for the Tag of an Act, and a slight Sketch for a Song, and as I take it, you are not over-fond of Paper Credit, where there is no Probability of Recovering the Debt: So wishing you better Customers, I expect no Return, but am proud of subscribing myself,

GENTLEMEN,

Your most obedient humble Servant

ᵂᵉᔥ

The Perplexed Lovers

SUSANNAH CENTLIVRE

[1712] ¹⁰

PREFACE

I am oblig'd to trouble my Reader with a Preface, that he may not
be carried away with false Notions, to the Prejudice of this Play, which
had the ill Fate to introduce a new Custom, viz. in being acted the first
Day without an Epilogue: It seems the Epilogue design'd wou'd not pass;
therefore the Managers of the Theatre did not think it safe to speak it,
without I cou'd get it licens'd,¹¹ which I cou'd not do that Night, with all
the Interest I could make: So that at last the Play was forc'd to conclude
without an Epilogue. Mr. Norris,¹² who is an excellent Comedian in his
way, was desired to speak six Lines Extempore, to intreat the Audience to
excuse the Defect, and promised them an Epilogue the next Night; but
they apprehending that that was the Epilogue design'd for the Play, were
pleas'd to shew their Resentment. It is plain the want of an Epilogue
caus'd the Hiss, because there had not been any thing like it during the
whole action; but on the contrary a general Clap attended the Conclusion
of the Play. The next Day I had the Honour to have the Epilogue Licens'd
by the Vice-Chamberlain, but by this time there was a Rumour spread
about Town, that it was a notorious whiggish Epilogue; and the Person
who design'd me the Favour of speaking it, had Letters sent her to
forbear, for that there were Parties forming against it, and they advis'd
her not to stand the Shock; here was a second Blow greater than the first:
The sinking of my Play cut me not half so deep as the Notion I had, that
there cou'd be People of this Nation so ungrateful as not to allow a single
Compliment to a Man that has done such Wonders for it. I am not
prompted by any private Sinister End, having never been oblig'd to the
Duke of Marlborough, otherways than as I shar'd in common with my
Country; as I am an English Woman, I think my self oblig'd to acknowledge my Obligation to his Grace for the many Glorious Conquests he has

attain'd, and the many Hazards he has run, to establish us a Nation free
from the Insults of a Foreign Power. I know not what they call Whigs, or
how they distinguish between them and Tories: But if the Desire to see my
Country secur'd from the *Romish* Yoke, and flourish by a Firm Lasting
Honourable Peace, to the Glory of the best of Queens, who deservedly
holds the Ballance of all Europe, be a Whig, then I am one, else not. I have
Printed the Epilogue, that the World may judge whether 'tis such as has
been represented. So much for that. Now I must acquaint my Reader, that
I shall not pretend to vindicate the following Scenes, about which I took
very little Pains, most of the Plot being from a *Spanish* Play, and assuring
my self Success from Mr. *Cyber's*[13] Approbation, whose Opinion was,
that the Business wou'd support the Play; tho' Mr. *Wilks* seem'd to doubt
it, and said, there was a great deal of Business, but not laughing Business;
tho' indeed I cou'd not have dress'd this Plot with much more Humour,
there being four Acts in the Dark, which tho' a *Spanish* Audience may
readily conceive, the Night being their proper time of intreaguing; yet
here, where Liberty makes Noon day as easie, it perplexes the Thought of
an Audience too much; therefore I shall take Care to avoid such Absur-
dities for the future; and if I live I will endeavour to make my Friends
amends in the next.

EPILOGUE

"Design'd to have been spoke the first Night by Mrs. Oldfield"
In these good Times when War is like to cease,[14]
And *Europe* soon expects a gen'ral Peace;
Ye Beaue Half-Wits, and Criticks, all may know
I from *Apollo* come a *Plenipo*;
Who well inclin'd to treat, by me thinks fit
To send Proposals from the State of Wit;
Against such strong Confederates engag'd,
An unsuccessful War he long has wag'd;
And now declares, if you will all submit   ]
To pay the Charges of his Box and Pit,   ]
He will no more Hostilities commit.   ]
In all their Works his Poets shall take Care
Never to represent you, as you are.
But on the Critick, Judgment shall bestow,
Sense on the Witling, Beauty on the Beau.

This for the Men; Next he assures the Fair,
He grieves that ever he with them made War;
Or ever in his Plays attack'd their Fame,
Or any thing disclos'd unfit to name;
Or Characters of faithless Women drew,
And show'd feign'd Beauties, so unlike the true.
But in all future Scenes the Sex shall see
Themselves as charming as they wish to be;
For them he will ordain new Comick Rules,
And never more will make them dote on Fools:
And when he rises to the Tragick Strain,
None but true Heroes shall their Favours gain;
Such as that Stranger who has grac'd our Land,
Of equal Fame for Council, and Command.
A Prince, whose Wisdom, Valour, and Success,
The gazing World with Acclamations bless;
By no great Captain in past Times outdone,
And in the present equal'd but by ONE.
These fair Conditions, will, I hope, compose
All Wars between the Poets and their Foes.
Come Sign the Peace, and let this happy Age
Produce a League in favour of the Stage:
But shou'd this fail, at least our Author prays
A Truce may be concluded for six Days.

NOTES

1. Jeremy Collier's *A Short View of the Immorality and Profaneness of the English Stage*, published in 1698, had attacked the theater in the strongest terms.

2. *The Perjur'd Husband* was produced at Drury Lane in October 1700, with a cast of mediocre and inexperienced actors. Playwrights were paid with the full house receipts of the third and, if the play was successful, the sixth nights.

3. Christopher Rich, manager of Drury Lane, produced George Farquhar's *The Constant Couple; or, A Trip to the Jubilee* in 1699. It was spectacularly successful and was popular through most of the eighteenth century.

4. *Love's Contrivance* opened at Drury Lane 4 June 1703 with an all-star cast. It was a hit and remained in the repertory for several seasons.

5. Robert Wilks (1670–1732), leading man and one of the best actors at Drury Lane.

6. Benjamin Johnson (1665–1742) was outstanding in comedy character roles.

7. *The Platonick Lady* opened at the Queens Theater 25 November 1706; it played four performances.

8. "Upholders" is an eighteenth-century term for funeral directors.

9. Referring to Jonathan Swift's famous hoax of 1708. Under the pen name of Isaac Bickerstaff, Swift pretended to forecast the death of the astrologer, John Partridge. Later, he claimed the prophecy had been fulfilled, and when Partridge insisted he was alive, Swift solemnly quoted an earlier Partridge statement that the stars never lied, adding that Partridge only thought he was living. The joke was a famous one in 1710.

10. *The Perplex'd Lovers* opened at Drury Lane 10 January 1712 and played three performances.

11. It was necessary for every part of a performance to be licensed by the crown, as represented by the Lord Chamberlain, before a public presentation.

12. Henry Norris, a favorite comedian with London audiences, who received the nickname "Jubilee Dicky" after his role in *The Constant Couple*.

13. Colley Cibber (1671–1757), star comedian and one of the three Drury Lane managers at this time.

14. Referring to the War of the Spanish Succession, which had begun in 1701. Peace rumors floated constantly, but the war did not end until the Treaty of Utrecht, 11 April 1713.

ELIZA HAYWOOD

1690(?)–1756

E LIZA HAYWOOD may have been born about 1693, although the christening register of St. Peter's Cornhill records an "Elizabeth, daughter of Robert ffowler and Elizabeth his wife" on 21 January 1689/90, and it is the more probable birth date. The facts of her early years are obscure, but it seems clear that her father was a London shopkeeper and that about 1710 she was married to Valentine Haywood, a clergyman at least fifteen years older than she. The marriage was not happy and eventually they separated, though whether Eliza left Haywood or he abandoned her and their two children is a matter of speculation. She is supposed to have been acting in Dublin at the Smock-Alley Theater in 1715, an unlikely place for a clergyman's wife if she were living with him, but not until 7 January 1720/1 did the following notice appear in *The Post-Boy:*

> Whereas Elizabeth Haywood, Wife of the Reverend Mr. Valentine Haywood, eloped from him her Husband on Saturday the 26th of November last past, and went away without his Knowledge and Consent: This is to give Notice to all Persons in general, That if anyone shall trust her with Money or Goods, or if she shall contract Debts of any kind whatsoever, the said Mr. Haywood will not pay the same.

There was no divorce; that was only for the aristocracy and, if granted at all, required an act of Parliament. Separation gave her personal freedom, but it was also hazardous; without husband, title, or independent income, she had no legal protection, few civil rights, and was an easy target for slander. She did have one advantage not shared by her less fortunate sisters: an energetic and inquiring mind. Unsatisfied with the usual rudiments of female education, she had managed to build a considerable acquaintance with the classics, a fair knowledge of French, and a solid background in the literature of her own tongue. When forced to earn her own living, she turned naturally to literature. One of the few avenues to quick cash was the theater, for the proceeds from the third night's performance of a new play went to the author, and success could provide almost a year's support. Her first opportunity came when John Rich, the manager of Lincolns-Inn-Fields, asked her to revise *The Fair Captive*, an unplayable tragedy by a Captain Hurst. It opened 4 March 1721, but unfortunately was a miserable failure, and the third night brought only about £46, from which forty were deducted for house expenses. It was not an auspicious beginning.

She found another, far more profitable field in writing romantic tales. *Love in Excess; or The Fatal Enquiry*, published late in 1719 or early 1720, was so popular that by 1725 it had gone into the sixth edition. It was followed by a flood of others: *Idalia* (1723), *The Fatal Secret* (1724), *The Mercenary Lover* (1726), *The Fruitless Enquiry* (1726), and *Phili-dore and Placentia* (1727) were the equivalents of modern bestsellers. She wrote with speed and ease—in one year she produced ten romances; within a decade, thirty-eight long works, several plays and a number of translations. Her circle of acquaintances included Sir Richard Steele, Aaron Hill, Richard Savage, and Daniel Defoe as well as more aristocratic patrons whose influence meant prestige and profit.

In 1730 the astonishing output suddenly and mysteriously ceased. She may have found another source of income, she may have travelled, or, no longer driven by financial need, she may simply have rested. It is equally possible, however, that other factors caused the change. As with Behn and Manley, her literary activities were regarded as "unfeminine" by her male contemporaries, and once she became successful she was severely attacked. Swift called her a "stupid, infamous, scribbling woman" (26 October 1731), and when she turned from straight narrative to a scandalous, thinly veiled satire of the court in *Memoirs of a Certain Island, adjacent to Utopia*, published with a key to identities in 1725, she outraged many. The scandal of her separation was publicized, her children were called illegitimate, and, although no infidelity was ever proved and she seems to have led an exemplary life, Pope heaped abuse on her in *The Dunciad* (1728).

Whatever the reason for her sudden silence, she broke it during the forties. Stories poured forth once again, but more interesting to the twentieth century is *The Female Spectator* (1722–46), the first magazine by and for women. Written almost solely by Haywood, it was no idle collection of romantic tales, but dealt with questions of female education, literature, the arts, and philosophy. Nine issues of *The Parrot*, more concerned with political gossip and satire, followed in 1746. The success she had enjoyed in her early years did not recur with these publications, and although she continued to write and publish at a rapid rate, she received little attention in the last decade of her life. She died in obscurity 25 February 1756, with two new novels ready for the press.

Her work follows the line of other narrative writers who predated Richardson. Her stories, however, differ from most romances; if she frequently uses the same love themes, she nonetheless is a moralist like Defoe, and his influence is especially clear in her later tales with their strong didactic note. Her strength is in her narrative techniques: vivid if undeveloped characters, scenes of romantic confrontation, and a rapid sequence of events. At her best she is highly entertaining, but the serious tone underlying even the lightest romance gives depth to her work. Her informal essays and commentaries are thoughtful, and in this excerpt from *The Female Spectator* she takes up one of her favorite themes, the education of women. Her arguments are cogent and pertinent; if they occasionally appear startling in their relevance to the twentieth century, it is perhaps because they are still part of a continuing debate, and her points remain tellingly sharp.

BIBLIOGRAPHY

Works

La Belle Assemblee; or, The Adventures of Six Days. 2 vols. London: D. Browne et al., 1724. Also published as *Poisson de Gomez,* tr. from French.
Clementina; or, The History of an Italian Lady. London: F. & J. Noble, 1768.
The Disguised Prince; or, the beautiful Parisian. 2 pts. London: T. Corbett et al., 1728.
Epistles for the Ladies. 2 vols. London: T. Gardner, 1729.
The Female Spectator. 4 vols. London: T. Gardner, 1746.
The Fortunate Foundlings. London: T. Gardner, 1744.
Frederick, Duke of Brunswick-Lunenburgh. London: W. Mears, 1729.
The Fruitless Enquiry. London: T. Lowndes, 1767.
The History of Jemmy and Jenny Jessamy. 3 vols. London: T. Gardner, 1753.
The History of Miss Betsey Thoughtless. London: T. Gardner, 1751.
The Husband. London: T. Gardner, 1756.
The Life of Madam de Villesache. London: W. Feales, 1727.
Love letters on all occasions. London: J. Brindley et al., 1730.
Mary, Queen of Scotland, tr. from French. London: D. Browne et al., 1725.
Memoirs of a certain Island adjacent to the Kingdom of Utopia. 2 vols. London: no publisher, 1725.

The Mercenary Lover, or the Unfortunate Heiresses. London: N. Dobb, 1726.
A Present for Women addicted to Drinking. London: W. Owen, 1750.
Reflections on the Various Effects of Love. London: N. Dobb, 1726.
Secret Histories, novels, and poems. 2 vols. London: D. Browne et al., 1724.
The Secret History of the . . . Court of Caramania. London: no publisher, 1727.
The Tea Table. London: J. Roberts, 1725.
The Unfortunate Princess. London: James Hodges, 1741.
The Virtuous Villager; or, The Virgin's Victory. 2 vols. London: F. Cogan, 1742.
The Wife. London: T. Gardner, 1756.
Works of Mrs. Eliza Haywood. 4 vols. London: D. Browne, 1724.

Related Readings

Whicher, George F. *The Life and Romances of Mrs. Eliza Haywood.* New York:
Columbia University Studies in English and Comparative Literature, Vol. 11,
1915.

Selections from

The Female Spectator

ELIZA HAYWOOD

[1746]

"To the Female Spectator"

Ladies,

Permit me to thank you for the kind and generous Task you have undertaken in endeavouring to improve the Minds and Manners of our unthinking Sex: —It is the noblest Act of Charity you could exercise in an Age like ours, where the Sense of Good and Evil is almost extinguish'd, and People desire to appear more vicious than they really are, that so they may be less unfashionable: This Humour, which is too prevalent in the Female Sex, is the true Occasion of the many Evils and Dangers to which they are daily exposed: —No wonder the Men of Sense disregard us! and the Dissolute triumph over that Virtue they ought to protect!

' Yet, I think it would be cruel to charge the Ladies with all the Errors they commit; it is most commonly the Fault of a wrong Education, which makes them frequently do amiss, while they think they not only act innocently but uprightly; —it is therefore only the Men, and the Men of Understanding too, who, in effect, merit the Blame of this, and are answerable for all the Misconduct we are guilty of: —Why do they call us *silly Women*, and not endeavour to make us otherwise? —God and Nature has endued them with Means, and Custom has established them in the Power of rendering our Minds such as they ought to be; —how highly ungenerous is it then to give us a wrong turn, and then despise us for it!

The Mahometans, indeed, enslave their Women, but then they teach them to believe their Inferiority will extend to Eternity; but our Case is even worse than this, for while we live in a free Country, and are assured from our excellent Christian Principles that we are capable of those refined Pleasures which last to Immortality, our Minds, our better Parts, are wholly left uncultivated, and, like a rich Soil neglected, bring forth nothing but noxious Weeds.

There is, undoubtedly, no Sexes in Souls, and we are as able to receive and practise the Impressions, not only of Virtue and Religion, but also of those Sciences which the Men engross to themselves, as they can be: —Surely our Bodies were not form'd by the great Creator out of the finest Mould, that our Souls might be neglected like the coarsest of the Clay.

O! would too imperious, and too tenacious Man, be so just to the World as to be more careful of the Education of those Females to whom they are Parents or Guardians! —Would they convince them in their Infancy that Dress and Shew are not the Essentials of a fine Lady, and that true Beauty is seated in the Mind; how soon should we see our Sex retrieve the many Virtues which false Taste has bury'd in Oblivion! —Strange Infatuation! to refuse us what would so much contribute to their own Felicity! —Would not themselves reap the Benefit of our Amendment? Should we not be more obedient Daughters, more faithful Wives, more tender Mothers, more sincere Friends, and more valuable in every other Station of Life?

But, I find, I have let my Pen run a much greater Length than I at first intended: —If I have said any thing worthy your Notice, or what you think the Truth of the Case, I hope you will mention this Subject in some of your future Essays; or, if you find I have any way err'd in my Judgment, to set me right will be the greatest Favour you can confer on,

Ladies,

Your constant Reader

And humble Servant,

Hampton-Court   CLEORA

Jan. 12, 1744–5

After thanking this Lady for the Favour of her obliging Letter, we think it our Duty to congratulate her on being one of those happy Few who have been blest with that Sort of Education which she so pathetically laments the Want of in the greater Part of our Sex.

Those Men are certainly guilty of a great deal of Injustice who think, that all the Learning becoming in a Woman is confined to the Management of her Family; that is, to give Orders concerning the Table, take care of her Children in their Infancy, and observe that her Servants do not neglect their Business: —All this no doubt is very necessary, but would it not be better if she performs those Duties more through Principle than Custom? and will she be less punctual in her Observance of them, after she becomes a Wife, for being perfectly convinced, before she is so, of the Reasonableness of them, and why they are expected from her?

Many Women have not been inspired with the least Notion of even those Requisites in a Wife, and when they become so, continue the same loitering, lolloping, idle Creatures they were before; and then the Men are ready enough to condemn those who had the Care of their Education.

Terrible is it, indeed for the Husband, especially if he be a Tradesman, or Gentleman of small Estate, who marries with a Woman of this Stamp, whatever Fortune she brings will immediately run out, and 'tis well if all his own does not follow: —Even Persons of the highest Rank in Life will suffer greatly both in their Circumstances and Peace of Mind, when she, who ought to be the Mistress of the Family, lives in it like a Stranger, and perhaps knows no more of what those about her do than an Alien.

But supposing her an excellent Oeconomist, in every Respect what the World calls a notable Woman, methinks the Husband would be yet infinitely happier were she endued with other good Qualities as well as a perfect Understanding in Household Affairs:—The Governess of a Family, or what is commonly call'd Houskeeper, provided she be honest and careful, might discharge this Trust as well as a Wife; but there is, doubtless, somewhat more to be expected by a Man from that Woman whom the Ceremony of Marriage has made Part of himself:—She is, or ought to be, if qualified for it, the Repository of his dearest Secrets, the Moderator of his fiercer Passions, the Softner of his most anxious Cares, and the constantly chearful and entertaining Companion of his more unbended Moments.

To be all this she must be endued with a consummate Prudence, a perfect Eveness of Temper, an unshaken Fortitude, a gentle affable Behaviour, and a sprightly Wit—The Foundation of these Virtues must be indeed in Nature, but Nature may be perverted by ill Customs, or, if not so, still want many Embellishments from Education; without which, however valuable in itself, it would appear rude and barbarous to others, and lose more than half the Effect it ought to have.

The younger Dryden's Translation of that admirable Satire of Juvenal has these Words:

Children, like tender Oziers, take the Bow,
And as they first are fashion'd always grow:
For what we learn in Youth, to that alone,
In Age we are by second Nature prone.[1]

How much therefore does it behove those who have the Care of Youth, to mould their tender Minds to that Shape which will best become those Stations in Life they may be expected to fill.

Our Sex, from their very Infancy, are encourag'd to dress and fondle their Babies; a Custom not improper, because it gives an early Idea of that Care and Tenderness we ought to shew those real Babes to whom we may happen to be Mothers: But I am apt to think, that without this Prepossession, Nature would inform us what was owing from us to those whom we have given Being: —The very Look and innocent Crys of those little Images of ourselves would be more prevailing than any Rules could be: —This the meerest Savages who live without Precept, and are utterly ignorant of all moral Virtues, may inform us; —nay, for Conviction in this Point, we may descend yet lower, and only observe the tender Care which the Beasts of the Field and the Fowls of the Air take of their young ones.

To be good Mothers, therefore, tho' a Duty incumbent on all who are so, requires fewer Lessons than to be good Wives: —We all groan under the Curse entail'd upon us for the Transgression of Eve.

"Thy Desire shall be to thy Husband, and he shall rule over thee."
(Genesis 3:16)

But we are not taught enough how to lighten this Burthen, and render ourselves such as would make him asham'd to exert that Authority, he thinks he has a Right to, over us.

Were that Time which is taken up in instructing us in Accomplishments, which, however taking at first Sight, conduce little to our essential Happiness, employ'd in studying the Rules of Wisdom, in well informing us what we are, and what we ought to be, it would doubtless inspire those, to whom we should happen to be united, with a Reverence which would not permit them to treat us with that Lightness and Contempt, which, tho' some of us may justly enough incur, often drives not only such, but the most innocent of us, to Extravagancies that render ourselves and those concern'd with us equally miserable.

Why then, as Cleora says, do the Men, who are and will be the sole Arbitrators in this Case, refuse us all Opportunities of enlarging our Minds, and improving those Talents we have received from God and Nature; and which, if put in our Power to exert in a proper Manner, would make no less their own Happiness than our Glory?

They cry, of what use can Learning be to us, when Custom, and the Modesty of our Sex, forbids us to speak in public Places? —'Tis true that it would not befit us to go into the Pulpit, nor harangue at the Bar; but this is a weak and trifling Argument against our being qualify'd for either, since all Men who are so were never intended for the Service of the Church, nor put on the long Robe; and by the same Rule therefore the Sons as well as Daughters of good Families should be bred up in Ignorance.

Knowledge is a light Burthen, and, I believe, no one was ever the worse for being skilled in a great many Things, tho' he might never have occasion for any of them.

But of all Kinds of Learning the Study of Philosophy is certainly the most pleasant and profitable: —It corrects all the vicious Humours of the Mind, and inspires the noblest Virtues; —it enlarges our Understanding; —it brings us acquainted with ourselves, and with every thing that is in Nature; and the more we arrive at a Proficiency in it, the more happy and the more worthy we are. —Mr. Prior tells us,

On its best Steps each Age and Sex may rise,
'Tis like the Ladder in the Patriarch's Dream.
Its Foot on Earth, its Height beyond the Skies.[2]

Many Examples have there been of Ladies who have attained to a very great Perfeciion in this sublime and useful Science; and doubtless the Number had been greatly increased but for the Discouragement our Sex meets with, when we aim at anything beyond the Needle.

The World would infallibly be more happy than it is, were women more knowing than they generally are; and very well worth the while of those who have the Interest of the Female Part of their Family at Heart, to instruct them early in some of the most necessary Rudiments of Philosophy: —All those little Follies now ascrib'd to us, and which, indeed, we but too much incur the Censure of, would then vanish, and the Dignity of Human Nature shine forth in us, I will venture to say, with at least as much Splendor as in the other Sex.

All that Restlessness of Temper we are accused of, that perpetual Inclination for gadding from Place to Place; —those Vapours, those Disquiets we often feel meerly for want of some material Cause of Disquiet, would be no more, when once the Mind was employ'd in the pleasing Enquiries of Philosophy: —a Search that well rewards the Pains we take in it, were we even to make no considerable Progress; because even the most minute Discovery affords Matter for Reflection and Admiration.

Whether our Speculations extend to the greatest and most tremendous Objects, or pry into the smallest Works of the Creation, new Scenes of Wonder every Moment open to our Eyes; and as Love and Reverence to the Deity is by every one allowed to be the Ground-Work of all Virtues and Religion, it is, methinks, no less impolitick than unjust to deny us the Means of becoming more good as well as more wise.

From the Brute Creation we may learn Industry, Patience, Tenderness, and a thousand Qualities, which tho' the Human Soul possesses in an infinitely larger Degree, yet the Observation how exercis'd by Creatures of inferior Specie, will oblige us to look into ourselves, and blush at the Remembrance, that for want of Reflection we have sometimes forgot what we are, and perhaps acted beneath those very Animals we despise, and think on as no more than the Dust from which they sprung.

It is certainly a very great Misfortune as well as a Fault in us, that we are apt to have Pride enough to value ourselves highly on the Dignity of our Nature, but yet have not enough to act up in any Measure to it: —This is, methinks, paying too great a Regard to Names, and neglecting Essentials.

The Men in this respect are, indeed, as much to blame as we, nay, much more so, those at least of a liberal Education, who having those Advantages of Learning, which are deny'd to us, behave as tho' they had never been instructed in any thing but how to indulge the Senses in the most elegant Manner.

The Women, at worst, could act as many of the Men do who are refused no Improvements: —they ought, therefore, to make Tryal of us, and not grudge the Expense of Books and Masters to the one Sex any more than to the other.

If, by the Texture of the Brain, as some pretend to alledge, we are less capable of deep Meditations, and have a Multiplicity of volatile Ideas, which, continually wandering, naturally prevent our fixing on any one Thing; the more Care should be taken to improve such as may be of Service, and suppress those that have a contrary Tendency.

That this is possible to be done, I believe, those who reason most strongly this way, and pretend to understand the Mechanism of our Formation best, will not deny.

But I agree no farther than in Supposition to this Common-Place Argument, made use of by the Enemies of our Sex: —The Delicacy of those numerous Filaments which contain and separate from each other what are call'd the Seats of Invention, Memory, and Judgment may not, for any thing they can prove to the contrary, render them less strong; but as I am not Anatomist enough to know whether there is really any such Difference or not between the Male and Female Brain, I will not pretend to reason on this Point.

I have an Opinion of my own, which, being approv'd of by Mira and Euphrosine, I will venture to declare, tho' our noble Widow laughs at us all for it. —It is this:

The Vivacity of our Ideas, —the Quickness of our Apprehensions, and those ready Turns which most Women, much more than Men, have on any sudden Exigence, seem to me to proceed from a greater Redundance of the animal Spirits; and if they sometimes appear too confus'd and huddled, as it were together, it is but like a Crowd of Mob round the Stage of a Mountebank, where all endeavouring to be foremost, obstruct the Passage of each other.

If this should happen to be the Case, as I shall always believe 'till convinced, by very good Reasons, of the contrary, it is easy to check the too great Velocity of these Particles by laying down one great Point, into which, as to a Center, they might all direct their Course.

The most Subtil Spirits may be fixed by that Sovereign Chymist, solid

Reflection: —Thought will give them a due Weight, and prevent their Evaporation; but then the Subject must be delightful as well as serious, or the Mind may be in Danger of an opposite Extreme, and from being too giddy, become irrecoverably mop'd.

Philosophy is, therefore, the Toil which can never tire the Person engag'd in it; —all its Ways are strewed with Roses, and the farther you go, the more enchanting Objects appear before you and invite you on.

That this Science is not too abstruse for our Sex to arrive at a great Perfection in, none can presume to deny; because many known Examples, both in ancient and modern Times, prove the Certainty of it.

Who had not heard of the fam'd Hypatia[3], who read Lectures of Philosophy in the Public Schools in Alexandria, and of whose Eloquence and Wisdom, St. Cyril, then Bishop of that Place, stood so much in Awe, that finding it impossible to bring her over to his Opinion in Matters of Religion, he never rested till he had found Means to take away her Life: —An Action for which he has been severely reproach'd by after, and less bigotted, Ages.

Many others acquired an equal Share of Reputation with this fair Greek, but there is no need of searching Antiquity for that which the present Age gives an unquestionable Proof of in the celebrated Donna Lawra, who has not only disputed with, but also confuted the most learned Doctors in Italy, in those Points on which they happen'd to differ from her.

Some Branches of the Mathematicks are also very agreeable and improving Amusements for young Ladies, particularly Geography, in which they may travel the World over, be acquainted with all its Parts, and find new Matter to adore the Infinite Wisdom, which presiding over and throughout such a Diversity of contrary Climes, suits every one so as to be most pleasing and convenient to the Inhabitants.

History must not be omitted, as it cannot fail engaging the Mind to Attention, and affording the strongest Precept by Example: —the Rise and Fall of Monarchies; —the Fate of Princes, the Sources from which their good or ill Fortune may be deduc'd; —the various Events which the Struggles for Liberty against arbitrary Power have produc'd, and the wonderful Effects which the Heroism of particular Persons has obtained, both to curb Oppression in the Tyrant, and Sedition in the Subject, affords an ample Field for Contemplation, and at the same time too much Pleasure to heave room for any Amusements of a low and trifling Nature.

These are what I would have the serious Employments of a young

Lady's Mind: —Music, Dancing, and the reading of Poetry and Novels may sometimes come in by way of Relaxation, but ought not to be too much indulg'd.

But any Study, any Amusement, should be suited to the Genius and Capacity of the Person to whom it's prescrib'd: —I only mention these as worthy Employments of the Mind; there are others which perhaps may be equally so, and are to be adhered to, or rejected, according to the Judgment of those who have the Government of Youth.

All I insist on, and all I believe that Cleora, or any other Well wisher to our Sex, and through us to the Happiness of Mankind in general, can desire, is that the Talents with which we are born may not be stifled by a wrong Education.

I cannot, however, take leave of this Subject without answering one Objection which I have heard made against Learning in our Sex, which is, that the politer Studies take us off from those that are more necessary, tho' less ornamental.

I believe many well-meaning People may be deceived into this Opinion, which, notwithstanding, is very unjust: —Those Improvements which I have mention'd, sublime as they are, will never be of Prejudice to our attending to those lower Occupations of Life, which are not to be dispensed with except in those of the great World. —They will rather, by making a Woman more sensible than she could otherwise be, of what is either her Duty, or becoming in her to do, that she will be doubly industrious and careful, not to give any Excuse for Reproaches, either from her own Conscience, or the Tongues of those who would suffer by her Transgression.

In a word, it is entirely owing to a narrow Education that we either give our Husbands room to find fault with our Conduct, or that we have Leisure to pry too scrutinously into theirs: —Happy would it be for both, were this almost sole Cause of all our Errors once reform'd; and I am not without some Glimmerings of Hope that it will one Day be so.

The Ladies themselves, methinks, begin to seem sensible of the Injustice which has long been done them, and find a Vacuum in their Minds, which, to fill up, they of their own accord invented the way of sticking little Pictures on Cabinets, Screens, Dressing-Tables, and other little Pieces of Chamber-Furniture, and then varnishing them over so as to look like one Piece of Painting; and they now have got into the Art of turning Ivory into whatever Utensils they fancy: —There is no doubt but a Pair of

Globes will make a better Figure in their Anti-Chambers than the Vice and Wheel; but great Revolutions are not to be expected at once, and if they once take it in their Heads to prefer Works of Ingenuity, tho' in the most trifling Matters, to Dress, Gaming and rambling Abroad, they will, it is to be hop'd, proceed to more noble and elevated Studies.

If the married Ladies of Distinction begin the Change, and bring Learning into Fashion, the younger will never cease soliciting their Parents and Guardians for the Means of following it, and every Toilet in the Kingdom be loaded with Materials for beautifying the Mind more than the Face of its Owner.

The Objection, therefore, that I have heard made by some Men, that Learning would make us too assuming, is weak and unjust in itself, because there is nothing would so much cure us of those Vanities we are accused of, as Knowledge.

A beautiful well dress'd Lady, who is acquainted with no other Merit than Appearance, never looks in her Glass without thinking all the Adoration can be paid to her, is too small a Tribute to her Charms; and even those of our Sex, who seem most plain in the Eyes of other People, never fail to see something in themselves worthy of attracting the most tender Homage.

It is meerly want of Consideration, and the living, as most of us do, in a blind Ignorance of what we truly are, or what we ought reasonably to expect from the World, that gives us that Pride, for which those, who to our Faces treat us with the greatest Respect, laugh at, and despise us for behind our Backs.

It has ever been agreed, by Men of the best Understanding, that the farther they go in the wonderful Researches of Nature, the more abash'd and humble they are: —They see the unfathomable Depth before them, and with it the Insufficiency of human Penetration: —The little they are able to discover convinces them that there are Things still out of their reach, and even beyond their Comprehension; and while it raises their Ideas of the Almighty Wisdom, puts an entire Check to all vain Imaginations of their own.

O but, say they, Learning puts the Sexes too much on an Equality, it would destroy that implicit Obedience which it is necessary the Women should pay to our Commands: —If once they have the Capacity of arguing with us, where would be our Authority!

Now will I appeal to any impartial Reader, even among the Men, if this very Reason for keeping us in Subjection does not betray an Arrogance and Pride in themselves, yet less excusable than that which they seem so fearful of our assuming.

I will also undertake to prove, not only by my own Observation but by that of every Person who has taken any Pains to examine the World, that those Women have always been the most domineering, whose Talents have received the least Improvement from Education.

It may happen, indeed, that some might grow overbearing on such Advantages, for there are Tempers too turbulent for any Bounds to restrain; but I will at the same time maintain, that they would have been still worse if kept in Ignorance that to be so was a Fault: —Nature will always be the same, and she who is prone to Pride and Vanity will give Testimonies of it, even tho' she has no one Perfection either of Mind or Body to serve as a Pretence.

But, as of two Evils the least is to be chosen, is it not better, therefore, for any Man who has the Misfortune to have a termagant or imperious Wife, that when People speak of her Behaviour they should say, *She is a Woman of an admirable Understanding and great Learning, she only knows her own Merit too well*; than to hear them cry, *What a vain, idle, ignorant, prating Creature she is*—I dare answer, there is not a Husband in all Great Britain that would not be glad to hear the first rather than the last Character given of the Woman to whom he is united.

This, however, is certain, that Knowledge can make the Bad no worse, and would make the Good much better than they could be without it.

If, therefore, the Parents of a young Lady thrust her out into the World unfinish'd, as I may venture to call it, when no Care is taken of her better Part, it would not, methinks, be unbecoming in her Husband to supply that Deficiency: —She would receive Instruction from his Mouth with double Pleasure, and it must certainly be an infinite Satisfaction to him to perceive the Improvement his fair Pupil daily made under his Tuition: —Nothing in my Opinion could more endear them to each other, nor be a greater Proof of their mutual Affection. Milton most elegantly expresses such a Circumstance in the Eighth Book of his Paradise Lost, where Raphael being in Conversation with Adam on Matters then above the Comprehension of Eve, she withdrew that she might afterwards hear it from her Husband. . . .

Where there is that Union of Hearts as well as Hands, which can

alone answer the Ends for which Marriage was first instituted, the
Husband in finding his Precepts effectual and delightful must feel no less
Rapture in himself, and Increase of Love for the dear Authoress of it, than
the same incomparable Poet, just now quoted, ascribes to the great Father
of Mankind, when speaking of Eve he defines the Passion he has for her,
and the Motives of it in these Terms:

> It is not
> Neither her outside Form so fair, nor aught
> In procreation common to all Kinds,
> (Tho' higher of the Genial Bed by far,
> And with mysterious Reverence I deem)
> So much delights me, as those graceful Acts,
> Those thousand Decencies that daily flow
> From all her Words and Actions, mix'd with Love
> And sweet Compliance, which declares unfeign'd
> Union of Mind, or in us both one Soul;
> Harmony to behold in wedded Pair. (595–605)

Methinks it would be no Difficulty for two People who love each
other as they ought, and some such there doubtless are, to practice over a
little of the Behaviour of our first Parents in their State of Innocence:
—'Tis true, they would incur a good deal of Ridicule from the more gay
and noisy World on first attempting such a thing, but that would wear off
in time by their Perseverance; and the Benefits accruing from it to all
belonging to them, as well as to themselves, would become so demonstra-
tive, as might, perhaps, induce the most Thoughtless to make tryal of
such a way of Life.

But all this, I doubt, will be look'd upon as visionary, and my Readers
will cry, that my Business as a Spectator, is to report such Things as I see,
and am convinced of the Truth of, not present them with Ideas of my own
Formation, and which, as the World now is, can never be reduc'd to
Practice: —To which I beg leave to reply that the Impossibility lies only in
the Will; —much may be done by a steady Resolution, —without it,
nothing.

I do not, indeed, flatter myself with living to see my Counsel in this
Point make any great Impression; the Mode is against me, and those who
may approve the most of what I say will yet be asham'd to confess it.

Custom a Second Nature grows,
And Law and Reason both o'erthrows.

Nothing certainly be more strange than that People, of even common Understanding, can suffer themselves to be sway'd to Actions and Behaviour repugnant to their own Hearts; and often unsuitable to their Circumstances, meerly because some Persons of Distinction have establish'd it into a Fashion; yet that it is so, every one knows, and any one who should undertake to put a Stop to this almost universal Propensity, at least in this Nation, might with equal Success, endeavour to turn the Wind from one Point of the Compass to another with a single Breath.

Monstrous Stupidity! —All Diseases, all Imperfections of the Body, which those in High Life would part with all their Grandeur to get rid of, are aped by the inferior World, and thought agreeable and genteel: —All the Vices and ill Qualities of the Mind are also sanctify'd by Title and Opulence: —Whatever is a Defect either in Nature or Principle, presently converts itself into the reverse, is copy'd after, and perhaps excell'd by those who care not what they are, so they are but like the Great.

But of all the Follies which this Passion for Imitation occasions, there is none more to be complained of by the Wellwishers of Mankind, than that which we daily see practised by married People; who, tho' they really have a sufficient Share of Tenderness for each other to answer all the Ends of that sacred Institution, and can neither of them find any Company abroad whose Conversation to them comes in any Competition with that they leave at Home, yet are hardly ever seen together in public Places: When one goes out of Town the other stays behind; so that they seem rather like Buckets of a Well, that are always in retrograde Motion, than Persons who are by Love and Law inseparably united: —And all this Violence they offer to themselves meerly to avoid being call'd unpolite.

We are often told, that all the Calamities under which this Nation at present groans, are owing to the general Corruption and Depravity among us; and I believe no Person of Understanding will pretend to deny so notorious and so melancholy a Truth; yet will all Exhortations, all Remonstrances, all Precepts be in vain to accomplish a Reformation, without some very great Examples lead the way, and once more bring Virtue and Good-Manners into vogue.

It is not from below we are to expect any illuminous Emanations, nor would they have the necessary Influence; but when darted upon us from above, all see their Light and partake of the Blessings they bestow. Virtue, tho' adorn'd with all the Graces, in mean Persons is no more than a dark Lanthorn giving Light only to him that carries it; but those who sit aloft wear a Sun upon their Breasts, which all behold, admire and are ambitious to follow.

NOTES

1. John Dryden, Jr., "The Fourteenth Satyr," in *Satires* (London: J. Tonson, 1702), 50–51 (first couplet) and 96–97 (second couplet).
2. "To Dr. Sherlock, on his Practical Discourse Concerning Death," 33–35.
3. Daughter of Theon of Alexandria, she held the chair of Platonic Philosophy at Alexandria. d. 415 A.D.

FRANCES BOSCAWEN

1719–1805

FRANCES EVELYN GLANVILLE was born 22 July 1719 at St. Clere, Kent. The great granddaughter of John Evelyn, the diarist, she was interested in literary matters from her earliest years and, although she did not become a professional writer, the fresh, spontaneous style of her letters earned her the title of "la Sévigné d'Angleterre."

In 1742 she married Captain Edward Boscawen, a rising young naval officer who eventually became Admiral of the Blue, and much of her life centered about the business of running a household and caring for her five lively children. From her letters she evidently enjoyed the domestic aspect of her life, but her interests did not stop there, and she reveals knowledge, taste, and enthusiasm for arts and ideas. In 1749 she met Elizabeth Robinson Montagu, the leader of the "bluestockings," as educated women came to be known. Elizabeth Montagu, herself an unashamed intellectual, was the focal point of literary London, and her "Assemblies" of authors and philosophers represented the elite of English letters. Such men as David Garrick, Edmund Burke, Sir Joshua Reynolds, and Dr. Samuel Johnson enjoyed the intelligent conversation of women like Fanny Boscawen, Hester Chapone, Elizabeth Carter, Fanny Burney, Hannah More, and Anna Laetitia Barbauld. There are several versions of the origin for the name "bluestocking"; one suggests that the Assemblies were so informal that Benjamin Stillingfleet, the naturalist, began the custom of wearing blue worsted hose in place of the usual formal white stockings, and that Admiral Boscawen amusedly remarked on the "bluestocking" group. The term, applied with some affection, became an insult in the nineteenth century.

Many of Mrs. Boscawen's letters were written to her husband. The combination of gossip, political events, and brief, witty sketches of friends not only kept Edward in touch with his family during the long months at sea, but provide us with a backstage view of history. Fanny, who claimed "Beauty and I were never acquainted," was a lively and literate correspondent. No matter was too trivial to relate; when George, the youngest, swallowed a shirt button, the event and the treatment were described crisply, concisely, and with evident delight.

The happy years came to an abrupt end with the Admiral's death in 1761. The children were still young: Edward Hugh was eighteen and at Oxford; Frances was seventeen; Elizabeth, the beauty, sixteen; William, twelve, was about to go to sea under Admiral Geary's tutelage; and George, the baby, was five. A wealthy widow, Boscawen was not faced with the problems of earning her living, and, though her income was reduced, there was never the slightest question of deprivation. She never remarried, but devoted herself to the welfare of her children. Both of her daughters married well: Elizabeth married Henry, fifth Duke of Beaufort in 1766, Frances married Captain (later Admiral) John Leveson-Gower in 1773. Yet Boscawen's later life was shadowed with tragedy. The beautiful Elizabeth was permanently lamed in a coach accident, and two of the boys died young: William, the adored family favorite, was drowned in Jamaica in 1769, when he was just seventeen; five years later, Edward Hugh died in France, ironically while on his way to a health spa. Only the youngest, George, carried on the name. He survived service during the American Revolution to become the third Viscount Falmouth.

Boscawen's later letters document her activities. She wintered in London, summered at her cottage—first Glan Villa near Enfield, then Rosedale near Richmond. She visited or entertained friends, and when they were away she maintained constant communication with them. Her life was not only full but long. She died in London on 26 February 1805, forty-five years after her husband's death.

If her literary endeavors were confined to letter writing, they were by no means inconsiderable. She took an informed and intense interest in the world about her; books, music, theater, and parties filled her social life. Through her husband she was aware of political developments almost as soon as they occurred, but it was her home at Hatchlands Park and her children that absorbed most attention. All of these interests are reflected in her voluminous correspondence. It is clear that she and her husband were devoted to each other and that he valued her strong, independent opinions. Unfortunately, editors interested in these same opinions have been of another mind and have disregarded her independence. Two volumes of her correspondence have been published under the titles *An Admiral's Wife* (1940) and *An Admiral's Widow* (1942). The letters here are from an unpublished collection at the Huntington Library, and a reading of the entire collection gives a comprehensive view of what it meant to be a woman in the eighteenth century.

BIBLIOGRAPHY

Letters

Aspinall-Oglander, Cecil, ed. *An Admiral's Wife.* London: Longmans, Green. 1940.

———. *An Admiral's Widow.* London: Hogarth Press. 1942.

Johnson, R. Brimley, ed. *Bluestocking Letters.* London: John Land, the Bodley Head Ltd. 1926, pp. 141–65.

The letters quoted in this text have not been published and are part of a collection of manuscripts belonging to the Huntington Library: MO 505–MO 563.

Letters to Elizabeth Robinson Montagu

FRANCES GLANVILLE BOSCAWEN

Portsmouth, 13 November 1755

Welcome! my Dearest Friend to your comfortable fireside in Hill Street if rather I shou'd not say to your shining Apartment in Peking where I envy all your Mandarines, that sit (cross leg'd or otherwise) in your Presence, while I am banish'd from it and know not alas! when my banishment will end, for we have had none but contrary Winds for this Week past, and more; till yesterday that they turn'd to the Westward, God be praised and remain so. Hitherto People have told me the Admiral *wou'd* come soon, now the Stile is he *must* come; and that I like the best, suspecting that while there is any good to be done he *would* not voluntarily leave it. It flatters me much to hear that they write from N. England they do not fear driving the French quite out of North America, and only demand three articles for that Service: viz: Money, Arms and Boscawen. This a Gentleman told me he saw in a Letter at Lisbon, from New England. Their own Johnson has, I flatter myself, by this time made a great Progress, for the French whom he defeated was *tout ce qu'ils avoient de meilleur* [the best of all they had] and I saw last Sunday a French letter out of one of the Prizes from Canada dated two days before the•Engagement in which I read these words: *nous n'avons plus ici que des Coiffes, tous nos Chapeaux sont allés à l'armée* [we no longer have anything but head-dresses (i.e. women) here, all our hats have gone to war]. Judge then whether this blow is not rather decisive. So much for American Politicks, as for those nearer home, I wait for you to give me the *branle* ["latest scoop"—French slang], and shall hardly form an Opinion till I hear yours; yet I think I rather incline to be of Mr. Montagu's Side, for why must I differ with Him always in Parliament. No, I think I must join with him in opposing a Continent war, and promoting only a truly British War by Sea; for which we never had so fair an Opportunity as now. I shall ask him whether Subsidies will not ruin us and where this Nation (*abimée* as it is) will find Money to pay and subsist such a vast body of forces. *Mais dites m'en les Sentimens de Madame aussi bien que ceux de Monsieur* [but tell me madam's feelings as well as monsieur's].

Yesterday as I was going out with Mrs Brett[1] in the Post Chaise, whom shou'd we behold but Mr Botham;[2] we brought him too, and adjudging him a lawful Prize order'd him home to dine with us, but in the Evening he made his Escape and as we are credibly inform'd set out this Morning with Mr Bendythe (a neighbouring Surrey-Vicar) for their respective homes. By him I received the Shells and shall thankfully obey your Commands, and by him I received too a very delightful account of your rustic air and rosy Health; which I heartily thank God for, and earnestly beseech you to preserve carefully. Mr Botham says 'twill be all gone by the time you have *rak'd* one fortnight in London, but I, who do not join with your Cousins West[3] and Botham in their Opinion of your *Rakery*, have only to fear your setting up late of Nights to read (for want of Opportunity in the day time) and your neglecting all airings and Motions of your Chaise of a Morning for want of the same Opportunity. I have only then to beg of you in general to take care of your Health, and in particular not to set up late, and not to remain always in your house without air or exercise, and this I do so earnestly, with join'd hands and bended knees, that you cannot be so obdurate as to refuse me. Botham and I have appointed to meet (together with our small fry assembled) at Hatchlands and at Albury in Christmas Holidays; but whether the troubles of these Times will permit me to keep my Word is, I think, uncertain. He proposes to have his Boys at home in the Holidays and we both propose to place Johnny at the Academy here, the first Week in

January. Sooner cou'd not well be as the Admiral has thus postponed his Arrival. Your little friend Harry grows. He din'd with me here on Sunday with his Brother. Botham has been at Wickham, thinks Mr West ill, and wishes him to go to Bath; thinks Miss Pitt[4] uneasy and dispirited, and I judge so too; for she does not write to me; I wrote to her a long time ago but have received no Answer. She grieves me!

I have demanded a tribute of feathers of many of my Sea-Vassals, but I cannot say they come in so kindly as I had expected. I am charm'd with Mr Berkeley's Hospitality and still more with your Description of it, and when I arraign his Chinese fence, it was not as a *fence*, but as Chinese, for it seems the gusto grande which reigns there, demanded a balustrade of Stone (*ou soi distant tel*) [or so they say].

I beseech you to go to, or rather send for Sir Sydney[5] and Lady Smythe; they will both come to you of a Sunday Evening. He cannot, on any other. 'Tis for all your Sakes that I thus become Procuresse, for I think you *made for each Other*. Shall I flatter my Self that you will wish for me, I'm sure I wish my Self with you. Come, the Westerly Winds blow hard, who knows how soon. *En attendant, aimer moi toujours ma très Chère Amie. Croyez que je suis penetrée de toute vos Bontés, et sera toute ma Vie tendrement à vous* [Meanwhile, love me always, my very dear friend. Know that I am struck with all your kindness, and will all my life be tenderly yours].

Hatchlands the 13th July 1756

You have fairly kept your Word, with us my dear Madam, and sent us such a quantity of Bingisms[6] as must content moderate Curiosity. They shall all go in terrorem to *our Brest Fleet*, not that I think any Commander there, will venture to try this new Method of *fighting safely*; at least I believe there is One who wou'd quickly undeceive such a Miscreant, and convince him it was of all others the most unsafe Method. From that One I have had a Letter this Morning, and I think in no great Spirits which I am sorry to perceive, however, that he had been harass'd with chasing all Night the Appearance of a French Squadron, and he had just perceived that it consisted of Ships of all Nations, France only excepted. His Letter is dated 5th July. The Royal George had not then join'd him; I hear of other Ships just about to go to him so that I must write today and borrow of my Friend the time which I ought to have employ'd in Thanks for her kind and agreeable Epistle. It wou'd be something, however, cou'd I execute your Commission; but of that too I am incapable, for my poor Wench has not had the Small pox, neither is there a Lass in my parish nor in the next (for I have inquir'd of a large body of haymakers) that has had it. Our Parson preaches against Inoculation so I do not suppose that benefit will ever be felt among them.

Adieu my dearest Friend—Madam Dolorida appears with the housebook, which I must dispatch. I shall not tell you how many good Wishes I send after you to Tunbridge nor how much I am

Affectionately faithfully gratefully yours

1756

My Dear Good Friend, I intreat you not to suppress the kind Notions you may have to write to me, who regret and want your Conversation more than all the Land beside: I write this at Mrs Cleveland's house, for I am as fanciful *lorsqu'il s'agit de ma Chère amie* [when it concerns my dear friend] as the Mother of a favourite heir can possibly be; I am just return'd with Mrs Clevland from the Country, so I thought this the most favourable Opportunity to send you Writing of mine with ink that is not mine. I shall say but little; for I must see poor Tweedle[7] before dinner, and it is now past four: When last I saw him, he seem'd quite easy and was much inclin'd to Play, has one Spot out and no more that we know of; they send me Word he has had a fine sleep since I have been gone and continues quite Well. The Damsels too, Mr Hawkins[8] says, are just as they shou'd be: so all is well here; and Mr Boscawen I hope is so, many Miles to the Westward. I had three Letters from him yesterday, two of which were the Produce of so many days Voyage between Portsmouth and Plymouth. I send you inclos'd a List of his Squadron that you may not expect more from him than mortal Man can do. I am in very good Spirits, I thank God, and hope to keep so. When I went to the Play it was not to dissipate, or run away from myself, but to amuse my own Girls and the Girls of my Friends, for I went to Mr Lalauze's benefit as well as to that of Mr Levier,[9] and I find a Play at this time of Year the quietest and most retired Scheme One can devise: it was very cool in the State box this Afternoon, and to Morrow I shall be at home, but I am perfectly easy in going out, because an excellent ancient (and yet active) Personnage who was my Mother's Servant and has been to me a Mother, has most generously convey'd herself hither out of Kent on purpose to be with me at this time of trouble. She looks upon my Children as her Grand-Children, and has all the Care of the Grand Mother without her folly: To this good Body I recommend my Sick Folk when I go out, and she has caused me to be informed (since I began this Letter) that Master has several more Spots; *à la bonne heure* [luckily] since he is so well. I hope this account so much in detail conveys to you an Idea of that happy Security in which I rest concerning your Friendship; I have no doubt of possessing that real Treasure, but how to deserve it is by no means so clear: let be a Gift, then, not a Purchase, for the Judges and Senates have been bought for gold. Esteem and love were never meant to be Sold.

Yet methinks I have something to bid—I have a heart that is most gratefully, most affectionately, and most faithfully Yours. *N'en doutez jamais ma très chère amie* [Never doubt it, my very dear Friend]!

Hatchlands, this cold Sunday
19th Jan 1757

How generous is my Dear Friend, to bestow upon me a second kind Letter without upbraiding me with Neglect of her First; a Neglect which has all the Appearance of Ingratitude, but in reality proceeds from a cause much less grave; no other than that my bureau stands at a distance from the fireside but cruel near a Window as a Cornish Man wou'd say and not improperly this Weather. This is the Cause my Dearest Friend that I have not wrote any Words, Syllables or Sentences since I was favour'd with Yrs except in extreme cases, such as Receiv'd in full of all demands of me, the X Mark of John a Nokes, etc. and even some of these necessary instruments have been drawn upon my lap; such and so severe is the Cold at this Place where we have little more than a Tent to cover us, our house in its last Moments having cold fits, or rather an universal Chill. Yet I thank God my Health is perfect, and my Spirits are also. Wishing to hear the like of you, it cannot but be a great trouble to Me to find that You have been visited with a Cholick and flux; your delicate frame must be shook with such rough companions. Pray, Dear Love, take Care of yourself and take Care of your Health and my Pleasure, for I intend to have much Comfort and much Mirth by your Fireside after this long Absence; but how? if I find the languid Eye, and all the benign Countenance of my precious Friend depress'd and worn with pain. I think a great deal upon this Subject (for it comes very near me) and it has occurr'd to me that Tar Water wou'd be a Noble Med'cine for you: you'll say 'tis the prescription of a Seaman's Wife, but read what a holy Bishop says about it, and then (after his Prescription) try it, in small quantities first, afterwards you may increase the dose if it agrees with your stomach, in which case I am almost sure it will do you no harm: if there be any Inflammation in your Case, then I withdraw my Prescription, for I suppose it to be a warm and a cordial Medicine. Tell me mean time (if it be but in two lines) whether you recover your Strength; and have found no ill Effects from this cold Weather; I charge you do not abandon your fireside, no, nor for that of Mrs Donellan,[10] at least she can't accuse me that this Advice is interested or that I profit by her loss, otherwise than in your Health *dont à la Vérité bien profiter, et sans peu* [from which, truthfully, I profit much]; for I take a final leave of this condemned Mansion to Morrow fortnight, and sooner it cannot well be consistent with the Arrangement preparatory to so great an Affair as Building a House; hundreds of Thousands of Bricks and Sands like a Sea Shore for Multitude must be brought in, for which my set of Bays are usefull Instruments, so that they must not yet be prefer'd to the less ignoble Employment of dragging me to Routs and Plays.

Our Society is good, Miss Van Sittart[11] and her Chearfulness remain, temper'd with a sage and very worthy Man, Major Burleigh; I have also my Brother, a useful Lieutenant without doors in the Absence of the Admiral, who from Friday to Monday is also *des Nôtres*; then I have his fine Boys and Girls as you say, who with the noble Game of Tagg and blind man's buff give our ancient fabrick many a Convulsion in the Evening: In the Morning they brave the Weather, and bring me home such frosty faces of rosy or rather of purple health as I cou'd wish to see you wear; I take a Walk too almost every day and have not as yet got the least Cold. Yesterday Mr Botham and his three Damsels walk'd hither, din'd and then trudg'd home again; I need not add that they are in good Health, but I must tell you that Mr Boscawen thinks your Missey improv'd in her Person: You will find her much grown. Thank you for your News—and Thank you for procuring me the Honor to be remember'd by Lady T. Williams and Lady Coningsby to whom I am much oblig'd.

I ought long ago to have told you what I know of Mr Codrington; from Inquiries that I made very soon after I saw Mrs Barnard, tho' in chatting with you so much as always it occurr'd that I forgot to mention it. Mr Codrington is Lieutenant in Admiral Saunders[12] own Ship, consequently is in a fair Way of preferment, as Admiral Saunders commands in the Mediterranean, and winters there. I have also heard that Mr Codrington is esteem'd a very good Officer and is a young Man that promises much. I hope Mrs Barnard comes often to you, and chiefly our Aimable Pitty[13] to whom my kind Love: I am glad she is settled so near me; and I am heartily glad Mr Pitt is recover'd, for his Sake and that of the Publick, in whose Favor I hope he will exert all his eminent Faculties. I must not expect a Letter from Miss Pitt, for she's ten times naughtier than I am that Way. Mrs Lane tells me the Operas are finer than ever were operated before, and so we have this day dispatch'd her to hear them, *dont nous ne sommes point trop marris* [for which we are not so very sorry]. We are in the line of Intelligence from Admiral Byng in whose Favor Capt. Hervey has so strongly depon'd, that his Evidence is diametrically Opposite to that of General Blakeney[14] and many other Deponents; for Mr Hervey[15] talk'd of his engaging fiercely with no less than three of the Enemy and of Shot flying about like hail: upon the whole it appear'd to the Auditors that the Evidence went much against the Prisoner and that his Cause seem'd desperate; what Weight Mr Hervey may have in the other Scale, time will show. You will not reveal this Intelligence as from me. I pity the Members of the Court who are all confin'd to the Ship without once going on Shore till the Trial is over. Adieu My Dearest Friend. My Fingers are froze, but my Heart is warm, and most tenderly

Yours

The Admiral sends you a thousand Douceurs, *mais je ne serai pas si sotte, moi que d'en etre le Porteur* [but I shall not be so foolish as to be the bearer].

Hatchlands Park, 1st August 1758

How does my Dear Friend and her agreeable Compagne do? I wonder. If they are but as well as I wish them, it is enough, for I wou'd conjur round them, like the Fairy Queen and bid Cramps and Spasms give no Offence: You got safe out of the Convoy of our trusty Botham, I understand. The said Botham hinder'd my Writing to you by Monday's Post, assuring me that he saw plainly I was only willing, whereas he was both willing and able. I hope he proved his Words and wrote his Letter. Will you have my History since we parted? I shall always have a Curiosity for yours, so I'll give myself a right to ask it of you.

Imprimis, I set out soon after you, and as soon perceiv'd I was no match for my Companions, being much more affected with the Loss I had sustain'd than they were at that which they were about to sustain; *aussi bien* I draw'd upon my Self many reproaches of *mon peu de diligence* [my lack of diligence] in the discovery of cats, hogs and magpyes in cages; however, we made shift to play four Games. Fortune decided equally between the Combatants and the testers return'd from whence they came.

Arriv'd at Kensington, I soon discover'd that you were in the Right, and I in the Wrong, which I suspect will generally be the case when we two dispute. Mr and Mrs Robert are departed *sans dire Mot* and mademoiselle Elin[16] reigns in their Stead. To her I consign'd my fair Daughters (entirely to *their* Satisfaction). I saw Miss Botham and have reported them ragged, not but that they were well drest when I inspected them and it was dancing day.

I proceeded to the Admiral Tree thro' the Parks, having announc'd my Self at Constitution Hill, Admiral Boscawen; upon which, the Gates flew open immediately, as I trust those of Louisbourg have done. The Moment I arriv'd, I was visited by Sir William Rowley[17] and Mr Cleveland, and at Dinner time produc'd my Self *à l'hôtel de Falmouth*, where *je m'ennuiois beaucoup quoique dans le beau Milieu de Londres* [I was never more bored than in the center of London], thence I transplanted my Self into Soho Square *où je me serai ennuiée pareillement* [where I was likewise bored] if I had not been prevented by a fit of Surprize on the sight of the Words Julia Sayer, and on the Reflection that I had lost my half crown, not without further proof of Mrs Montagu's always putting me in the Wrong. Saturday Morning I took a Walk round the Park, but cou'd not allow that the *London* Park was so pretty as this same Hatchlands Park. At one, Lady Smythe arriv'd much to her Satisfaction, and I'm sure to Mine, she left her Sister recover'd (strength excepted). She accompany'd me to Lee (five Miles out of Town) where we din'd with Mr and Mrs Clevland and talk'd America with the former. Sunday we went to Church, walk'd in the Park, were caught in *London* rain, which has dirty'd my white cloak and *enfin* we left this dear old odious London at four in the afternoon.

Chemin faisant, I thought within my Self, what if I shou'd meet an Express from America, and sure enough upon Cobham Common I met a Post Chaise containing an Officer. On him I star'd Attentive. He star'd again; then he cry'd Stop, I echo'd Stop. *Enfin* I heard him ask, Is Admiral Boscawen's Lady in that Coach? I made quick reply in the Affirmative, and soon he produc'd himself at my Coach Window and told me he was express sent by the Governor of Nova Scotia with News of our Troops having taken the Forts of Beau Sejour and Chignecto, that he attended Admiral Boscawen for his Orders twenty-three Days ago and left him in perfect Health. He added, with a Politeness not unusual among the Scots (for he is of that Nation), that Admiral Boscawen had saved North America, where all our Colonies were in the utmost Danger as well as Consternation till he came. Papers having been found which shew'd the French had a Design to destroy Hallifax where the People imagin'd French would let in the Indians to massacre them. Accordingly, when our Squadron appear'd, they took them for French Ships, and the Panic Terror was inexpressible, but when they found not only that it was Friends, but Successful Friends, who had taken Ships and Troops and Officers from the Enemy, there was a sudden Transition to such unbounded Joy and Confidence that now they were sure they should entirely drive the French from that Continent. Mr. Cunningham likewise spoke many other Words in praise of your Toast, Words not "unpleasing to the married Ear."

He added that Mr. B. had taken (or as the Phrase there is, *detain'd*) six French Merchant Ships and had Blockaded Louisbourg, but of this I had no Advice in his Letters to me. Concerning those Letters, think of my Self-Denial! Mr Cunningham had them with him in the Chaise, but as they were directed to Mr Clevland, I wou'd not *detain* them, and was oblig'd to content my Self with sending black Tom after the Post Chaise, who brought them hither the following day. They contain'd little of publick News, but much of private Friendship, and what was best of all, a Prayer that I wou'd not go into Kent, for indeed he wou'd come home in August. So to Morrow Se'enight, being the Ninth of August, I shall take as many Steps towards meeting him as the Bounds of the Land will permit. Please to direct for me at Charles Brett's[18] Esquire, at the Dock Yard, Portsmouth. Tell Miss Pitt Mrs Brett has been here on her Way home and inquired much how she did and how she liked Dorsetshire. I said as well cou'd be expected from a Woman that resided in Surrey and Berkshire.

Saturday Evening 7 o'clock
13 December 1760

My Dear Friend
Do not think about me, it disturbs your Quiet and lessens not my case. Suppose me in Cornwall, and my poor Dear Husband at Sea, contending with the French, not with a fever, not the Cesar that says give me some drink Titinius, like a sick Girl. Indeed, my Dear Friend, I have been very miserable. I am easier now, God be prais'd, my Patient is gone to bed (for he cannot *keep* his bed) and there he seems to sleep quietly. I sit by his

fireside, his sole Nurse, Occupations new to both of us. In eighteen Years, I have never known him to have an illness beyond a Cold, in one of which last Year he let Duncan[19] visit him, but, as I remember, 'twas only to keep out a Physician that Lady Falmouth threatened him with, for if I don't mistake, *you* visited him too. However, I urg'd this Precedent to let me send for Dr. Duncan now, and yesterday my Brother was so kind to attend the Doctor hither. I kept the Apothecary to meet him, to whom I hope he gave full Instructions and Directions. It appears to me that he greatly alter'd the Method pursu'd by the latter, and the Event seems to have justify'd him, for Mr. Boscawen is considerably amended this Evening. The Apothecary gave Astringents, the Doctor forbade them, and even added Rhubarb to his Draughts, the Effect of which, tho it may bring him low, yet I trust has carry'd off part of his Illness, for the Pain in his head and back is remov'd, he is less loaded and said himself just now that he believ'd he shou'd have a good Night, which I am sure he has never had yet in his Illness, so that I hope his Prophecy proceeded from feeling himself better, the rather as he is what wou'd be call'd very low Spirited. I think Strong Men unus'd to Illness generally are so, tho I never saw him so before, indeed I never saw him very ill till now. I will tell you more to Morrow. Mean time Good Night to you, my Dear Friend! 'Tis a great Satisfaction to me that you seem so well; of all human Blessing, Health is surely the first.

Sunday Afternoon

No, not a good Night, and yet rather better than worse today, at least my Patient says so, and I must hope so.

Grosvenor Street

the 30th December 1766

Je reprendrai le fil de votre Histoire, ma Chère Ami [I shall take up again the thread of your story, my dear friend], and will just where you left off, which I mistake not was with these Words, "little Marquess of Worcester." The little Marquess of Worcester[20] then is a very pretty Child with fine blue Eyes, a fair Skin, sucks heartily, roars lustily and is now situate, lying and being in his Cradle in the next Room fast asleep. His happy Mother is sitting bolt upright in her great Chair at my Elbow, passing like a mummy, to be sure, but in perfect Health, I thank God, tho, indeed, she was full twenty-four hours in Labour. Very safe, however, and already I think we have forgot the Anguish for Joy that a Man is born in the World. He has indeed brought much Joy with him, and his noble Father, who is now writing on the Table by me, seems to have as many Congratulations to answer as wou'd employ a dozen clerks. Come then, and partake my Joy, an Invitation I have not often made you of late. I saw Lord Lyttleton[21] this Morning, he was so good to bring me his Congratulation. We talk'd of you. He said you wou'd not be above a fortnight a-coming, I don't think you will have Patience to march so slow when your face is set towards London, at least I hope not, tho' I wou'd not have you make more haste than good speed. You bid me tell you news mean time—as for Politicks—Lord Chatham is at Bath; in short, the Players are gone to dinner on their respective Mince pyes till the 16 January, by which time I hope you will hear with Ears and see with Eyes. For private News, Mr Burdett, eldest Son to Sir Robert Burdett[22] was marry'd this Morning to Miss Jones, an heiress. So was Lord Barrymore to Lady Emily Stanhope. Lady Guilford is dead and has left all her own Family (of Sir Johns) extremely disappointed, she having given all to Lord Guilford,[23] not for life only, but *in seculo seculorum* (in perpetuity). Some legacies, *viz.* £3000 to Mrs. Gabott, £2000 each to Lord Bolingbroke's[24] sons, and a few other trifling legacies, but I hear that Lord Guilford, who was extremely affected with such a Mark of her Affection and Confidence that he declar'd if he knew which way she wou'd have chose to dispose it among her Family, he wou'd do it immediately, being really distress'd with her Goodness to him.

Mr. Norris of Berkeley Square, his only Son has marry'd Kitty Fisher,[25] which is very horrid and grievous to the best of Parents, for so indeed are the Father and Mother of this wretched young Man. Lady Dalkeith[26] (I hear) is to be an English Baroness and to proceed to her Townshend—Children. They talk of more Irish Dukes, *viz.* Lord Hertford and Lord Shelbourne, whose Lady asked me t'other day, when you wou'd return from your northern Expedition.

My Grandson cries—I must visit him, and you have no loss for—I have been so islanded, as our Friend Cambridge[27] says, that I shou'd not be able to give you any more Intelligence but that the Caudle is good and so is the Cake. Adieu then, my Dear Madam, I long very much for your Arrival. Take care of yourself that you may come *saine et sauve* to your very Affectionate.

Hatchlands Park the 1st October 1767

You may go as far North as you please, my Dear Madam; your friends in the South will be apt to follow you with their Souvenirs and

Enquiries. I should like to have mine answer'd by means of a pigeon who shou'd *soon* bring me your Letter (for at all events I choose a Letter) to say you are well and have been so. I know Travelling always agrees with you, and as to Climate, I defy you to have seen less of the Sun than we have this past Summer, for alas, it is past without our suspecting it (you cannot once have found Occasion for your Summer Cloak, substantial as it is.) No, you will have said, the fur is better, just now indeed, we have *un petit été St. Michel* [i.e., Indian summer], but the Shortness of the Days makes it but poor amends for *la St. Jean. Mais, c'est assez parlez du Temps. Mort hélas! après etc.* [but that is enough talk about the weather. Death, alas! after all . . .] has not respected, you see, the Gayety, Vivacity, Activity or Royalty of the Duke of York! His Aunt, the Princess of *Our Times*, Mary of Hesse, had not found such flowery Paths as his; many Thorns were mix'd among her Roses, so that if she shares our Mourning, I think she has less claim to our Regret.

I imagine you have had good Intelligencers from London of the News, Politicks and Changes that have and have not been. For me, that have not stir'd from my Retirement, I know Nothing but what I pay for in the Shape of Newspaper. I am sure you lamented monsieur de Guerchy,[28] I pity poor Madame. Lord Albermarle,[29] I hear, is dying, his Riches then will not bribe, no more than the Eloquence of Mr Townshend persuade Death to respite the Sentence. Marriage is a pleasanter Subject, but not pleasant (*dit-on*) to your Cousin Lord Bute[30] at this time, whose second Son your rich Namesake is suppos'd to be secretly marry'd to a Scotch Lady, niece to Lord Eglintoun and nam'd Cunningham. That she is near thirty years old is perhaps the most extraordinary circumstance, if Lord Palmerston's[31] Choice had not lately brought another instance of Love's knowing no Register. If I misinform you with respect to Mr Montagu's marriage, *ce n'est pas ma faute au moins* [at least it is not my fault]. Every word that I tell you I have heard very positively. So have I heard too, much Scandal *en Sujet d'une belle et Noble Dame* Lady Bolingbroke. You have heard the same, probably, and will not believe even the half of it. *Mais revenons à nos Moutons* [But let us return to the subject]. Your Cousin, Mrs Stewart, comported herself with much matronly Dignity and Propriety at a certain Guilford breakfast to which she went *en famille* three Days after she was marry'd and because I found Lady Onslow[32] wou'd not go to meet her, I went myself, tho' it is seven years since I have thought of such a thing, but I judg'd it wou'd be very unpleasant and awkward to her not to meet one Matron of her Acquaintance, and accordingly she and her Family were much pleas'd with this mark of my Attention. I plac'd her at the head of the Table, the Bridegroom on her right hand, Mr Boscawen[33] on her left. The latter offer'd her his Service to dance, but she declin'd Dancing, so Dancing was not, and the young People play'd Cards a round table, the Aged at Quadrille. My Son, Daughter and Self were decorated with her *Favours*. It is so long since I have seen Mr Botham that I conclude he is still absent from Albany. He and his daughters din'd with me just before they left, and I was sorry to observe Miss Botham looks *so* as to give one very little Idea of her Recovery.

I have just heard that the Princess Mary is not dead, and I have just heard too such Particulars of the Duke of York's Death as much increase my Sense of his Loss. I will transcribe my Letter as I am assur'd it is from good Authority. After heating himself by Dancing, he went upon the Water. This was the Stroke—and his People soon observ'd an Alteration in his looks, but he held up some Days without attending at all to his Complaints. When he took to his bed, he declar'd it was over with him. Mr Schutz was in that part of the World and carry'd him James's Powder, which he took, contrary to his Physicians' Opinion. It did him much good, but he soon relaps'd. He had Prayers by his own Request constantly and desir'd all his Servants (even the meanest) to attend and pray by him, and with him. The last time he had Prayers, he took leave of each Servant, thank'd them and said he was sorry they wou'd have so melancholy a Voyage home with his Corpse. He then call'd for Wrottesley[34] and told him he wou'd have him go with the news of his Death to England. Go with it to Mr LeGrand and beg him to break it tenderly to his Mother. To the Prince of Brunswick,[35] he order'd an Express, with a Desire that the Princess might not hear it, till the Prince himself told her. To the King he wrote, lamenting his Opposition and Misconduct towards him and recommending Mr Wrottesley. To the Duke of Gloucester[36] he wrote, but had not Ability to finish regretting again his Behaviour to the King whom he call'd the Best of Brothers! He dy'd in great Agonies in his Bowels and was a day and a half in the Pangs of Death, but was sensible to the last. He said, "Life made great Resistance. It was hard work to die!" This detail (which is very affecting and must have made a deep impression on his Servants) I have copy'd from a Letter, thinking it worth your knowing, but as it is a Copy, I do not pretend to vouch the Truth of it, but (as I have said before) my Correspondent assures me it is from good Authority.

Adieu my Dear Friend. I hope it will not be long before you turn your face Southward. I am ready to obey an early Summons to Hill Street, for the Duke and Duchess of Beaufort set out for this Place next Week, and when the former has deposited the latter safe into my Hands, he will return to his Militia and I shall not think I discharge my Trust well if I keep her long out of the reach of Dr. Ford. My eldest Son is in Cornwall (so I venture to direct him to Mr Montagu). *Vous avez vu cette chienne d'Ecriture* [You have seen that scrap of writing] I am going to dispatch a Cousin to Newcastle nam'd William Glanville Evelyn, a Lieutenant in Brudennel's. We are sorry to part with him, for he is our Reader aloud, and tho' he has finish'd Lord Lyttelton's History, yet we shou'd find him something Else to read while we work round the fire, for I (*afin que Vous le sachier*) [as you know] net venerable Hoods fit for a Grandmother, but I had almost forgot my Cousin. Pray recommend him to the Hospitality of your Neighbours, but by no means stay to do him any yourself. He is very amiable and Dr. Evelyn's Son, you will believe, is sensible. From Newcastle, the Regiment marches on to Scotland, where he wou'd be very proud to carry any Commands of yours to the numberless Admirers you have in that Kingdom. Were it but a Glove to Lord Kaimes,[37] etc. etc. I hope Mrs Carter[38] is very well.

I wish you a very good Summer, and am always with the greatest Sincerity, your affectionate

faithful friend

Excuse these blots. I have wrote on till I am sleepy and it is the hour of sleep.

NOTES

1. Probably the wife of Charles Brett, the Admiral's flag lieutenant.
2. Rev. John Botham, friend of the Montagus and the Boscawens.
3. Temple West, Vice Admiral and second in command to Admiral Byng at Minorca, but not charged with the defeat there.
4. Mary Pitt, sister of William Pitt, the elder.
5. Sir Sydney Smythe (1705–1778) was the great-grandson of Edmund Waller's "Sacharissa," and called "the ugliest man of his day." At this time he was Baron of the Exchequer.
6. John Byng (1704–1757), appointed Admiral of the Blue in 1751 and sent to relieve Minorca, then threatened by the French fleet. During the engagement, Byng stopped to dress his line; the first line of ships was cut to pieces and the British were defeated. Byng was courtmartialed and shot on the quarterdeck of his flagship, the *Monarque*.
7. Her son, William, who had been inoculated for smallpox.

8. Dr. Caesar Hawkins (1711–1786), surgeon at St. George's Hospital and a fashionable physician.

9. *Lalauze*: ballet-master at Covent Garden. *Levier*: dancer at Drury Lane. His last season was 1754–55.

10. Anne Donellan, one of the "bluestockings."

11. Susannah Vansittart was Maid of Honour to the Princess of Wales.

12. Admiral Sir Charles Saunders (1713?–1775) was present at the victory of Quebec.

13. Mary, daughter of the elder Pitt and a favorite of all the bluestockings.

14. General William Blakeney (1672–1761) was in charge of the army garrison at Minorca. He withstood the French for seventy days, during which time he never went to bed; he surrendered honorably on condition his troops were not taken prisoner. He was 81 years old at the time.

15. Admiral Augustus John Hervey (1724–1779). Third Earl of Bristol. He took part in the Minorca engagement with Byng.

16. *Mr. and Mrs. Robert*: servants of Mrs. Boscawen who departed "without a word." *Mademoiselle Ellin*: Mrs. Boscawen's housekeeper.

17. Sir William Rowley (1690–1758) was Admiral of the Fleet in 1752, knighted in 1753.

18. Charles Brett was Admiral Boscawen's flag lieutenant.

19. Duncan was a local physician.

20. The Marquess of Worcester was the first child of Mrs. Boscawen's daughter Elizabeth, Duchess of Beaufort.

21. George, Lord Lyttleton (1709–1773) was Privy Councillor and Under Treasurer at this time.

22. Sir Robert Burdett, fourth Baronet of an ancient family, was active in government.

23. Lord Guilford, the Second Earl of that title, opposed William Pitt the younger.

24. Henry St. John, Viscount Bolingbroke (1678–1751) had been a friend of Alexander Pope's.

25. John Norris, M.P. Kitty Fisher was a notorious courtesan but devoted the rest of her life to repairing her husband's small fortune.

26. Caroline, widow of the Earl of Dalkeith, married Charles Townshend in 1755. He was Chancellor of the Exchequer.

27. Richard Cambridge (1717–1802) was a poet, author of *The Scribleriad*.

28. Monsieur de Guerchy was the French minister charged with attempted poisoning by the Chevalier d'Eon. De Guerchy was sent home by the English government.

29. George Keppel, Third Earl of Albermarle (1724–1772) was the general who captured Moro Castle at the Battle of Havana. He lived another five years.

30. Lord John Bute (1713–1792) was Prime Minister and First Lord of the Treasury, 1762–63.

31. Henry Temple, Second Viscount Palmerston (1739–1802) was Lord of the Admiralty.

32. Lady Henrietta Onslow was the wife of the first Earl, George, Lord of the Treasury.

33. Mrs. Boscawen's eldest son, Edward Hugh.

34. Sir Richard Wrottesley, Dean of Worcester.

35. Charles William Frederick, Hereditary Prince of Brunswick, a cousin.

36. His brother, William Henry.

37. Henry Home, Lord Kames (1696–1782), Scottish judge and philosophic writer.

38. Elizabeth Carter, one of the bluestocking circle.

ANNA LAETITIA BARBAULD

(1743–1825)

ANNA LAETITIA BARBAULD was born at Kibworth, Leicestershire, on 20 June 1743, the eldest child and only daughter of Dr. John Aikin, a brilliant Dissenting clergyman and teacher. A precocious child who could read with ease before she was two, she was taught Greek, Latin, Italian, and French by her father. In 1758 the family moved to Warrington, where Dr. Aikin was engaged as a classical and divinity tutor at the Dissenting academy there, and his children, surrounded by academic tradition, were trained in literary discipline. John, the son, later turned to medicine, but Anna Laetitia began writing early, although she did not publish anything until her volume of *Poems* in 1773, when she was thirty years old. It gave her an immediate success, entree into Elizabeth Robinson Montagu's bluestocking circle, and the admiration of Dr. Samuel Johnson.

The following year she married Rochemont Barbauld, six years younger than she, the son of a French Huguenot. Barbauld was a Dissenting minister and at this time had just been assigned a congregation in Palgrave, Suffolk. The income from the living was small and intermittent; to add to their resources they opened a boys' boarding school. It did well, and for the next twelve years Anna Laetitia kept house, wrote lectures on history and geography, and personally looked after the welfare of each student. It was an occupation that did not impress her friend Dr. Johnson, who commented acidly, "Miss Aikin was an instance of early cultivation, but in what did it terminate? In marrying a little Presbyterian parson, who keeps an infant boarding-school, so that all her employment now is

To suckle fools and chronicle small beer

... If I had bestowed such an education on a daughter, and had discovered that she thought of marrying such a fellow, I would have sent her to the Congress." The contemptuous reference to the Continental Congress in Philadelphia indicates the intensity of his disapproval.

It is obvious she did not concur with this view, for she took her teaching seriously and clearly enjoyed it. Her practice differed sharply from that of most eighteenth-century teachers. In an age when fear of caning was the common motivation for scholarship, she advocated the gentle approach of reason. Educators may not have agreed with her, but they had to admit that her methods produced excellent results.

She was very close to her brother, John Aikin, and when it became obvious that her marriage would be childless, she asked him if she and her husband could rear one of his rapidly increasing family. Accordingly, in 1777, the Barbaulds took two-year-old Charles Aikin into their home. For him, she wrote *Lessons for Children* (1778), a primary text that became very popular and soon replaced the ABC and hornbooks previously used. *Hymns in Prose* (1781), equally well received, established her as the first serious writer for children. Her educational theories anticipated the Montessori system, for she firmly believed that reading lessons should begin at the age of two.

In 1785, Rochemont Barbauld's health broke down. They closed the Palgrave school and set out for a visit to the Continent. It was more extended than they had planned; they did not return until 1796. Barbauld accepted a congregation at Hampstead and Anna Laetitia returned to teaching. Mothers were particularly eager to have her educate their daughters, and, without establishing a formal Academy, she took a few students. Again her approach differed from the standard: in place of deportment and fine needlework, her students compared Pope and Boileau, construed Horace, and read Gibbon's *Decline and Fall of the Roman Empire*.

They remained in Hampstead until 1802, when Barbauld was given the ministry of the Chapel in Stoke Newington, and at long last Anna Laetitia could be in daily contact with her brother John, who had moved there four years earlier. Here she continued to write and was an outspoken pamphleteer of unpopular causes: against the Test Act, against slavery, for abolition and, until the Terror, for the French Revolution. During these years, Rochemont Barbauld's mental condition began to deteriorate, and he became more and more alienated. He was unable to fulfill his duties to the congregation and eventually required constant care. Twice he tried to kill his wife, and at last, in 1808, he ended his life by suicide. Meanwhile, as a means of support, Anna Laetitia had edited Akenside's *Pleasures of the Imagination* (1795) and William Collins's *Odes* (1797), both with fine critical prefaces; in 1804 she produced a selection of essays from eighteenth-century journals and an edition of Samuel Richardson's *Letters* that is still a standard reference work.

Barbauld's death left her inconsolable, and she attempted to ease her sorrow by work: a fifty-volume edition of *British Novelists* (1810); a book of essays, *The Female Speaker* (1811); and one final poem, *One Thousand Eight Hundred Twelve* (1812), which was severely criticized. She wrote no more but remained in Stoke Newington near her brother and his family until her death on 9 March 1825.

Anna Laetitia Barbauld's letters reveal a lively and inquiring mind, not only well informed but alert to new experiences. Her personality was warm, and if she was not so gay or giddy as some of her sisters, she nonetheless enjoyed herself immensely. Her views on the education of girls in "On Female Studies" may appear hopelessly out of date to the modern woman, but they seem almost radical when set in the context of such contemporaries as Hannah More, who follows her. Without false modesty or militancy, Anna Laetitia destroyed the popular eighteenth-century notion that women could not be educated without irreparable damage to their brains.

BIBLIOGRAPHY

Works

The British Novelists. 50 vols. ed. Anna Laetitia Barbauld. London: F. C. and
    J. Rivington, 1810.
*Epistle to William Wilberforce, Esq. on the rejection of the Bill for abolishing the
    Slave Trade.* London: J. Johnson, 1791.
The Female Speaker. London: J. Johnson, 1811.
Hymns in Prose for Children. London: n.p., 1781.
Instructive Lessons for Children. London: Hamilton, Adams & Co., 1835.
A Legacy for Young Ladies. London: Longman & Co., 1826.
Lessons for Children. 4 vols. London: J. Johnson, 1812.
Letters of Maria Edgeworth and Anna Laetitia Barbauld. Selected and edited by
    Walter Sidney Scott. London: Golden Cockerell Press, 1953.
Poems. London: J. Johnson, 1773.
Works. With a Memoir by Lucy Aikin. 2 vols. London: Longman, Hurst, Rees,
    Orme, Brown, and Green, 1825. The letters in this book are from this edition.

Related Readings

Balfour, C. L. *A Sketch of Mrs. Barbauld.* London: W. and F. G. Cash, 1854.
Ellis, Grace A. *Memoir, Letters and a Selection from the Poems and Prose
    Writings of Mrs. Barbauld.* 2 vols. Boston: J. R. Osgood, 1874.

Le Breton, A. L. *Memoir of Mrs. Barbauld*. London: n.p., 1874.
Murch, Jerom. *Mrs. Barbauld and her Contemporaries*. London: n.p., 1877.
Oliver, G. A., ed. *Tales, poems & essays by Mrs. Barbauld . . . With a biographical sketch*. Boston: Roberts Bros., 1884.
Rodgers, Betsy. *Georgian Chronicle. Mrs. Barbauld and her Family*. London: Methuen, 1968.

❧

Letters

ANNA LAETITIA BARBAULD

Palgrave, 1774

To Dr. John Aikin

Thanks to my dear brother for his letter, and the copy of verses, which Mr. B. and I admire much. As to your system, I do not know what to say; I think I could make out just the contrary with as plausible arguments: as thus, Women are naturally inclined not only to love, but to all the soft and gentle affections, all the tender attentions and kind sympathies of nature. When, therefore, one of our sex shows any particular complacency towards one of yours, it may be resolved into friendship; into a temper naturally caressing, and those endearing intercourses of life which to a woman are become habitual. But when man, haughty, independent man, becomes sensible to all the delicacies of sentiment, and softens his voice and address to the tone of *les manières douces*, it is much to be suspected a stronger power than friendship has worked the change. *You* are hardly social creatures till your minds are humanized and subdued by that passion which alone can tame you to "all the soft civilities of life." Your heart requires a stronger fire to melt it than ours does; the chaste and gentle rays of friendship, like star-beams, may play upon it without effect; it will only yield to gross material fire. There is a pretty flight for you! In short, women, I think, may be led on by sentiment to passion; but men must be subdued by passion before they can taste sentiment. Well! I protest I think I have the best of the argument all to nothing. I'll go ask

Mr. Barbauld. Yes; he says my system will do. I beg I may have Dr E.'s[1] upon it, as I take him to be a pretty casuist in these affairs. I hope I am by this time richer by a nephew or niece: if it is a boy, I claim it;[2] if a girl, I will be content to stay for the next. I am afraid *my poor child*[3] is tossing upon the waves, for I have not heard yet of its arrival in London; and I cannot help feeling all a parent's anxiety for its fate and establishment in the world; several people here are so kind as to inquire after it, but I can give them no satisfaction.

To Mrs. Elizabeth Robinson Montagu, c. 1774

A kind of literary academy for ladies (for that is what you seem to propose), where they are to be taught in a regular, systematic manner the various branches of science, appears to me better calculated to form such characters as the *Précieuses* or the *Femme Sçavantes* of Molière than good wives or agreeable companions. Young gentlemen, who are to display their knowledge to the world, should have every motive of emulation, should be formed into regular classes, should read and dispute together, should have all the honours, and, if one may say so, the pomp of learning set before them, to call up their ardor. It is their business, and they should apply to it as such. But young ladies, who ought only to have such a general tincture of knowledge as to make them agreeable companions to a man of sense, and to enable them to find rational amusement for a solitary hour, should gain these accomplishments in a more quiet and unobserved manner; subject to a regulation like that of the ancient Spartans, the thefts of knowledge in our sex are only connived at while carefully concealed, and, if displayed, punished with disgrace. The best way for women to acquire knowledge is from conversation with a father, a brother, or a friend, in the way of family intercourse and easy conversation, and by such a course of reading as they may recommend. If you add to these an attendance upon those matters which are usually provided in schools, and perhaps such a set of lectures as Mr. Ferguson's, which it is not uncommon for ladies to attend, I think a woman will be in a way to acquire all the learning that can be of use to those who are not to teach or engage in any learned profession. Perhaps you may think that, having myself stepped out of the bounds of female reserve in becoming an author, it is with an ill grace I offer these sentiments; but, though this circumstance may destroy the grace, it does not the justice, of the remarks; and I am fully convinced that to have a too great fondness for books is little favorable to the happiness of a woman, especially one not in affluent circumstances. My situation has been peculiar, and would be no rule for others.

I should likewise object to the age proposed. Their knowledge ought to be acquired at an earlier period; geography, those languages it may be proper for them to learn, grammar, etc., are best learned from about nine to thirteen or fourteen, and will then interfere less with other duties. I should have little hopes of cultivating a love of knowledge in a young lady of fifteen, who came to me ignorant and untaught; and if she has laid a foundation, she will be able to pursue her studies without a master, or with such a one as only Rousseau gives his Sophie! It is too late then to *begin* to learn. The empire of the passions is coming on, a new world opens to the youthful eye; those attachments begin to be formed which influence the happiness of future life; the care of a mother, and that alone, can give suitable attention to this important period. At this period they have many things to learn which books and systems never taught. The grace and ease of polished society, with the established modes of behavior to every different class of people; the detail of domestic economy, to which they must be gradually introduced; the duties, the proprieties of behavior, which they must practise in their own family, in the families where they visit, to their friends, to their acquaintance; lastly, their behavior to the other half of their species, with whom before they were hardly acquainted, and who then begin to court their notice, the choice of proper acquaintance of that sex, the art to converse with them with a happy mixture of easy politeness and graceful reserve, and to wear off by degrees something of the girlish bashfulness without injuring virgin delicacy. These are the accomplishments which a young woman has to learn from fourteen or fifteen till she is married, or fit to be so; and surely these are not to be learned in a school. They must be learned partly at home, and partly by visits in genteel families; they cannot be taught where a number are together; they cannot be taught without the most intimate knowledge of a young lady's temper, connections, and views in life, nor without an authority and influence established upon all the former part of her life. For all these reasons, it is my full opinion that the best public education cannot at that period be equally serviceable with—I had almost said—an indifferent private one.

My next reason is, that I am not at all qualified for the task. I have seen a great deal of the manner of educating boys, and know pretty well what is expected in the care of them; but in a girls' boarding-school I should be quite a novice; I never was at one myself, have not even the advantage of younger sisters; indeed, for the early part of my life I conversed little with my own sex. In the village where I was, there were none to converse with; and this, I am very sensible, has given me an awkwardness in many common things which would make me most peculiarly unfit for the education of my own sex. But suppose I were tolerably qualified to instruct those of my own rank; consider that *these* must be of a class far superior to those I have lived amongst and conversed with. Young ladies of that rank ought to have their education superintended by a woman perfectly well-bred, from whose manner they may catch that ease and gracefulness which can only be learned from the best company; and she should be able to direct them, and judge of their progress in every genteel accomplishment. I could not judge of their music, their dancing, and, if I pretended to correct their air, they might be tempted to smile at my own; for I know myself remarkably deficient in gracefulness of person, in my air and manner, and in the easy graces of conversation. Indeed, whatever the kind partiality of my friends may think of me, there are few things I know well enough to teach them with any satisfaction, and many I never could learn myself. These deficiencies would soon be remarked when I was introduced to people of fashion; and were it possible that, notwithstanding, I should meet with encouragement, I could never prosecute with any pleasure an undertaking to which I should know myself so unequal; I am sensible the common boarding-schools are upon a very bad plan, and believe I could project a better, but I could not execute it.

Hampstead, February 1788

To Dr. John Aikin

We are waiting with great impatience for two things, your book and my sister,—your child and your wife, that is to say. . . .

I have been reading an old book, which has given me a vast deal of entertainment, —Father Herodotus, the father of history, and the father of lies too, his enemies might say. I take it for granted the original has many more beauties than Littlebury's humble translation, which I have been perusing; but, at any rate, a translation of an original author gives you an idea of the times totally different from what one gains by a modern compilation. I am much entertained in observing the traces of truth in many of his wildest fables; as where he says it was impossible to proceed far in Scythia on account of vast quantities of feathers which fell from heaven and covered all the country.

We are reading, too, Sir T. More's "Utopia." He says many good things; but it wants a certain salt, which Swift and others have put into their works of the same nature. One is surprised to see how old certain complaints are. Of the frequent executions, for instance: twenty men, he says, being hung upon one gibbet at a time; of arable land turned to pasture, and deserted villages in consequence.

I hope that the exertions which are now making for the abolition of the slave-trade will not prove all in vain. They will not, if the pleadings of eloquence or the cry of duty can be heard. Many of the most respectable and truly distinguished characters are really busy about it, and the press and the pulpit are both employed; so I hope something must be done. I expect to be highly gratified in hearing Mr. Hastings[4] trial, for which we are to have tickets some day. This impeachment has been the occasion of much pomp, much eloquence, and much expense; and there, I suppose, it will end. As somebody said, It must be put off for the judges to go their circuit, resumed late, and so it will fall into the summer amusements.

Hampstead, 1791

To Dr. John Aikin

. . . I do not know whether I said so before, but I cannot help thinking that the Revolution in France will introduce there an entire revolution in education, and particularly be the ruin of classical learning, the importance of which must be lessening every day; while other sciences, particularly that of politics and government, must rise in value, afford an immediate introduction to active life, and be necessary in some degree to everybody. All the kindred studies of the cloister must sink, and we shall live no longer on the lean relics of antiquity.

Apropos of France, Mrs. Montagu, who entertains all the aristocrats, had invited a marchioness of Boufflers and her daughter to dinner. After making her wait till six, the marchioness came, and made an apology for her daughter, that just as she was going to dress she was seized with a *dégoût momentance du monde* [sudden distaste for society], and could not wait on her.

There is a little Frenchman here at Hampstead who is learning the language, and he told us he had been making an attempt at some English verses. "I have made," says he, "four couplets in masculine and feminine rimes." "O sir," says I, "you have given yourself needless trouble; we do not use them." "Why, how so?" says he; "have you no rules, then, for your verse?" "Yes, sir; but we do not use masculine and feminine rimes."

Well, I could not make him comprehend there could be any regular poetry without these rimes.

Mr. Brand Hollis[5] has sent me an American poem, "The Conquest of Canaan,"—a regular epic in twelve books; but I hope I need not read it. Not that the poetry is bad, if the subject were more interesting. What had he to do to make Joshua his hero, when he had Washington of his own growth?

We are at present reading Anacharsis, and are much pleased with it. There is nothing of adventure, nothing like a novel; but the various circumstances relating to the Greeks are classed and thrown together in such a manner as to dwell on the mind. It has just the effect which it would have if in the Museum, instead of being shown separately the arms and dresses of different nations, you had figures dressed up and accoutred in them: the Otaheitan mourner walking to a *morai*; the warrior full armed in the attitude of attack; and the priest with all the various instruments of sacrifice before the altar. Thus they become grouped in the mind.

I want you to propose a metaphysical question to your society, which Mr. B——— and I have had great debates upon; and I want to know your opinion and my sister's. It is this: If you were now told that in a future state of existence you should be entirely deprived of your consciousness, so as not to be sensible you were the same being who existed here,— should you or should you not be now interested in your future happiness or misery? or, in other words, Is continued consciousness the essence of identity?

On Female Studies

ANNA LAETITIA BARBAULD

LETTER I

My dear young friend, —

If I had not been afraid you would feel some little reluctance in addressing me first; I should have asked you to begin the correspondence between us; for I am at present ignorant of your particular pursuits. I cannot guess whether you are climbing the hill of science, or wandering among the flowers of fancy; whether you are stretching your powers to embrace the planetary system, or examining with a curious eye the delicate veining of a green leaf and the minute ramifications of a sea-weed; or whether you are toiling through the intricate and thorny mazes of grammar. Whichever of these is at present your employment, your general aim, no doubt, is the improvement of your mind; and we will therefore spend some time in considering what kind and degree of literary attainments sit gracefully upon the female character.

Every woman should consider herself as sustaining the general character of a rational being, as well as the more confined one belonging to the female sex; and therefore the motives for acquiring general knowledge and cultivating the taste are nearly the same to both sexes. The line of separation between the studies of a young man and a young woman appears to me to be chiefly fixed by this, —that a woman is excused from all professional knowledge. Professional knowledge means all that is necessary to fit a man for a peculiar profession or business. Thus men study in order to qualify themselves for the law, for physic, for various departments in political life, for instructing others from the pulpit or the professor's chair. These all require a great deal of severe study and technical knowledge; much of which is nowise valuable in itself, but as a means to that particular profession. Now, as a woman can never be called to any of these professions, it is evident you have nothing to do with such studies. A woman is not expected to understand the mysteries of politics, because she is not called to govern; she is not required to know anatomy, because she is not to perform surgical operations; she need not embarrass herself with theological disputes, because she will neither be called upon to make nor to explain creeds.

Men have various departments in active life; women have but one, and all women have the same, differently modified indeed by their rank in life and other incidental circumstances. It is to be a wife, a mother, a mistress of a family. The knowledge belonging to these duties is your professional knowledge, the want of which nothing will excuse. Literary knowledge, therefore, in men, is often an indispensable duty; in women, it can be only a desirable accomplishment. In women it is more immediately applied to the purposes of adorning and improving the mind, of refining the sentiments, and supplying proper stores for conversation. For general knowledge women have, in some respects, more advantages than men. Their avocations often allow them more leisure; their sedentary way of life disposes them to the domestic, quiet amusement of reading; the share they take in the education of their children throws them in the way of books. The uniform tenor and confined circle of their lives makes them eager to diversify the scene by descriptions which open to them a new world; and they are eager to gain an idea of scenes on the busy stage of life from which they are shut out by their sex. It is likewise particularly desirable for women to be able to give spirit and variety to conversation by topics drawn from the stores of literature, as the broader mirth and more boisterous gayety of the other sex are to them prohibited. As their parties must be innocent, care should be taken that they do not stagnate into insipidity. I will venture to add that the purity and simplicity of heart which a woman ought never, in her freest commerce with the world, to wear off, her very seclusion from the jarring interests and coarser amusements of society, fit her in a peculiar manner for the worlds of fancy and sentiment, and dispose her to the quickest relish of what is pathetic, sublime, or tender. To you, therefore, the beauties of poetry, of moral painting, and all, in general, that is comprised under the term of polite literature, lie particularly open, and you cannot neglect them without neglecting a very copious source of enjoyment.

Languages are on some accounts particularly adapted to female study, as they may be learned at home without experiments or apparatus, and without interfering with the habits of domestic life; as they form the style, and as they are the immediate inlet to works of taste. But the learned languages, the Greek especially, require a great deal more time than a young woman can conveniently spare. To the Latin there is not an equal objection; and if a young person has leisure, has an opportunity of learning it at home by being connected with literary people, and is placed in a circle of society sufficiently liberal to allow her such an accomplishment, I do not see, if she has a strong inclination, why she should not make herself mistress of so rich a store of original entertainment: it will not in the present state of things excite either a smile or a stare in fashionable company. To those who do not intend to learn the language, I would strongly recommend the learning so much of the grammar of it as will explain the name and nature of cases, genders, inflection of verbs, etc.; of which, having only the imperfect rudiments in our own language, a mere English scholar can with difficulty form a clear idea. This is the more necessary, as all our grammars, being written by men whose early studies had given them a partiality for the learned languages, are formed more upon those than upon the real genius of our own tongue.

I was going now to mention French, but perceive I have written a letter long enough to frighten a young correspondent, and for the present I bid you adieu.

LETTER II

French you are not only permitted to learn, but you are laid under the same necessity of acquiring it as your brother is of acquiring Latin. Custom has made the one as much expected from an accomplished woman, as the other from a man who has had a liberal education. The learning French, or indeed any language completely, includes reading, writing, and speaking it. But here I must take the liberty to offer my ideas, which differ something from those generally entertained, and you will give them what weight you think they deserve. It seems to me that the efforts of young ladies in learning French are generally directed to what is unattainable; and if attained, not very useful, —the speaking it. It is utterly impossible, without such advantages as few enjoy, to speak a foreign language with fluency and a proper accent; and if even by being in a French family some degree of both is attained, it is soon lost by mixing with the world at large. As to the French which girls are obliged to speak at boarding-schools, it does very well to speak in England, but at Paris it would probably be less understood than English itself.

I do not mean by this to say that the speaking of French is not a very elegant accomplishment; and to those who mean to spend some time in France, or who, being in very high life, often see foreigners of distinction, it may be necessary; but in common life it is very little so: and for English people to meet together to talk a foreign language is truly absurd. There is a sarcasm against this practice as old as Chaucer's time: —

"... Frenche she spake ful fayre and fetisely,
After the schole of Stratford atte Bowe,
For Frenche of Paris was to her unknowe." [6]

But with regard to reading French, the many charming publications in that language, particularly in polite literature, of which you can have no adequate idea by translation, render it a very desirable acquisition. Writing it is not more useful in itself than speaking, except a person has foreign letters to write; but it is necessary for understanding the language grammatically and fixing the rules in the mind. A young person who reads French with ease and is so well grounded as to write it grammatically, and has what I should call a good English pronunciation of it, will, by a short residence in France, gain fluency and the accent; whereas one not grounded would soon forget all she had learned, though she had acquired some fluency in speaking. For speaking, therefore, love and cultivate your own: know all its elegancies, its force, its happy turns of expression, and possess yourself of all its riches. In foreign languages you have only to learn; but with regard to your own you have probably to unlearn, and to avoid vulgarisms and provincial barbarisms.

If, after you have learned French, you should wish to add Italian, the acquisition will not be difficult. It is valuable on account of its poetry—in which it far excels the French—and its music. The other modern languages you will hardly attempt, except led to them by some peculiar bent.

History affords a wide field of entertaining and useful reading. The chief thing to be attended to in studying it is to gain a clear, well-arranged idea of facts in chronological order, and illustrated by a knowledge of the places where such facts happened. Never read without tables and maps: make abstracts of what you read. Before you embarrass yourself in the detail of this, endeavor to fix well in your mind the arrangement of some leading facts which may serve as landmarks to which to refer the rest. Connect the history of different countries together. In the study of history the different genius of a woman, I imagine, will show itself. The detail of battles, the art of sieges, will not interest her so much as manners and sentiment; this is the food she assimilates to herself.

The great laws of the universe, the nature and properties of those objects which surround us, it is unpardonable not to know: it is more unpardonable to know, and not to feel the mind struck with lively gratitude. Under this head are comprehended natural history, astronomy, botany, experimental philosophy, chemistry, physics. In these you will rather take what belongs to sentiment and to utility than abstract calculations or difficult problems. You must often be content to know a thing is so, without understanding the proof. It belongs to a Newton to prove his sublime problems, but we may all be made acquainted with the result. You cannot investigate; you may remember. This will teach you not to despise common things; will give you an interest in everything you see. If you are feeding your poultry, or tending your bees, or extracting the juice of herbs, with an intelligent mind, you are gaining real knowledge; it will open to you an inexhaustible fund of wonder and delight, and effectually prevent you from depending for your entertainment on the poor novelties of fashion and expense.

But of all reading, what most ought to engage your attention are works of sentiment and morals. Morals is that study in which alone both sexes have an equal interest; and in sentiment yours has even the advantage. The works of this kind often appear under the seducing form of novel and romance: here, great care and the advice of your older friends is requisite in the selection. Whatever is true, however uncouth in the manner or dry in the subject, has a value from being true; but fiction in order to recommend itself must give us *la belle Nature*. You will find fewer plays fit for your perusal than novels, and fewer comedies than tragedies.

What particular share any one of the studies I have mentioned may engage of your attention will be determined by your peculiar turn and bent of mind. But I shall conclude with observing that a woman ought to have that general tincture of them all which marks the cultivated mind. She ought to have enough of them to engage gracefully in general conversation. In no subject is she required to be deep, —of none ought she to be ignorant. If she knows not enough to speak well, she should know enough to keep her from speaking at all; enough to feel her ground and prevent her from exposing her ignorance; enough to hear with intelligence, to ask questions with propriety, and to receive information where she is not qualified to give it. A woman who to a cultivated mind joins that quickness of intelligence and delicacy of taste which such a woman often possesses in a superior degree, with that nice sense of propriety which results from the whole, will have a kind of *tact* by which she will be able on all occasions to discern between pretenders to science and men of real merit. On subjects upon which she cannot talk herself, she will know whether a man talks with knowledge of his subject. She will not judge of systems, but by their systems she will be able to judge of men. She will distinguish the modest, the dogmatical, the affected, the over-refined, and give her esteem and confidence accordingly. She will know with whom to confide the education of her children, and how to judge of their progress and the methods used to improve them. From books, from conversation, from learned instructors, she will gather the flower of every science; and her mind, in assimilating everything to itself, will adorn it with new graces. She will give the tone to the conversation even when she chooses to bear but an inconsiderable part in it. The modesty which prevents her from an unnecessary display of what she knows, will cause it to be supposed that her knowledge is deeper than in reality it is: as when the landscape is seen through the veil of a mist, the bounds of the horizon are hid. As she will never obtrude her knowledge, none will ever be sensible of any deficiency in it, and her silence will seem to proceed from discretion rather than a want of information. She will seem to know everything by leading every one to speak of what he knows; and when she is with those to whom she can give no real information, she will yet delight them by the original turns of thought and sprightly elegance which will attend her manner of speaking on any subject. Such is the character to whom professed scholars will delight to give information, from whom others will equally delight to receive it: —the character I wish you to become, and to form which your application must be directed.

NOTES

1. Dr. Enfield, a friend of John Aikin.
2. Refers to the birth of Charles, the child they adopted.
3. Her *Devotional Pieces*, sent from Norfolk by sea, to be printed at Warrington.
4. The "trial of the century" was the impeachment of Warren Hastings (1732–1818), who was charged with exploiting his post as Governor General of India for personal gain. After a trial lasting seven years, he was unanimously acquitted, but was left penniless, having spent his entire fortune on his defense. Later, he was given a pension, and in 1813, when he appeared before a Parliamentary committee, the entire House of Commons stood bareheaded in his honor.
5. Thomas Brand took the name Hollis when Thomas Hollis left him his estate.
6. Referring to the nun in the Prologue to *Canterbury Tales*.

HANNAH MORE

1745–1833

H ANNAH MORE was born 2 February 1745 at Stapleton, Gloucestershire, the fourth of Jacob and Mary More's five daughters. Her father was master of the free school at Fishponds, and Hannah was trained early in intellectual pursuits. At the age of four, she could read well, and by the time she was eight, she was learning Latin and mathematics under her father's tutelage, although the latter subject was discontinued because her progress was so rapid that it seemed "unfeminine" to her worried parents.

At Bristol in 1757, her three older sisters, Mary, nineteen, Elizabeth, seventeen, and Sarah, fourteen, began what was to become the best-known girls' school of the eighteenth century. Hannah and her younger sister, Martha, joined them first as students, later as teachers. The curriculum, which included Italian and Spanish in addition to the usual French, was considered extremely advanced in an age when most girls' schools offered little more than housekeeping skills.

In 1767 Hannah was engaged to William Turner, an elderly local squire, but the engagement was terminated by mutual agreement. Hannah was not physically robust, and Turner settled £200 a year on her to relieve her of the necessity for teaching; he left her £1000 in his will besides. Neither of them ever married. She had been writing and publishing since 1762, and in 1773 her first play, *The Inflexible Captive*, a translation of Metastasio's *Attilio Regolo*, was well received in Bath; David Garrick saw it there and wanted it for Drury Lane. Though the play was never produced there, this premiere was the beginning of a long friendship between More and the Garricks.

In the winter of 1774–75 she visited London and was at once caught up in the literary life of the capital. She met and became friends with Edmund Burke, Sir Joshua Reynolds, Dr. Burney, and Dr. Samuel Johnson, who once called her "the most powerful versificatrix in the English language." In addition, she was added to the circle of bluestock-

273

ings that surrounded Mrs. Montagu, a circle she celebrated in her poem "Bas Bleu."

In 1777, when her tragedy *Percy* met with great success at Covent Garden, she herself became a "literary lion," a position she retained for the rest of her life. She often used the status to help others, and when she met Anna Yearsley, the poetical milkmaid in 1784, she arranged with Mrs. Montagu to have the lady's work published. As the excerpts from her letters indicate, she was not in the least prepared for the storm that followed her attempts to assist "Lactilla."

It was not the last controversy in which she was involved. Although she claimed she wanted only a quiet existence, her writings frequently caused considerable stir, especially her *Cheap Repository Tracts* (1799), a series of moral lessons and tales permeated with her own strong antislavery sentiments. She was criticized even more sharply when she and her sisters became interested in education for the poor. In 1790, after retiring from the management of their own school, they implemented their interest in the poor by establishing eleven schools in various villages near Bristol. Such an undertaking required courage and strength, for few saw much purpose in educating the lower classes. The More sisters fought prejudice, agreeing to teach on Sundays after church, since that was the only time the children were not working; they gave of their strength—even the frail Hannah would walk ten miles from one village to the next. They taught only the rudiments—they regarded higher education, particularly for females, as the prerogative of the upper classes—but their efforts were recognized as the results became clear: the crime rate dropped and the attainment of literacy bred neither discontent nor revolution among the poor.

In 1779 Hannah set forth her ideas in *Strictures on the Modern System of Female Education with a View to the Principles and Conduct of Women of Rank and Fortune.* Compared to young Mary Wollstonecraft's *Thoughts on the education of daughters* (1787), More's emphasis on traditional decorum, propriety, and morality might seem old-fashioned and outmoded. The major difference between them, however, was only that the kind of education More felt was basic to the moral health of society, Wollstonecraft claimed as a woman's right. The village schools were eventually closed or replaced by the state schools, but More's interest in education did not subside. Her *Hints toward forming the Character of a Young Princess* (1805) was extremely popular and was said to have influenced the Prince of Wales' daughter Charlotte, the princess who, had she lived, would have become queen instead of Victoria.

More's novel *Coelebs in Search of a Wife* (1818) was an immediate success despite its severe moralizing and its static plot. It gives an image of the "ideal" female as seen by the late eighteenth-century. More did not pursue novel writing further, but turned instead to tracts on practical religion: *Practical Piety* (1811), *Christian Morals* (1812), and *The Character and Practical Writings of St. Paul* (1815). In 1812 she and her sisters settled at Barley Wood, where the tight family circle was broken by the death of Mary the following year. Deaths of the other sisters followed one by one until Hannah alone remained. For several years she was an invalid, but in 1828 she recovered enough to move to Clifton Wood, where she died on 7 September 1833.

Active to within a few weeks of her death, she carried on a voluminous correspondence all her life, and there is ample evidence that she took her letter writing seriously. When not involved in a specific problem, her letters were long and thoughtful and displayed a remarkable range of interests, especially when she was communicating with people like Elizabeth Montagu or Horace Walpole. Her reputation declined rapidly in the nineteenth century. The Romantics were intolerant of her religious views and her strict interpretation of morality. Few critics were as charmed by her as Johnson had been, and the last edition of her *Works* was published a year after her death. Yet Hannah More has much to offer; if in many ways she is a product of her times, it is equally true that often she steps beyond them, demonstrating a new range of interests and achievements was possible for the properly educated woman.

BIBLIOGRAPHY

Works

Bible Rhymes. London: n.p., 1821.
Bishop Bonner's Ghost. Strawberry Hill: Thomas Kirgate, 1789.
Cheap Repository Tracts. 3 vols. London: J. Marshall, 1799.
Christian Morals. London: n.p., 1813.
Coelebs in Search of a Wife. 2 vols. London: T. Cadell & W. Davies, 1808.
Essay on the Character and practical writings of St. Paul. 2 vols. London: T. Cadell & W. Davies, 1815.
Essays on various subjects. London: J. Wilkie, T. Cadell, 1777.
Florio and *Bas Bleu.* London: n.p., 1786.
The Inflexible Captive. Bristol: n.p., 1774.

Letters of Hannah More. Edited by R. Brimley Johnson. London: John Lane, 1925.
Letters of Hannah More to Zachary Macaulay, Esq. Edited by A. Roberts. Edinburgh: n.p., 1860.
The Miscellaneous Works of Hannah More. 2 vols. London: n.p., 1840.
Moral Sketches. London: T. Cadell, 1830.
Observations on the effect of Theatrical Representations with respect to Religion and Morals. Bath: J. Hume, 1804.
Percy. London: n.p., 1778.
The Pilgrims. London: Religious Tract Society, 1830.
Sacred Dramas. London: n.p., 1782.
Sir Eldred of the Bower and the Bleeding Rock. London: n.p., 1776.
Strictures on the Modern System of Female Education. London: T. Cadell and W. Davies, 1799.
The Twelfth of August, or The Feast of Freedom. London: J. & T. Clarke, 1819.
The Works of Hannah More in prose and verse. Cork: n.p., 1778.
The Works of Hannah More. 11 vols. London: T. Cadell, 1830.

Related Readings

Balfour, C. L. *A Sketch of Hannah More and her sisters.* London: W. and F. G. Cash, 1854.
Buckland, A. J. *The Life of Hannah More.* London: R. T. S., [1882].
Cropper, Margaret B. *Sparks among the Stubble.* London: Longmans Green, 1955.
Harland, Marion. "Hannah More," in *Literary Hearthstones.* New York: G. P. Putnam's Sons, 1900.
Hopkins, Mary Alden. *Hannah More and her Circle.* New York: Longmans Green, 1947.
Jones, M. G. *Hannah More.* Cambridge: Cambridge University Press, 1952.
MacSarcasm, Rev. Archibald [William Shaw]. *The Life of Hannah More, with a critical review of her writings.* Bristol: T. Hurst, 1802.
Meakin, Annette M. B. *Hannah More.* London: Smith, Elder & Co., 1911.
More, Martha. *Mendip Annals.* Edited by A. Roberts. London: n.p., 1859.
Roberts, William. *Memoirs of the Life and Correspondence of Mrs. Hannah More.* 4 vols. London: R. B. Seeley & W. Burnside, 1834.
Silvester, James. *Hannah More, Christian philanthropist.* London: Thynne & Co., 1934.
———. *The Story of Hannah More.* Stirling: Drummond's Tract Depot, [1928].
Tabor, Margaret E. *Pioneer Women.* London: Sheldon Press, 1925–33.
Thompson, Henry. *The Life of Hannah More.* London: T. Cadell, 1838.
Walford, Lucy B. *Four Biographies from 'Blackwood'.* Edinburgh: W. Blackwood & Sons, 1888.
Weiss, Harry B. *Hannah More's Cheap Repository Tracts in America.* New York: New York Public Library, 1946.
Yonge, C. M. *Hannah More.* London: Allen & Co., 1883.

Letters to
Elizabeth Robinson Montagu

HANNAH MORE

Bristol Aug 27 1784

My dear Madam

I have had a great struggle in my mind whether I should write to you or not; I could not easily settle if it were better to be troublesome or ungrateful; however, as most people had rather be thought wicked than foolish, I had determined to let Ingratitude triumph, rather than break in on your precious moments by troubling you with my thanks for the most pleasant, most profitable, most delightful fortnight I ever passed. I can truly say that if to have the liveliest admiration of your wit, and the keenest sensibility of your goodness be in any degree to deserve the blessing I enjoy'd, then am I not quite as unworthy of it, as I appear to be: —But my dear Madam, tho' I wou'd have done violence to my *own* gratitude by my silence, yet I do not find it easy or just to forbear returning you the warm and lively acknowledgments of the *Poetical Milkwoman*.[1] She was inexpressibly affected at your generous bounty; and I believe you wou'd have thought her silence and her tears as touching as the most elaborate expressions that ever flowed from the "rattling tongue of saucy and audacious Eloquence."

I have enquired into her life and Conversation, which I find to be very blameless. She is about seven and twenty, and what will excite your compassion for a Woman of *Sentiment*, was sacrificed for *money* at seventeen to a silly man whom she did not like; the Husband had an Estate of near *Six pounds* a year, and the marriage was thought too advantageous to be refused. But misfortunes, six Children, and the Poet's vice, want of Oeconomy, have dissipated this *ample* Patrimony; so that in the severity of last Winter, herself, husband, babes, and her aged Mother all got together into a Stable—to die of hunger! —the Mother actually perished; the rest were saved by a gentleman accidentally looking into the stable; they are now in a flourishing way, have nine Pigs and a Cow. I had a great deal of Conversation with her, she discovers great strength of understanding and uncommon fortitude. She assured me she wou'd not change the pleasures of a contemplative mind for all the advantages the world cou'd give and that tho' she never allowed herself to look into a book till her work was done and her children asleep, yet in those moments she found that reading and writing cou'd allay hunger and subdue calamity. She told me it wou'd look like affectation were she to describe the tranquility of her spirit, and her entire self-possession when famine and death stared her in the face. I told her I envied the state of her mind; don't envy me, ma'am, she reply'd, for I have great doubts as to my Motives; I am afraid my mind is rather *hardened* than *subdued*. It is a calm temper and a lively Imagination which support rather than the religious confidence which my dear Mother had. I have too much imagination to have a proper delight in serious books; I read them but not with proper delight! (I give you her own words). I asked who were her favorite authors? "Among the Heathens," said she, "I have met with no such Composition as in Virgil's Georgics." How I stared! besides the choice was so *professional*. Of English Poets her favorites are Milton and Dr Young, the latter she said has an ardour and boldness in his Imagination that was very delightful to her. —I asked her why she did not apply for relief in her distress; this was her answer, "To hard hearts it is useless to apply, and I cannot bear to afflict tender ones."

I make no apology for this minute account, for independent of the pleasure you will feel at having relieved so singular a person you will like to know she is not an unworthy one. I will send you some of her verses the first opportunity. I wou'd have done it now, had not Mr. Pitt, that Toe to Phoebus who taxes *light* and *letters*, put it out of my power. I beg my best Compliments to Mr. Montagu—indeed he is right pleasant, in spite of that barbarous German. I implore you not to give yourself the trouble to answer this; but my Conscience is easier now I have sent you the thanks of the poor Poetess. You may think I mean myself if you please.

Dear Madam your ever oblig'd

27 September [1784]

I am but just returned from a long and pleasant Excursion into Somersetshire. —A thousand, and ten Thousand thanks, dearest Madam, for the delightful letter you have done me the honour to write me. Your proposal is very tempting; I believe irresistible. But I am so *genée* in point of time, and so hampered with less agreeable engagements that I hardly dare to take the liberty to propose to you, Madam, the only time I have to dispose of—This must be if you please, either from the eighth to the sixteenth, or from the twelfth to the nineteenth or thereabouts, a week being my utmost limit; the latter time most suitable to me, if it will not interfere with the Primate's visit.

I hear my little eccentric, extraordinary friend (of whom Mrs Garrick[2] and I said so much to you) is in these quarters: I have not yet seen him, nor do I know any thing of his plans and projects; but if your curiosity and that of Mr Montagu continues for seeing this very great little genius, perhaps I might be able to pack him in a corner of my valise, for he does not occupy half the space of a Balloon Hat, being more diminutive than either Ibad, Syahouk or Bobekon, the three Crumps of Damascus. Now, my dear madam, I beg you will speak with the plainest truth, and not imagine that I shall be in the smallest degree hurt if tis not quite convenient and agreeable to you to see this odd but ingenious animal. I know how you are circumstanced about beds, etc. and shall not breathe a syllable to him till I have your commands; and even then I am by no means sure that he is to be come at, for he is much *fêté* and invited out to my great regret, as he loses all that precious time in *being agreeable* which he ought to devote to severer employments. He is idle but virtuous, if idle people can ever be called so, no, if indeed he can be called idle, who has amass'd such a fund of knowledge, good and bad. —

Our poetical milkwoman drinks tea here this afternoon. I shall examine her more thoroughly. All that you say on her subject is dictated by Wisdom itself. I am *utterly* against taking her out of her station. *Stephen*[3] was an excellent Bard as a *Thrasher*, but as the Court Poet, and rival of Pope, detestable. I will get Ossian[4] for her; as she has never read Dryden's, I have given her his Tales, and the most decent of the Metamorphoses. Best Compliments to Mr Montagu. I hope he is quite recovered. I rejoyce at your continued health and am most gratefully,

Dear Madam

October 22 1784

It was said, I think, of the Duke of Buckingham,[5] that he wasted more wit at a supper than wou'd have lasted other men a year: I never had the honour to sit down to supper with you, without secretly applying this remark to you; and never receive a letter from you but that I think the wit of it wou'd last a good Manager full as long; and yet all his correspondents think his letters very ingenious too. In your last letter I admired a quality which almost effaced the wit of it, I mean your humanity towards our poor Poetess. All I see of her, raises my opinion of her genius. You judge with your usual wisdom in saying that she shou'd not be corrupted by being made *idle* or *useless*, but in order to soften the rigours of the approaching Winter, I have hired for her a *little* Maid, to help her feed her pigs, and nurse the little ones, while she herself sells her Milk, and have desired her to put one or two of her children out to learn to read; the idea of bringing them up in ignorance being to her more terrible than their being hungry. When I have the happiness of seeing you, dear Madam, I shall shew you her verses, and talk her over more at large. In the mean time I send you a passage or two from a longer Poem, which you will allow to be extraordinary for a milker of Cows, and a feeder of Hogs, who has never even *seen* a Dictionary.

Speaking of Conscience, she says:

"That secret Arbitrator
Shall give thee self-applause, or deep remorse;
Heav'n guard thee from that Harpy never fill'd
Still, still insatiate as the bird of Jove,
That deeply gores the breast for Meals eternal
Nor knows a glut from ever grazing food."

And yet she has never heard of Eschylus. —again

"O say, for strong-ey'd Faith has borne *you* far,
Beyond the gloomy Chambers of the grave,
Speak loudly to my late corrected Soul,
That sure reward awaits the blameless mind,
Else will I give the strenuous struggle o'er,
Throw up your angel mind as painted Shade,
Or notion strong, from early precept caught,
Rove thro' the maze of all-alluming Sense,
And this side Jordan every hope shall fix,
Mere ravings all—these crude ideas die,
As Faith to Calvary's Mount directs my view;
Nor will I lose, thus humbled as I am,
My dear bought claim to immortality.
    Excuse me, Stella! lo! I guideless stray,
No friendly hand assists my wilder'd thought,
Uncouth, unciviliz'd, and rudely rough,
Not with completion, or the artists hand
To add a something more. —Such is the Mind
Which thou mayst yet illumine: tis a task
For angels thus to raise the groveling Soul

And bid it pant for more than earthly bliss.
Then shew Heaven's op'ning glories to my eyes,
And I will view thee as the fount of light
Which pierc'd old Chaos to his depths profound,
While all his native horrors stood reveal."

Confess, dear Madam, that you and I know many a head competently stored with Greek and Latin which cou'd not have produced better verses. I never met with an Ear more nicely tuned.

You must charge this trouble to the Account of your own goodness, and *that* is a Treasury on which the demands are so general and so large that you need have little to do but answer them. Best Compliments to Mr Montagu

Dearest Madam, your ever oblig'd

7 December 1784

Allow me to thank you, as I do most cordially, for the happy days you caused me to spend at Bath; they were the very reverse of the good Patriarch's, for they were "few and full of *pleasure.*" I cannot help being anxious to know if you have recovered your fine Sandleford health and countenance which you brought with you to Bath, and which I most warmly wish you may take with you to London.

I cannot help troubling you, dear Madam, with a new production of Lactilla, which I am the more impatient you shou'd see because it betrays totally new Talents, for I think you will agree with me that there is in it, wit, ease and pleasantry; and what sounds quite ridiculous, the Poem appears to me to have the tone of good Company and a gentility that is wonderful in a milker of Cows and a feeder of Hogs. I have begun my Subscription, at the head of which stands the honour'd name of Mrs Montagu. I think to fix the Price at five Shillings; I mean that shall be the *legal* demand, for the Poems, which I fear will be but a mince Brochure for the money. Any names you can get you will do me the honour to transmit to me, to swell my list.

I have no news from the Vesey; I hope you have better luck; and that the last letter is found.

As I have made a Party to go to Town from hence, I shall not be able to stop a minute at Bath, by which I shall lose the happiness of seeing you. I shall set out at six on Friday morning, and if you will send any pacquet before eight inclosed to me at the Christopher Inn near the Market, it shall be safely convey'd and delivered in London. In the mean time, is it

too much just to beg the favour to know how you do, which I am very
solicitous to know. My sisters join in best respects with, dearest Madam
your much obliged

                                                        and very obedient

                                                    Adelphi, Wednesday 3 a clock
                                                            [June, 1785]

I arrive this morning in Town after vagabonding about the Country for
three weeks; part of the time in Kent, part with our friend, Mrs Boscawen, at her little Villa. I have not yet seen Mrs Garrick, but I have had
another great pleasure, that of receiving your most agreeable Letter,
which came the moment I did. I never again will believe Rumour nor any
of her hundred tongues. This same lying Deity has said from day to day
and week to week that Mrs Montagu was expected in Portman Square
and that alone prevented my writing as in duty bound, after all your great
goodness to Lactilla. In truth, I waited for that history till I knew exactly
the amount of her *fortune*. Were you not surprised, dear Madam, to see
so magnificent a book? Really, the Crown subscribers have a bargain, to
my great regret. We printed 1250 copies, and are obliged to sell the
supernumerary copies at six to indemnify us a little; I paid near fourscore
pounds *all* expenses, have lodged 350 in the Five per Cents which will
produce about £18 a year, and shall take her down about £20 to cloathe
her family and furnish her House. As I wished to have the honour of *your*
name to sanction my own, I have laid out the money in your name,
madam, and mine, having first had an instrument drawn up by the
Lawyer signed by Yearsley and his wife, allowing us the controul of the
money, and putting it out of the Husband's power to touch it. All the
trouble this will ever give you, my dear Madam, will be when you come to
Town next Winter, to have the goodness to let me wait on you to the
Bank, where it seems it is necessary we shou'd appear in person to accept
it. —Mrs E. Hervey was so good as to bring me the names of eleven
persons (too late to be printed) and the Money, three pounds, fifteen. I
hope you will not disapprove of what I have done, and who knows but
one day or another you will have the bounty to tell me so in a letter
directed to Bristol? for I am on the wing thither, I set out tomorrow, but as
I have promised a little visit at Oxford, I cannot, alas, accept of your
delightful proposal to call at Sandleford. Wou'd I cou'd!

Mrs Garrick is come in—I find she has at last had the good fortune to
get your letter, and has answer'd it; so I have nothing to say further but to

repeat that she impatiently waits commands and longs to see you at Hampton. O dear! and I shall be quite *another where*. We have just learnt that the incurable Vesey has left that dear woman[6] *nothing* but that hole of a house and the old Coach! The plate to Lord Lucan after the death of the heir. What an absurd fellow! and £1000 to his W————. He was determined to make his memory hated as well as despised.

I am in all the horrors of packing up, which I hope will be some excuse for this abominable scrawl; but the fairest hand and the finest eloquence wou'd tell but very imperfectly how much I am, my dear

Madam, your ever

obliged and faithful

Bristol, 21 July 1785

My dear Madam

Accept, I beseech you, the warmest congratulations that the highest esteem, and the most grateful affection can offer on the present joyful occasion;[7] by the concurring testimony of all parties, and of all persons, indifferent or interested, there never was a marriage of happier, brighter prospects. May He in whose hand is the disposal of all events realize and perpetuate them. I have always been particularly struck with that passage of David, where he considers it is an Act of Omnipotence itself, "That he maketh men to be of one mind in an house." This, I take it, is the great secret of human happiness; and I reall think *vos mariés* are as likely to find it out as any two young people I ever saw, as they both seem to be possessed of that genuine good temper without which all the talents and I had almost said, all the virtues will not make them happy. Do me the favour, dear Madam, to present my most cordial respects and good wishes.

I envied Mrs Garrick the sole possession of you at Hampton; it was a shameful monopoly and such as no fair Trader shou'd engross to herself. However, she had one claim which I won't pretend to dispute, she *does* know and feel the value of the blessing she enjoy'd.

It is with sorrow, that I stain a paper, which I had intended to consecrate to joy and congratulation with an unworthy, and to me, a painful subject. Your exquisite penetration and deep knowledge of the world will prepare you to hear, with less pain than I can write it, that our unhappy Milkwoman has treated me with the blackest ingratitude. There is hardly a species of calumny with which she does not load me; the second time she saw me after my return here, when I had invited her to supper and was treating her with all imaginable tenderness, she accused me in the openest and fullest manner of a design to defraud her of the money, and demanded it. She had before cheerfully signed the deed which impower'd you, Madam, and me to be Trustees for her Children, lest her Husband shou'd spend it. When I recovered my Speech, I told her the money was in the Bank of England, that Mrs Montagu had condescended to be joint Trustee, but nothing wou'd appease her fury but having the money to spend, and which she expected in a fit of vulgar resentment, I shou'd give her, but my sense of duty will not allow it. Her other charges against me are that I have spoilt her verses by my corrections, and that she will write another book directly to show I was of no use to her, that I have ruined her reputation by the Preface which is full of falsehoods, that it was the height of insult and barbarity to tell that she was poor and a Milkwoman. —My dear Madam, I cou'd weep over our fallen human Nature. What wretched creatures are we when our natural pride is unsubdued by religious principle! But what shall I say to *you* whose bounties to her have been so manifest, so noble? —As her gratitude was not my motive of action, I am not so much touched in that view, and I pray that it may not harden my heart to the next object which presents itself: *You* have been used to these sorts of recompences. I have spent above eight months entirely in this business, I have written above a thousand pages on her subject and with your generous concurrence have got near five hundred pounds; I believe it will be more, for I am preparing a second Edition, and am trying to get the husband a place. I do not see her, of which she is very glad, as she says I am such a Tyrant; I hear she wears very fine Gauze Bonnets, long lappets, gold Pins etc. Is such a Woman to be trusted with her poor Children's money?

Dear Madam ever Yours

Bristol, 16 September 1785

My dear Madam

It is grievous to me to disturb your elegant and happy retirement with the turbulent wickedness of the wretched object of your bounty. The Peace of my life is absolutely broken by her revenge. As I refuse to see her, I had a letter from her lately, of which I must torment you with an extract—*le voici*:

"Had your protection arisen from humanity, my gratitude wou'd not have been erased, or had you been activated by a disinterested desire to serve me; but your late treatment has set a narrow bound to my gratitude;

which cannot be avowed for favours which circumstances convince me arise more from your vanity than generosity. You tax me with ingratitude, for why? You found me poor yet proud, if it can be called pride to feel too much humbled by certain obligations, and above submitting to servility. You helped to place me in the public Eye; my success you think beyond my abilities, and purely arising from your protection, but granting this to your vanity, surely mine does not *soar*, in thinking the singularity of my situation wou'd have secured me some success. This will soon be tried. And let me ask you what I have gain'd by your professed friendship? I find myself deprived of the money which my Poems, and the torturing tale of my distress have raised. My feelings and gratitude is traduced, but the public may yet discover my despised situation. —I cannot think it ingratitude to disown as obligation a proceeding which must render me and my children your poor dependents for ever. I have trusted more to your *probity* than the event justifies. You have led me to sign a settlement which defrauds me of my right, and makes it ever received your peculiar gift. Your bankruptcy or death may lose it for ever, and let me ask you Miss More what security you have ever given my children whereby they may prove their claim? I am sorry remonstrance is needful, or your motives less bare to doubt and suspicion. My mind is too haughty not to glory in being grateful for obligations it cou'd stoop to receive. If you are judged wrong, confute my opinions. On this depends my raising a *Monument* in my second Publication either to your just or unjust proceeding. The choice be yours. —As it's necessary for *my* character to be *wrecked* to do justice to *yours*, I submit to it; in this it is your turn to be grateful. Ann Yearsley."

Methinks, my dear Madam, I see your noble indignation at reading this curious Epistle. To give up the Trust of the Funded Money just now, wou'd be sacrificing a duty to a fear, and appear, to *her*, at least, as if I were afraid to stand the scrutiny. Do not think, dear Madam, that she will ever venture to abuse *you*, she has more sense. I shall be infinitely obliged to you to write me a few lines which may be reported to her, to say that you condescend to retain the Trust, till we can both rid ourselves of it by placing it in the hands of some responsible Person. I feel for you, dear Madam, too exalted a veneration and love to let you be brought into any scrape; grieved enough that I have been the means of your wasting your patronage and money on such a Wretch. You see she affects to name *me* only in the trust, and indeed I very imprudently told her that *you* wou'd have nothing to do with her, which she affected to call very noble, and to be persuaded that you wou'd give it up to her. I laid out for her £318 to buy £350 on the five per cents. It is bought, as you were pleased to permit, in your name and mine. I will send you the Bank Receipt for it and the state of my accounts for this woman, if you will allow me; but I dread to give you trouble. I hear they have put me in the Papers. I take not the least notice of any of *their* Scurrilities (for she has a low fellow, one Shiells, a Gardener in London, who assists her). Nor shall I answer any of their letters. I take care of her affairs in the mean time, and am bringing out a second Edition in the Advertisement to which I have made this alteration note:

"The Editor has raised a very handsome sum of money which is placed in the Public Funds, vested in Trustees hands for the benefit of the Author's Family." This is all the answer I think it necessary to make. —My dear Madam, have the goodness to assure me that you will strengthen my hands by letting your name stay for the present, and I shall rejoyce to renounce it as soon as it can be done with dignity.

Your ever obliged and faithful

NOTES

1. Anna Yearsley (1756–1822), Bristol milkwoman and poet.

2. Eva Marie Violetti (1724–1822) was a dancer until she married the most popular actor of the day, David Garrick (1717–1779). She was a close friend of Miss More.

3. Stephen Duck (1705–1756), "the Thresher Poet." A Hampshire farmer, he had been considered for the post of Poet Laureate in 1730.

4. A legendary early Scottish bard. In 1762 James Macpherson published fradulent "translations" that were exposed by Dr. Johnson, but were nonetheless admired.

5. George Villiers, Duke of Buckingham (1628–1687). Restoration rake and writer.

6. Mrs. Elizabeth Vesey, a member of the bluestocking circle.

7. The marriage of Mrs. Montagu's nephew, Lord Rokeby.

‿ؤ

The Practical Use of Female Knowledge, with a Sketch of the Female Character and a Comparative View of the Sexes

HANNAH MORE

The chief end to be proposed, in cultivating the understandings of women is to qualify them for the practical purposes of life. Their knowledge is not often, like the learning of men, to be reproduced in some literary composition, and never in any learned profession, but it is to come out in conduct: it is to be exhibited in life and manners. A lady studies, not that she may qualify herself to become an orator or a pleader; not that she may learn to debate, but to act. She is to read the best books, not so much to enable her to talk of them, as to bring the improvement which they furnish to the rectification of her principles and the formation of her habits. The great uses of study to a woman are to enable her to regulate her own mind, and to be instrumental to the good of others.

To woman, therefore, whatever be her rank, I would recommend a predominance of those more sober studies, which, not having display for their object, may make her wise without vanity, happy without witnesses, and content without panegyrists; the exercise of which may not bring celebrity, but will improve usefulness. She should pursue every kind of study which will teach her to elicit truth; which will lead her to be intent upon realities; will give precision to her ideas; will make an exact mind. She should cultivate every study which, instead of stimulating her sensibility, will chastise it; which will neither create an excessive nor a false refinement; which will give her definite notions; will bring the imagination under dominion; will lead her to think, to compare, to combine, to methodise; which will confer such a power of discrimination, that her judgment shall learn to reject what is dazzling, if it be not solid; and to prefer, not what is striking, or bright, or new, but what is just. That kind of knowledge which is rather fitted for home consumption than foreign exportation is peculiarly adapted to women.

It is because the superficial nature of their education furnishes them with a false and low standard of intellectual excellence, that women have too often become ridiculous by the unfounded pretensions of literary vanity; for it is not the really learned, but the smatterers, who have generally brought their sex into discredit, but an absurd affectation, which has set them on despising the duties of ordinary life. . . . There have not been wanting ill-judging females, who have affected to establish an unnatural separation between talents and usefulness, instead of bearing in mind that talents are the great appointed instruments of usefulness; who have acted as if knowledge were to confer on woman a kind of fantastic sovereignty, which should exonerate her from the discharge of female duties; whereas, it is only meant the more eminently to qualify her for the performance of them. A woman of real sense will never forget, that while the greater part of her proper duties are such as the most moderately gifted may fulfil with credit, —since Providence never makes that to be very difficult which is generally necessary; —yet that the most highly endowed are equally bound to fulfil them; and let her remember that the humblest of these offices, performed on Christian principles, are wholesome for the minds even of the most enlightened, as they tend to the casting down of those "high imaginations" which women of genius are too much tempted to indulge.

For instance, ladies whose natural vanity has been aggravated by a false education may look down on *economy* as a vulgar attainment, unworthy of the attention of a highly cultivated intellect; but this is the false estimate of a shallow mind. Economy, such as a woman of fortune is called on to practise, is not merely the petty detail of small daily expenses, the shabby curtailments and stinted parsimony of a little mind, operating on little concerns; but it is the exercise of a sound judgment exerted in the comprehensive outline of order, of arrangement, of distribution; of regulations by which alone well-governed societies, great and small, subsist. She who has the best regulated mind will, other things being equal, have the best regulated family. . . . The difference is, that to a narrow-minded vulgar economist the details are continually present; she is overwhelmed by their weight, and is perpetually bespeaking your pity for her labours, and your praises for her exertions; she is afraid you will not see how much she is harassed. She is not satisfied that the machine moves harmoniously, unless she is perpetually exposing every secret spring to observation. Little events and trivial operations engross her whole soul; while a woman of sense, having provided for their probable recurrence, guards against the inconveniences, without being disconcerted by the casual obstructions which they offer to her general scheme. Subordinate expenses and inconsiderable retrenchments should not swallow up that attention which is better bestowed on regulating the general scale of expense, correcting and reducing an overgrown establishment, and reforming radical and growing excesses.

Superior talents, however, are not so common, as, by their frequency, to offer much disturbance to the general course of human affairs; and many a lady, who tacitly accuses herself of neglecting her ordinary duties because she is a *genius*, will perhaps be found often to accuse herself as unjustly as good St. Jerome, when he laments that he was beaten by the angel for being too Ciceronian in his style.

The truth is, women who are so puffed up with the conceit of talents as to neglect the plain duties of life will not frequently be found to be women of the best abilities. And here may the author be allowed the gratification of observing, that those women of real genius and extensive knowledge, whose friendship has conferred honour and happiness on her own life, have been, in general, eminent for economy and the practice of domestic virtues; and have risen superior to the poor affectation of neglecting the duties and despising the knowledge of common life, with which literary women have been frequently, and not always unjustly, accused.

A romantic girl with a pretension to sentiment, which her still more ignorant friends mistake for genius, —for in the empire of the blind the one-eyed are kings, —and possessing something of a natural ear, has, perhaps, in her childhood exhausted all the images of grief, and love, and fancy, picked up in her desultory poetical reading, in an elegy on a sick linnet, or a sonnet on a dead lap-dog; she begins thenceforward to be considered as a prodigy in her little circle; surrounded with fond and flattering friends, every avenue to truth is shut out; she has no opportunity of learning that her fame is derived not from her powers but her position; and that when an impartial critic shall have made all the necessary deductions, such as, that she is a neighbour, that she is a relation, that she is a female, that she is young, that she has had no advantages, that she is pretty, perhaps; when her verses come to be stripped of all their extraneous appendages, and the fair author is driven off her 'vantage ground of partiality, sex, and favour, she will commonly sink to the level of ordinary capacities; while those more quiet women, who have meekly sat down in the humble shades of prose and prudence, by a patient perseverance in rational studies, rise afterwards much higher in the scale of intellect, and acquire a much larger stock of sound knowledge, for far better purposes than mere display: —and though it may seem a contradiction, yet it will generally be found true, that girls who take to scribble are the least studious, the least reflecting, and the least rational; they early acquire a false confidence in their own unassisted powers; it becomes more gratifying to their natural vanity to be always pouring out their minds on paper, than to be drawing into them fresh ideas from richer sources. The original stock, small perhaps at first, is soon spent. The subsequent efforts grow more and more feeble, if the mind which is continually exhausting itself, be not also continually replenished, till the latter compositions become little more than reproductions of the same ideas, and fainter copies of the same images, a little varied and modified, perhaps, and not a little diluted and enfeebled.

It will be necessary to combat vigilantly that favourite plea of lively ignorance, that study is an enemy to originality. Correct the judgment, while you humble the vanity, of the young untaught pretender, by convincing her that those half-formed thoughts and undigested ideas, which she considers as proofs of her invention, prove only that she wants taste and knowledge; that while conversation must polish, and reflection invigorate, her ideas, she must improve and enlarge them by the accession of various kinds of virtuous and elegant literature; and that the cultivated mind will repay with large interest the seeds sown in it by judicious study. Let it be observed, I am by no means *encouraging* young ladies to turn authors; I am only reminding them that

Authors before they write should read

I am only putting them in mind that to be ignorant is not to be original.

These self-taught and self-dependent scribblers pant for the unmerited and unattainable praise of fancy and of genius, while they disdain the commendation of judgment, knowledge, and perseverance, which would probably be within their reach. To extort admiration, they are accustomed to boast of an impossible rapidity in composing; and while they insinuate how little time their performances cost them, they intend you should infer how perfect they might have made them had they condescended to the drudgery of application; but application with them implies defect of genius. They take superfluous pains to convince you that there was neither learning nor labour employed in the work for which they solicit your praise. Alas! the judicious eye too soon perceives it! though it does *not* perceive that native strength and motherwit, which, in the works of real genius, make some amends for the negligence which yet they do not justify. But instead of extolling these effusions for their facility, it would be kind in friends rather to blame them for their crudeness; and when the young candidates for fame are eager to prove in how short a time such a poem has been struck off, it would be well to regret either that they had not taken a longer time, or had refrained from writing at all. In the former case, the work would have been less defective, and in the latter, the writer would have discovered more humility and self-distrust.

. . . But there is one *human* consideration which would perhaps more effectually tend to damp in an aspiring woman the ardours of literary vanity—I speak not of real genius, though there the remark often applies—than any which she will derive from motives of humility, or propriety, or religion; which is, that in the judgment passed on her performances, she will have to encounter the mortifying circumstances of having her sex always taken into account, and her highest exertions will probably be received with the qualified approbation *that it is really extraordinary for a woman.* Men of learning, who are naturally disposed to estimate works in proportion as they appear to be the result of art, study, and institution, are inclined to consider even the happier performances of a fruitful but shallow soil, and to give them the same kind of praise which we bestow on certain salads, which often draw from us a sort of wondering commendation, not, indeed, as being worth much in themselves, but because, by the lightness of the earth, and a happy knack of the gardener, these indifferent cresses spring up in a night, and therefore we are ready to wonder they are no worse.

As to men of sense, however, they need be the less hostile to the improvement of the other sex, as they themselves will be sure to be gainers by it; the enlargement of the female understanding being the most likely means to put an end to those petty and absurd contentions for equality which female smatterers so anxiously maintain. I say smatterers, for between the first class of both sexes the question is much more rarely and always more temperately agitated. Cooperation, and not competition, is indeed the clear principle we wish to see reciprocally adopted by those higher minds in each sex which really approximate the nearest to each other. The more a woman's understanding is improved, the more obviously she will discern that there can be no happiness in any society where there is a perpetual struggle for power; and the more her judgment is rectified, the more accurate views will she take of the station she was born to fill, and the more readily still she accommodate herself to it; while the most vulgar and ill-informed women are ever most inclined to be tyrants, and those always struggle most vehemently for power who, at the greatest distance from deserving it, would not fail to make the worst use of it when attained. Thus the weakest reasoners are always the most positive in debate; and the cause is obvious, for *they* are unavoidably driven to maintain their pretensions by violence, who want arguments and reasons to prove that they are in the right. . . .

But *they* little understand the true interests of woman who would lift her from the important duties of her allotted station, to fill, with fantastic dignity, a loftier but less appropriate niche. Nor do they understand her true happiness, who seek to annihilate distinctions from which she derives advantages, and to attempt innovations which would depreciate her real value. Each sex has its proper excellences, which would be lost were they melted down into the common character by the fusion of the new philosophy. Why should we do away distinctions which increase the mutual benefits and enhance the satisfactions of life? Whence, but by carefully preserving the original marks of difference, stamped by the hand of the Creator, would be derived the superior advantage of mixed society? Is either sex so abounding in perfection, as to be independent of the other for improvement? Have men no need to have their rough angles filed off, and their harshnesses and asperities smoothed and polished by assimilating with beings of more softness and refinement? Are the ideas of women naturally so *very* judicious, are their principles so *invincibly* firm, are their views so *perfectly* correct, are their judgments so *completely* exact, that there is no occasion for additional weight, no superadded strength, no increased clearness, none of that enlargement of mind, none of that additional invigoration, which may be derived from the aids of the stronger sex? What identity could advantageously supersede such an enlivening opposition, such an interesting variety of character? Is it not, then, more wise, as well as more honourable, to move contentedly in the plain path which Providence has obviously marked out to the sex, and in which custom has for the most part rationally confirmed them, rather than to stray awkwardly, unbecomingly, and unsuccessfully in a forbidden road? Is it not desirable to be the lawful possessors of a more limited domestic territory, rather than the turbulent usurpers of a wider foreign empire? to be good originals instead of bad imitators? to be the best thing of one's own kind rather than an inferior thing, even if it were of a higher kind? to be excellent women rather than indifferent men?

. . . Natural propensities best mark the designations of Providence as to their application. The fin was not more clearly bestowed on the fish that he should swim, nor the wing given to the bird that he should fly, than superior strength of body and a firmer texture of mind were given to man, that he might preside in the deep and daring scenes of action and of council; in the complicated arts of government, in the contention of arms, in the intricacies and depths of science, in the bustle of commerce, and in those professions which demand a higher reach and a wider range of powers. The true value of woman is not diminished by the imputation of inferiority in those talents which do not belong to her, of those qualities in which her claim to excellence does not consist. She has other requisites, better adapted to answer the end and purposes of her being, from "Him who does all things well," who suits the agent to the action; who accommodates the instrument to the work.

Let not, then, aspiring, because ill-judging, woman view with pining envy the keen satirist, hunting vice through all the doublings and windings of the heart; the sagacious politicians leading senates, and directing the fate of empires; the acute lawyer, detecting the obliquities of fraud; and the skilful dramatist, exposing the pretensions of folly; but let her ambition be consoled by reflecting that those who thus excel, to all that Nature bestows and books can teach, must add besides that consummate knowledge of the world to which a delicate woman has no fair avenues, and which, even if she could attain, she would never be supposed to have come honestly by.

In almost all that comes under the description of polite letters, in all that captivates by vivid imagery or warms by just and affecting sentiment, women are excellent. They possess in a high degree that delicacy and quickness of perception, and that nice discernment between the beautiful and defective which comes under the denomination of taste. Both in composition and in action they excel in details; but they do not so much generalise their ideas as men, nor do their minds seize a great subject with so large a grasp. They are acute observers, and accurate judges of life and manners, as far as their own sphere of observation extends, but they describe a smaller circle. A woman sees the world, as it were, from a little elevation in her own garden, whence she makes an exact survey of home scenes but takes not in that wider range of distant prospects which he who stands on a loftier eminence commands. Women have a certain *tact* which often enables them to feel what is just more instantaneously than they can define it. They have an intuitive penetration into character bestowed on them by Providence, like the sensitive and tender organs of some timid animals, as a kind of natural guard, to warn of the approach of danger, beings who are often called to act defensively.

In summing up the evidence, if I may so speak, of the different capacities of the sexes, one may venture, perhaps, to assert that women have equal *parts*, but are inferior in *wholeness* of mind, in the integral understanding: that though a superior woman may possess single faculties in equal perfection, yet there is commonly a juster proportion in the mind of a superior man: that if women have in an equal degree the faculty of fancy which creates images, and the faculty of memory which collects and stores ideas, they seem not to possess in equal measure the faculty of comparing, combining, analysing, and separating these ideas that deep and patient thinking which goes to the bottom of a subject, nor that power of arrangement which knows how to link a thousand connected ideas in one dependent train, without losing sight of the original idea out of which the rest grow, and on which they all hang. The female, too, wanting steadiness in her intellectual pursuits, is perpetually turned aside by her characteristic tastes and feelings. Woman, in the career of genius, is the Atalanta, who will risk losing the race by running out of her road to pick up the golden apple; while her male competitor, without, perhaps, possessing greater natural strength or swiftness, will more certainly attain his object by direct pursuit, by being less exposed to the seductions of extraneous beauty, and will win the race, not by excelling in speed, but by despising the bait.

Here it may be justly enough retorted, that, as it is allowed the education of women is so defective, the alleged inferiority of their minds may be accounted for on that ground more justly than by ascribing it to their natural make. And, indeed, there is so much truth to the remark, that till women shall be more reasonably educated, and till the native growth of their mind shall cease to be stinted and cramped, we have no juster ground for pronouncing that their understanding has already reached its highest point, than the Chinese would have for affirming that their women have attained to the greatest possible perfection in walking, while the first care is, during their infancy, to cripple their feet. At least, till the female sex are more carefully instructed, this question will always remain as undecided as to the *degree* of difference between the masculine and feminine understanding, as the question between the understandings of blacks and whites; for until men and women, as well as Africans and Europeans, are put more nearly on a par in the cultivation of their minds, the shades of distinction, whatever they be, between their native abilities can never be fairly ascertained. . . .

And as the final hope of the female sex is equal, so are their present means, perhaps, more favourable, and their opportunities often less obstructed than those of the other sex. In their Christian course women have every superior advantage, whether we consider the natural make of their minds, their leisure for acquisition in youth, or their subsequently less exposed mode of life. Their hearts are naturally soft and flexible, open to impressions of love and gratitude; their feelings tender and lively; all these are favourable to the cultivation of a devotional spirit. Yet, while we remind them of these native benefits, they will do well to be on their guard lest this very softness and ductility lay them more open to the seductions of temptation and error. . . .

And as women are naturally more affectionate than fastidious, they are likely both to read and to hear with a less critical spirit than men; they will not be on the watch to detect errors, so much as to gather improvement; they have seldom that hardness which is acquired by dealing deeply in the books of controversy; but are more inclined to the perusal of works which quicken the devotional feelings, than to such as awaken a spirit of doubt and scepticism. They are less disposed to consider the compositions they read as materials on which to ground objections and answers, than as helps to faith and rules of life. With these advantages, however, they should also bear in mind that their more easily received impressions being often less abiding, and their reason less open to conviction from the strong evidences which exist in favour of the truth of Christianity, "they ought, therefore, to give the more earnest heed to the things which they have heard, lest at any time they should let them slip." Women are also, from their domestic habits, in possession of more leisure and tranquillity for religious pursuits, as well as secured from those difficulties and strong temptations to which men are exposed in the tumult of a bustling world. Their lives are more regular and uniform, less agitated by the passions, the businesses, the contentions, the shock of opinions, and the opposition of interests which divide society and convulse the world.

If we have denied them the possession of talents which might lead them to excel as lawyers, they are preserved from the peril of having their principles warped by that too indiscriminate defence of right and wrong, to which the professors of the law are exposed. If we should question their title to eminence as mathematicians, they are happily exempt from the danger to which men devoted to that science are said to be liable, namely, that of looking for demonstration on subjects which, by their very nature, are incapable of affording it. If they are less conversant in the powers of nature, the structure of the human frame, and the knowledge of the heavenly bodies than philosophers, physicians and astronomers, they are, however, delivered from the error into which many of each of these have sometime fallen, —I mean from the fatal habit of resting in second causes, instead of referring all to the first; instead of making "the heavens declare the glory of God, and proclaim his handy-work;" instead of concluding, when they observe "how fearfully and wonderfully we are made, marvellous are thy works, O Lord, and that my soul knoweth right well."

And let the weaker sex take comfort, that in their very exemption from privileges, which they are sometimes foolishly disposed to envy, consists not only their security but their happiness. If they enjoy not the distinctions of public life and high offices, do they not escape the responsibility attached to them, and the mortification of being dismissed from them? If they have no voice in deliberative assemblies, do they not avoid the load of duty inseparably connected with such privileges? Preposterous pains have been taken to excite in women an uneasy jealousy, that their talents are neither rewarded with public honours nor emoluments in life; nor with inscriptions, statues, and mausoleums after death. It has been absurdly represented to them as a hardship, that, while they are expected to perform duties, they must yet be contented to relinquish honours; that they must unjustly be compelled to renounce fame, while they must sedulously labour to deserve it. . . .

If women should lament it as a disadvantage attached to their sex, that their character is of so delicate a texture as to be sullied by the slightest breath of calumny, and that the stain once received is indelible; yet are they not led by that very circumstance to shrink, as if instinctively, from all those irregularities to which the loss of character is so certainly expected to be attached, and to shun, with keener circumspection, the most distant approach towards the confines of danger? Let them not lament it as a hardship, but account it to be a privilege, that the delicacy of their sex impels them more scrupulously to avoid the very "*appearance* of evil," let them not regret that the consciousness of their danger serves to secure their purity, by placing them at a greater distance, and in a more deep intrenchment, from the evil itself. . . .

ANNA SEWARD
1742–1809

ANNA SEWARD, born 12 December 1742 at Eyam, Derbyshire, was the eldest child of Dr. Thomas Seward, former chaplain and tutor to the Duke of Grafton, and Elizabeth Hunter Seward, whose father had been the tutor of Dr. Samuel Johnson. Introduced to poetry early in life, at the age of three Seward could repeat passages from "L'Allegro," and by the time she was nine she had memorized the first three books of *Paradise Lost*. She began to write poems before she was twenty; at age forty she had earned the title, "The Swan of Lichfield."

While still quite young she had two romances; one came to an end because her father disapproved, the other because the young man married someone else. There is no suggestion that either romance left her heartbroken; she was devoted to her family, and they in turn considered her their young genius. She was capable of intense feelings, however; in 1764 she was devastated when her twenty-year-old sister Sarah died a few weeks before she was to have married Dr. Johnson's stepson, Joseph Porter. Seward turned for consolation to Honora Sneyd, a young girl who had lived with the family since she was a small child, but her attachment gradually became extremely possessive.

In 1769, Anna encouraged a romance between Honora, then nineteen, and a young local man, John Andre, later the notorious Major Andre hanged as a spy in America. Seward, who regarded the matter as a tragic love affair, celebrated him as a hero in her "Monody on the Death of Major Andre" (1781). It was extremely popular, and her excoriation of George Washington was so severe that the future president was moved to write and explain his inability to alter the sentence of the court-martial. Shortly afterward, Honora married Richard Lovell Edgeworth, father of the novelist Maria. Seward disapproved strongly, and the relationship with Honora was permanently shattered. Honora died five years later without ever seeing Seward again.

Seward's life was sheltered and centered around the home; after her mother's death in 1780, she rarely travelled far from Lichfield and devoted herself to caring for her father until he died in 1790. But, although she remained far from the cultural center of London, her retired life gave her ample opportunity for reading and writing. With a comfortable income, she did not have to write for a living as had Behn, Manley and Centlivre, and her poems reveal a cultivated, literate mind working at a leisurely and thoughtful pace. Nevertheless, she was prolific. Almost every issue of *The Gentleman's Magazine* during the mid-eighties contained her verses, and in the judgment of the editors, she was an author "in whom almost every poetical excellence seems to be united."

Almost everything she wrote was successful. Her poetic novel *Louisa*, written in 1782, published in 1784, went into five editions and brought her acclaim in London. She was admired by bluestockings and critics alike and was consulted for literary advice, which she gave freely. Her correspondence included a long interchange with Sir Walter Scott, whose work she admired. Romney's portrait of her shows a tall, handsome woman with auburn hair and blue eyes, perhaps "a bit affected" as Southey found her, but also, as he added, likeable, warm, and sincere. For all her conservative background, her politics were liberal and her religious views unusually tolerant.

Lichfield was always the core of her existence and provided her with almost all her social contacts. During her father's lifetime, she lived in the Bishop's Palace; later she moved to the Cathedral Close where she spent the rest of her years. Her attachments were deep; her friendship with John Saville, a singer in the Cathedral choir, lasted forty-eight years. She knew, but did not like, Dr. Johnson, and she furnished Boswell with several Lichfield stories of the great critic. Boswell, perhaps suspicious of her obvious hostility, did not use them, and Seward was deeply offended.

In 1799 she published a collection of original sonnets. Although published a year after Wordsworth's *Lyrical Ballads*, the dates and subjects of the collection indicate that she had been writing in the form long before he began to re-popularize it. Her language is not that of the Romantics, but these early attempts show definite Romantic concepts—particularly her sense of nature—struggling to break through the rigidified eighteenth-century diction.

She published little after this except for the *Memoirs* of her friend Dr. Erasmus Darwin, one of her few works unfavorably received. She continued a voluminous correspondence with the major literary figures of the day until her death on 25 March 1809. In her will, she named Scott her literary executor, and he edited a three-volume collection of her works that same year.

Among her correspondents, Edward Jerningham (1727–1812) occupies a minor place. A serious, second-rate poet and dramatist, he nonetheless had a great love of literature and admired Seward greatly. These unpublished letters to him, now in the Huntington Library, are less self-consciously literary than those to more famous writers; they show a warm, friendly nature often hidden in her formal works and clearly set forth the eighteenth-century standards for criticism. Neither as perceptive nor as experienced as Dr. Johnson, Seward nevertheless gives an accurate view of the kind of experience that shaped most authors of the time, and in nonliterary matters she frequently rises to a surprising level of timelessness.

BIBLIOGRAPHY

Works

The Beauties of Anna Seward. Edited by W. C. Oulton. London: n.p., 1813.
Blindness. Sheffield: J. Montgomery, 1806.
Elegy on Captain Cook. London: n.p., 1780.
Letters. 6 vols. Edited by A. Constable. Edinburgh: George Ramsay, 1811.
Llangollan Vale. London: n.p., 1796.
Louisa. Lichfield: n.p., 1784.
Memoirs of the Life of Dr. Darwin. London: J. Johnson, 1804.
Miss Seward's Enigma. London: R. Theobald, [1855].
Monody on Major André. Lichfield: n.p., 1781.
Ode on General Eliott's Return from Gibraltar. London: n.p., 1787.
Original Sonnets on various Subjects. London: n.p., 1799.
The Poetical Works. 3 vols. Edited by Sir Walter Scott. Edinburgh: Joseph Ballantyne, 1810.

Related Readings

Ashmun, Margaret. *The Singing Swan.* New Haven: Yale University Press, 1931.
Lucas, E. V. *A Swan and her Friends.* London: Methuen, 1907.
Myers, Robert Manson. *Anna Seward. An Eighteenth-Century Handelian.* Williamsburg, Va.: Manson Park Press, 1947.
Pearson, Hesketh. *The Swan of Lichfield.* London: Hamish Hamilton, 1936.

The letters in this volume are from an unpublished correspondence in the Huntington Library, JE 758–768.

ᘐᦗ

Letters to Edward Jerningham

ANNA SEWARD

1 August 1789.

Ignorant as I yet am of your address, nor knowing at present where to find my Cottonian channel to you, yet I cannot suffer the obliging letter before me to remain unacknowledged. Directing my letter to Mr. William Jerningham's it will probably circle round to you.

Nothing can be more reciprocal than the flattering wish you express that we were in each other's vicinity, but the *advantages* of its realization wou'd be *mine*.

You have rightly divined my lot—that I live amongst those who, if I *do* possess any thing intellectual worth the least attention, I must cautiously *veil* it, if I wou'd not be much less agreeable to *them* than they are to *me*.

It is very soothing that you wish to see me again as an author. I have materials, in prose and verse, which added to the things of mine already published, wou'd fill several Volumes; but many are the obstacles to such a collective appearance. First, and chiefest, the want of leisure to prepare them. The few hours I can abstract, thro' the swiftly fleeting day, from nursing a feeble Parent, household cares, and visiting intercourses, are swallowed up in the inevitable duties of a too extended correspondence.

The less am I disposed to make *sacrifices* to Authorism, from dislike to the idea of running the gauntlet amongst the critical Hornets, who live, not to extract honey, but to sting.

I am ashamed of this egotism—but it seemed due to the kind interest you avow in my destiny, social and poetic. The generous desire is, I perceive, hereditary with *you*,

"To warm the timid, and exalt the low."

I remain, with a thousand good wishes, and with that lively regard which I have found very possible to exist without personal consciousness, Sir

Your obliged Friend

and Servant

P.S. I shall soon hope to have an opportunity of perusing Sir J. Reynold's[1] last Treatise. It will give me pleasure to see our Apelles doing generous justice to the merits of our lost Protogenes.

16 March 1790.

You had earlier received my acknowledgements for the obliging paquet, and for the poetical present it contained, if I had not been unhappily prevented by the threatning aspect my dear Father's disease began to assume. It has terminated fatally. His long-enduring infirmities and gradually darkening intellects, had rendered his existence of but little value to himself; or to any body but *me*, his Child, who passionately loved him; —yet, as he was insensible to his own deprivations, and not afflicted with bodily pain, to tend, to sooth, to protect him formed the dear tho' anxious blessing of my life—I have *lost* it—*You* can pity, for you have *felt* the affliction of *such* a loss.

I had seen your Verses, upon Sir Joshua's resignation in the Newspapers, before I was honored by receiving them from yourself. They had charmed me. Their questions of reproach are highly animated, and their description of the Painter's Eye eclipsing over his *own* creation, is very fine indeed.

Ah! Sir, how little can any production of my pen deserve to inspire the ardor of expectation! I have long wanted spirits to encounter the trouble and solicitude of passing the Press—*Now* I want them more than ever. Few things possess more power to rekindle the obtrusive courage of female authorism than the consciousness that Mr. Jerningham will take up whatever I may publish with a generous desire to be pleased.

The death of my excellent Friend, Mr. Howard,[2] perishing at last in his angelic Ministry, afflicts, and wou'd have deeper afflicted me had not a still more heart-piercing Sorrow sat on my Spirit. He passed the Evening of February the 7th, 1789 with me, beneath this roof. At parting he expressed a tender and solemn presentiment that we shou'd meet no more on *Earth*. O! tha his generous wish of our renewed interviews in happier Regions may be fulfilled!

Adieu Sir!—pardon the mournful egotism of my letter!
Your ever obliged and

obedient Servant
This letter, folded up, and directed to go by the Post lay on my table when Mrs. Sneyd[3] obliging offered to inclose it in a frank to Lord Vernon.[4]

9 December 1791.

I grieve that it is not in my power to serve Mr. Colls. I have been, and still continue so much out of health as to prevent all ideas of going to our Plays this Winter. My illness is so heavy on my spirits as often to prevent my being able to see my *Friends*. It obliges me totally to decline the visits of Strangers—but the loss of Mr. Colls[5] is all *ideal*; my patronage wou'd not serve him, but the contrary. Our Play-Goers are very tenacious about what they call *judging for themselves*. They made such Parties against the two last dramatic Performers, for whose reputation and emolument they perceived me anxious, that I made a firm resolve never again to attempt supporting the claim of Talents in that line. You know enough of human Nature not to wonder at this operation when you recollect that I have lived here these hundred years. A *new Author* might have influence with them, but there are certain dispositions which will make a very Cassandra of one they are *used* to, who, if she prophesies of expanding powers, and rising genius, must prophesy in vain. I will however make mention of Mr. Jerningham's recommendation of this young Man, and *that*, I think, may serve him.

I remain, with much esteem, and many good wishes.

15 January 1792.

Your attention to me is very flattering, and the present of your ingenious Poem truly welcome. Amid the interest I feel in its general spirit, and in the beauty of particular passages, permit me to object to Abelard giving himself the appellation of *Youth*, which he repeats three times in the course of six lines. The *repetition* however had been, or rather is in *itself* graceful but the use of the word at *all* militates most revoltingly against the consciousness impressed upon the mind of every poetic reader, that Abelard was in *middle* life when he *first* saw his Eloisa. Mr. Berington has exactly ascertained their mutual ages at *that* period, he 40, she 16. We learn, from the prose letters, that she took the veil at 22. We must suppose a twelvemonth at least to have elapsed from that epoch when this letter of Abelard's, first paraphrased by Mr. Cawthorne, and now by yourself, was written. It is not at 47 that ingenious Men lose their power over the female heart, and its passions; but if they style themselves *youths* the effect must be ludicrous. Taking a real, and *known* story for the basis of our Poem, however, it is allowed as to heighten and embellish, surely we shou'd abstain from every word that violates the truth of situation. We find Pope judiciously guarding the pen of Eloisa from every expression that might convey a false idea of Abelard's juvenility. Angelica's[6] picture of these Lovers, separating at the gate of the Convent, always displeases me from the stripling appearance of Abelard.

Your account of that miraculous degree of perfection to which Lady Hamilton[7] has carried the power of countenance and attitude confirms the truth of the news-paper account. No exhibition cou'd have had greater charms for me. I thought *Mrs. Siddons*[8] had attained the ne plus ultra of expression in all the *graver* passions that no silence *cou'd* be more eloquent than *her* silence.

Miss Vernon's remembrances do me honor—I beg leave to return my best compliments to that Lady. I *hope* she is as *well* as I am *sure* she is *good* and ingenious.

The concern you express for the decline of my health is kind—I have grown considerably better within these three weeks—and purpose venturing to the Theatre, for the *first* time, on Wednesday next, the night of Mrs. Coll's Benefit. She is thought a pleasing actress I find. Mr. Coll does not appear on the Boards. That depravity of public Taste in the general preference it shows of flimsy modern Comedies to Shakespear's Plays, having almost banished them the *Stage*, completely sickens me of its exhibitions.

But I am delighted with your allusion to the veil of Isis—for the unimpersonality of our mutual regard. This is *true*, and what is more, *natural* platonism.

Adieu! —with the increasing influence of long predilection, and perfect esteem, I am

Your obliged and faithful
humble Servant

"Iron extirpation"—is good, but is not "cloud of iron" a false metaphor?

8 January 1794.

I think myself honored and obliged by the new poetical gift you have sent me. The incident of this Play, tho' single, is interesting, and considerable poetic genius appears in several of the passages. It is perhaps desirable that you had paid more attention to the structure of the verse. Surely even a Tragedy had better be written in *prose* than in measure which loses its nature by perpetual violation of the requisite verbal quantities. The redundant syllable at the end of the line is the utmost licence allowed to dramatic verse as to quantity—and I apprehend that we ought never to allow ourselves a separation of the adjective from the substantive, by ending a line with the epithet, and beginning the next with its substantive. It is an habit *fatal* to the grace of the poetry, and to that of the voice in recitation. I believe scarce a single instance will be found in the whole Paradise Lost of such division, nor even in Shakespear's *best* writing. To have the pauses float thro' the lines by incessant variation forms the excellence of blank verse; —yet that variation must not sin against certain cadences, which to violate destroys the very nature of verse, even where the verbal quantities are preserved. Many a line may *scan* as verse, that will not *read* as such. Thus

> "She gave it to Love, a tender present—and in this Play
> We shou'd not have found the name of Cressy"

"O! we shou'd ne'er have found the name of Cressy"—had satisfied the ear—

> "Say what *paternal*
> "*Bosom* will not feel a warm renew'd affection."

That line, and also a number more, has twelve syllables, besides utter neglect of cadence

> At Windsor did I first behold that *matchless*
> *Woman*, tho' attractive, yet not dazzling;
> As looks the softer green amid the *radiant*
> *Colours* of the vernal bow, so Ethelberta &c.

The second line of that passage has but nine, the fourth twelve syllables, besides putting asunder what the God of Verse joins together. What pity that the ear shou'd be revolted in a passage which so beautiful a simile adorns.

Excuse my ingenuousness. I have given way to it in the hope of seeing your next dramatic Work in numbers chaste, elevated, and harmonious as the sentiments will be great, as the allusions will be ingenious, as the imagery will be striking, as the story will be pathetic.

Thank you for enquiring after my health. It is far from being good tho' I meditate a month's visit to Nottingham very soon. May the new-born Year prove auspicious to all your hopes!

It is grievous to see public affairs wear so dark an aspect—to feel how much in vain the swords of just chastisement have been drawn by the surrounding Nations against Tyranny, Anarchy, Blasphemy and Murder.[9]

    Adieu

Your obliged and

obedient Servant

I like the prologue and Epilogue much.

3 April 1794.

I cannot bear but *seem* ungrateful, or even regardless of any mark of Mr. Jerningham's attention—therefore, tho' I have this past fortnight sat in darkness and inaction from a violent inflammation in one eye, which does not seem to yield at all to medical application, yet I must, however briefly, endeavor to express my thanks for the new effusions of his poetic talent with which he has honored me. Tho' I cannot see to read them, or any thing else at present, they have been read to me, and I have listened with pleasure. The little Negro is pathetically sweet—the fables elegant. With the interesting graces of the Album verses I have long been acquainted. My criticisms are honored by your attention.

France has ever been habituated to take the lead in dictating to the customs and manners of the surrounding Nations, and I fear there is too much probability in your finely-expressed apprehension. The rational consequence of the mind being familiarized to cruelty shou'd and necessarily must render true Wisdom more than ever cautious to guard the remotest outworks of our political establishment from innovation. If the stationary point cannot be exactly preserved it is, of the two evils, certainly the least to tighten the reins of Monarchy, rather than, in the smallest degree, to give way to the many-headed Monster; with whom, inherently sick and envious of superiority, claim will inevitably lead to claim, "till all things meet in meer oppugnancy."

Love of the arts and attention to them is fading fast away beneath the contemplation of those bloody and momentous deeds that take preoccupying hold of the general mind. So far has the Gallic Comet *already* tinged us—Oh! that its extinction may be effected ere the dark hue deepens, and becomes indelible!

Adieu! —with pain and difficulty have I kept my burning eyes thus long on this paper. Maladies of various species hover, like dark clouds, over my waning life. May yours be long golden and serene! If that benediction was not animated and sincere, I should ill deserve the pleasing marks of regard and prepossession with which Mr. Jerningham has long honored

his obliged and obedient Servant

17 February 1796. "Written . . . after reading Southey's *Joan of Arc*."

I thank you for remembering me, and am glad that resistance to impulses lost its power at last. Your Poetry is always welcome to me, from consciousness that it will prove the genuine product of *Genius*. It never leaves the Friends of your Muse any thing to wish for on the score of *ideas*—nothing but that a little freer use had been made of the chisel. I chiefly mean as to those hard abbreviations, as *I'd* and *I'm* and *he'd*, which to me appear great blemishes in Verse that, like the Poem before me, takes an high heroic tone.

My aversion to the ignorant cant of Reviewers banishing [i.e., having banished] their pamphlets [from] this roof, kept me in ignorance that you had recently published till I received your letter—else would not this Work have been *new* to me on its arrival last Thursday. It does not exactly breathe my *politics*—but *that* circumstance veils not to my imagination one ray of its poetic beauty. Those passages which appear to me the richest in this splendor are, that which begins "Oh, my loved Country," and the ensuing one, which involves the *incantation*; next the apotheosis of Voltair; that on prostrate Education, closing with a metaphor at once beautiful, just and *new*, the description of the Infant initiation in Massacre.

If I were not convinced that we had irretrievably lost the opportunities we had of closing this unavailing, this ruinous Contest, which alone cou'd have united France in that strong *internal compact* which has rendered her omnipotent; if I were not sure that those human Friends now by their success in Flanders and Italy on fire with ideas of the rich plunder of England, will not listen to *any* terms of accommodation till they have risqued the experiment of invasion; if I were not sure of *this*, I shou'd be extremely sorry to see a Friend of mine (I hope I am not too presumptuous in deeming *you* so) stimulating this desperate *Crusade*.

Under the outraged name of Liberty, France is become, by her Revolution, the most tyrannous and despotic Power on the Globe. Arrogating absolute dominion over the property and lives of her exhaustless Population, she sends forth the Myriads she has maddened, resistless as the Goths of old, to find the means of life, which France cannot afford, by the plunder of every Nation with which she is at War, or that she has vanquished. You have a right, exclaims the Monster, to do unto *them* as we have done unto you.

If England comes to exert at full such force upon the wills of her Subjects, which the dire effects of this War has already obliged her to *commence*, the free spirit of this Nation will not endure it, and Rebellion will ensue. The demands of Government upon private property are already very near *Requisition*, and are very reluctantly borne. They must be doubled and trebled, over and over again, if the War is to be *continued*—The hard pressure of pecuniary distress upon the Peasantry, and upon a large Class whose incomes are so limited that a considerable reduction will plunge them into that penury, to which habit has not inured them, must naturally weaken their attachment to a Government which no longer affords them the means of *comfortable life*.

Mr. Burke's[10] system, which you adopt in your Poem, pronounces upon this fruitless War the dreadful word *eternal*—if not *verbally* by inevitable *implication*. Its meaning results unequivocally from the two assertions he makes, viz. "while France maintains her present System, England must not sheath the Sword."—"The system of Jacobinism is laid too deep in the corruption of human Nature to afford rational hope that it will ever be renounced by any State which has adopted it." Thus that great Man, so much more eloquent than wise, pronounces eternal War the duty of this Country, and you echo his edict in Verse. I confess I think no Man ought to utter such a decision to England unless he was in possession of the grand chymical arcanum, to avoid *requisitions*,—and if he *was* our Population, so very inferior to that of France, would not bear *us* out in never ending warfare. Therefore is it that I think, if it can be made the *interest* of France to give peace to us and to Europe, *he* cou'd not be his Country's Friend that shou'd seek to rephrenzy her into the *continued* sacrifice of her *safety* to what you call her *glory*. Alas! what an ignis fatuus has that word proved to England in the American War, and in *this*. The love of War is a fatal passion for this Country to entertain. That proud jealousy of authority, which sent our armies over the Atlantic in '75, eventually ruined Europe. I see something severely retributing in the chain of events. The Courts of France and Spain and the Dutch, were treacherous to *us* in joining America, in violation of their Treaty. The regal Power of France, thro' jealousy of this Country, was, you well know, the Ring-Leader of that infidelity. In their faithless Fraternity her People learnt to hate Kings and Courts. —Severely has this treachery been visited upon the *French* king and Court. —Spain, humbled, and on the brink of Ruin, has been obliged to purchase her very existence as a nation by humiliation to a Democracy; Holland is completely enslaved; and England, whose oppressive severity to her Colonies was the original cause of all this wide wasting mischief—England, joining the impotent struggle to coerce that Demoniac spirit of Anarchy which unassaulted from without must have been self-destroying within, has sacrificed the flower of her army to the sword and the Pestilence—has drained her national resources till Requisition commences—has lost her Commerce, at least all rational prospect of its duration—while every object has melted from her grasp which was, in succession, held out as the motive for protracting the War—Invasion is attempted, which would have taken place if the Winds had slept as soundly as our Admiral. O! it is more than time that we tried to heal the bleeding World with Peace, whose veins our American War unsluiced; —but if, as I fear, no balm of ours will be found effectual, at least let us not resume our *crusading* spirit, and seek only to defend our Country against the certain invasion of a mighty and terrible Foe.

I conclude you are determined to go into the Army. I dare assure myself you would not brand your Country with cowardice for wishing to terminate a War, from the fatigues and dangers of which you yourself kept aloof. It is *that* which has always disgusted me in the disposition of the King. Since his People hold his personal *safety* dearer than his personal *glory*, in not permitting him to lead his Armies into the Field of Battle as was the custom of our former Kings, he surely ought to have prized *their* safety too dearly to have lavished their lives and properties in the phrenzied ardor of Glory—sacrificing substances for a shadow.

I am glad you do not like that vulgar insensible Block in the Monthly Mirror, who stares upon the page, and calls itself *me*, tho' it has not even the lineaments of my face and features. Shewn to my Servants with the name concealed, not one of them cou'd guess for whom it was designed. Every Body here reprobates it as a likeness. I neither expected nor desired to see that beauty and grace which not even my juvenile years cou'd boast, but some expression of countenance, some air of a Gentlewoman, I thought I had a right to expect. This Abigal Engraving has not an atom of either and almost as little resembles Romney's[11] picture of me drawn fourteen years ago as it does my present self. My head and face are small proportioned to my height and size. Dark and heavy is the head of this Beast of an Engraving. Thro' the past ten years I had resisted various applications made to me for permission to engrave Romney's picture from a presentiment that some clumsy artist might be employed who would quiz me. I have enough of the woman about me to dislike the idea of going down to Posterity a confirmed Quiz. One of the Editors of the Monthly Mirror is a Friend of my Cousin, Mr. White of this Town—and found means to engage his interest warmly on the subject, so, in an evil hour for my vanity, I complied. After slow leave had been wrung from me for the Engraving, they wrote for *anecdotes*. Had I been aware of *that* request it would have influenced me strongly to refuse the *first*. Mr. White then persuaded me that unless I permitted him to write them I shou'd certainly have the mortification of seeing a fulsome history of my self, abounding with mistaken circumstances, which I shou'd not only have the vexation to see but the trouble to contradict. He therefore, by my consent, took care that my mind's portrait shou'd be somewhat less unfaithful than that of my face—but a living History, even from the hand of a Friend, can never be a grateful contemplation to its object. I believe one has always reason to repent compliances granted against strong presentiment.

I have half promised Mr. Bookseller to let him publish this spring my large *family of Sonnets* as you call them, to which will, I believe, be subjoined twenty-five paraphrases of the Odes of Horace. I gave away a hundred and thirty *Llangollen Vales*, and more than half that number of my acquaintance were affronted that I had not included *them* in the list of donation. Therefore is it that I am advised to make no presents of my next Publication.

I inclose a few lines, written lately, after reading the *Joan of Arc*—a poetic miracle, considering the youth of its author, now in his twentieth year. An opportunity of sending this paquet post-free has tempted me to swell it thus largely—but the minute of my Friend's departure for Town approaches. Adieu therefore, and believe me, Sir

Your obliged and obedient Servant

Anna Seward

NOTES

1. Sir Joshua Reynolds (1723–1792), painter. She probably refers to his fourteenth *Discourse on Art*, published in 1788.

2. John Howard (1726?–1790), philanthropist, improved prison conditions in England.

3. Mother of Anna's beloved Honora.

4. Sir Edward Vernon (1723–1794), admiral who served under Admiral Boscawen.

5. J. H. Colls was a provincial actor and playwright.

6. Angelica Kauffman (1741–1807), historical and portrait painter.

7. Lady Emma Hamilton (1761?–1816), notorious for her affair with Admiral Nelson.

8. Sarah Kemble Siddons (1775–1831), most famous tragic actress of the day.

9. The reference is to the French government. Under Robespierre, Danton, etc. Marie Antoinette had been beheaded in October 1793; the French armies were winning victories against the Poles, the Austrians, the Prussians, *and* the English. In addition, the French had conquered Holland and Belgium and had driven off the foreign armies.

10. Edmund Burke (1729–1797), statesman. She probably refers to his *Reflections on the Revolution in France* (1790).

11. The great portrait artist George Romney (1734–1802), who painted her portrait.